keywords in sound

keywords

in sound

david novak and matt sakakeeny, editors

DUKE UNIVERSITY PRESS   Durham and London 2015

© 2015 Duke University Press
All rights reserved
Printed and bound by CPI Group (UK) Ltd,
Croydon, CR0 4YY
Designed by Amy Ruth Buchanan
Typeset in Quadraat
by Westchester Book Group

Library of Congress Cataloging-
in-Publication Data
Keywords in sound / David Novak and
Matt Sakakeeny, eds.
pages cm
Includes bibliographical references and index.
ISBN 978-0-8223-5903-6 (hardcover : alk. paper)
ISBN 978-0-8223-5889-3 (pbk. : alk. paper)
ISBN 978-0-8223-7549-4 (e-book)
1. Sound—Terminology. I. Novak, David, 1969–
II. Sakakeeny, Matt, 1971–
QC225.15.K499 2015
152.1'5—dc23
2014041994

Cover art: Lissajous curves created by Mark McCombs.

contents

David Novak and Matt Sakakeeny

introduction

Sound is vibration that is perceived and becomes known through its materiality. Metaphors for sound construct perceptual conditions of hearing and shape the territories and boundaries of sound in social life. Sound resides in this feedback loop of materiality and metaphor, infusing words with a diverse spectrum of meanings and interpretations. To engage sound as the interrelation of materiality and metaphor is to show how deeply the apparently separate fields of perception and discourse are entwined in everyday experiences and understandings of sound, and how far they extend across physical, philosophical, and cultural contexts.

The OED defines sound strictly as matter, "that which is or may be heard; the external object of audition, or the property of bodies by which this is produced." The physical forms of sound—as impulses that move particles of air and travel through bodies and objects—provide the fundamental ground for hearing, listening, and feeling, which in turn enable common structures of communication and social development, as well as elemental survival skills. The raw "stuff" of sound is the tangible basis of music, speech, embodiment, and spatial orientation, and a substantive object of scientific experimentation and technological mediation. We analyze language with phonemes, we locate ourselves in spaces through reverberation, we distribute sound and capture it as sound waves on vinyl or magnetic tape, or as binary codes in digital compression formats, and we feel it in our bodies and vibrate sympathetically.

But the conceptual fields used to define sound—for example, silence, hearing, or voice—circulate not as passive descriptions of sonic phenomena but as ideas that inform experience. Metaphors "have the power to define reality," as Lakoff and Johnson influentially argued, "through a coherent network of entailments that highlight some features of reality and hide others" (1980: 157). To "hear" a person is to recognize their subjectivity, just as to "have a voice" suggests more than the ability to speak or sing, but also a manifestation of internal character, even essential human consciousness. Sound, then, is a substance of the world as well as a basic part of how people frame their knowledge about the world.

This book is a conceptual lexicon of specific keywords that cut across the material and metaphorical lives of sound. A lexicon is not just a catalog of language but a vocabulary that is actualized in use. The keywords here have been chosen for their prevalence and significance in both scholarship and in everyday perceptions of sound. Contributors approach their keywords differently, but each begins by addressing the etymology or semantic range of his or her keyword and then goes on to reveal how these terms develop conceptual grammars and organize social, cultural, and political discourses of sound. To reexamine these words is, first, to invoke them as artifacts of rich and diverse histories of thought, and second, to attend to the existential and even mundane presence of sound in everyday life.

In this, and in many other ways, we take inspiration from Raymond Williams, whose *Keywords* (1985) remains the central reference for students of culture, literature, materialism, and more. Williams's taxonomy does not end with description and classification; he integrates the historical meanings that cluster around a particular term into a relational field of interpretation. We can see the utility of this approach in his famous reading of the term "culture," which he distinguishes as one of the most complicated words in the English language. "Culture" is a noun of process for tending of natural growth, even as this process is linked to the material product of animal and plant husbandry; "culture" becomes an independent noun that, in turn, indicates a separate kind of matter yet to be "cultivated." These practical and material meanings extend into metaphors of social cultivation that reinforce a progressive linear history of "civilization." This universal model of human culture was pluralized and rematerialized in the Romantic separation between multiple national and traditional cultures (such as "folk-culture") and "high cultural" productions of music, theater, art, and education (symbolic forms that could now be capitalized as "Culture"). Williams shows how these simultaneous meanings of "culture"— as a human developmental process, as a way of life for a particular people, and as a set of artistic works and practices—cannot be usefully clarified in distinction from one another. Despite producing discrete and sometimes radically incommensurable interpretations, "it is the range and overlap of meanings that is significant" (Williams 1985: 91).[1]

Williams was interested in the many possibilities not only for defining culture but also for studying culture, and his work was foundational to the field of cultural studies, which did not exist as such when Williams published his seminal *Culture and Society* in 1958. *Keywords* provided a point of intersection and a unifying discourse for scholars applying various research methods to diverse topics under the banner of cultural studies. While *Keywords in Sound* is a different book, from a different time, for an interdisciplinary field that is already relatively established, Williams offers us a model for taking up a topic so vast and familiar ("sound") and situating it within and against a field that is necessarily narrower and more fragmented ("sound studies"). As with "culture," the links between terms of sonic discourse and their conceptual genealogies require critical interrogation. We have adopted the keyword format in an attempt to directly lay out the foundational terms of debate and map the shared ground of sound studies.[2]

The intellectual histories within each keyword are entwined in ways that destabilize and denaturalize sound as a distinct object of research. For example, after articulating together the terms silence, deafness, noise, and echo, it becomes apparent that attempts to define them as the negation of sound or mere artifacts of sound "itself" are narrowly limited. In both silence and deafness, the presumed absence of sound is shown to be the impetus for a host of sound-oriented developments, including new forms of composition (e.g. John Cage's 4'33"), communication (e.g. lip-reading, braille, sign language), technology (e.g. Bell's telephone, the audiometer, the hearing aid), and metaphysical theories of acoustic multinaturalism. Noise was repeatedly reconceptualized through the Industrial Revolution and the growth of urban centers, and noise continues to mean very different things for audio engineers, city and country residents, and avant-garde composers; for animals, birds, and insects; and for recording machines and networks of transmission. In their attempts to reanimate the past, historians have devised methodologies for excavating echoes that are never fully retrievable, piecing together traces from decontextualized sound recordings or, more commonly, working in silent archives of textual description. Far from being constructed against noises, echoes, and silences, the domain of sound is constituted by them.

The entries in this book draw on an enormous variety of approaches to the study of sound, each of which carries its own conceptual genealogy. But their referential fields are not self-contained, and each keyword links to the others in ways that disrupt linear histories of inquiry. Identifying a keyword such as noise does not mean that there is something discrete out there in the world that is containable within the term itself, or that it could be conceived as a category without reference to its opposites (i.e., silence, music, order, meaning). In illuminating specific keywords, then, our intention is not to produce a centralized frame of reference or a canonical list of conceptual terms. Instead, we elucidate the philosophical debates and core problems in the historical development of studies of sound, both during and prior to their reconfiguration under the banner of sound studies.

Words for sound can also interanimate one another. In positioning two keywords with such radically different legacies as transduction and acoustemology into a relationship of complementarity, the conceptual whole becomes greater than the sum of its referential parts. Proceeding through a social critique of science and technology, Stefan Helmreich wonders if the utility of transduction as the material transformation of energy reaches a limit in the sonic ecologies of the rainforest, where Steven Feld developed his theory of acoustemology, a phenomenological approach to sound as a way of knowing. And yet virtually every aspect of Feld's research required processes of transduction—from the listening practices adopted by the Kaluli to navigate the soundscape of birds and waterfalls to the microphones used to capture those sounds for the recording *Voices of the Rainforest*, to the headphones and loudspeakers that allow a distant listener to access and interpret representations of this world of sound. In juxtaposing two very different keywords, our hope is that the reader will not only recognize them each as constituent elements of sound studies but also reconsider how the integration of such discrepancies and overlaps might allow for the emergence of new concepts of sound.

Following from this logic, we do not include a separate entry for "sound." Instead, this über-keyword emerges as a semiotic web, woven by the complementarities and tensions of its entanglements in different intellectual histories. Sound has been conceptualized as a material unit of scientific measurement subject to experimentation and manipulation as acoustic data. Sound can also be conceived through its resonance in space as a nonsemantic, nonexpressive environmental context. On the other hand sound is analyzed as a purely semantic object of language that distinguishes humans from other animals, and then again as the perceptual ground for subjectivities formed through feeling, embodiment, and the reception of listening. The central reference point of sound binds together these disparate approaches, even as they break its meanings down and partition its effects into different subareas. But sound studies cannot become an interdisciplinary field by insisting on a holistic object that can hold together across these historical gaps and ruptures. Instead, scholars can expand sound studies by knowing and saying more about what we mean when we reference sound, and becoming more reflexive about how its meanings are positioned within a range of interpretations.

As editors, our own perspective derives in part from our affiliations with music and anthropology. The differences between these approaches are instructive for considering their interventions in sound studies: the former represents a legacy of historical systems of sonic production and analysis, and the latter an emergent program of social constructivism that reframes sound as an object of culture and human agency. There are, of course, points of overlap and intersection between these and many other disciplines, yet each has developed unique lines of inquiry in the development of sound studies.

Historically, music has stood as the most distinct object in studies of sound, partly because it elicits a heightened attention to sound and a widespread recognition of its characteristics, and partly because it represents a robust and established literature about sound, touching on its creative organization and social valuation. Along with speech, the study of music subsumed the study of sound until the Scientific Revolution, resulting in the first attempts to scientize sound in relation to the "harmony of the spheres," to entextualize sound as graphical notation, and to philosophize sound as an aesthetic art form. Having congealed over centuries, the thematic frames of music studies—style and repertoire, aesthetic appreciation and biography, along with the proprietary tools used to formally analyze musical texts—have been productively questioned in sound studies. For example, recent work by David Suisman and Susan Strasser (2009), Mark Katz (2010), Jonathan Sterne (2012), and others has foregrounded the technological production and social consumption of music, revealing how these processes of mediation have conditioned reception, aurality, and the creative agency of listening. Collections edited by Georgina Born (2013), Michael Bull (2013), and Sumanth Gopinath and Jason Stanyek (2014) demonstrate how music in spatial environments is subject to interpretations that extend far beyond music as it has been socially constructed as an autonomous art form. As another indicator, the Special Interest Group for Sound Studies formed within the Society for Ethnomusicology in 2009 to represent an increasing interest in sound and aurality.

But if sound studies has presented specific challenges to the field of music studies and offered productive paths forward, the repositioning of "music" within the domain of "sound" has sometimes minimized or obscured the vastly different histories of these terminological concepts. Music studies predates sound studies by two millennia yet maintains an amorphous presence in the new order. The more we follow the trail of sound studies, the more often we bump into things that had always been called music, walking like a ghost through the gleaming hallways of the house that sound built. "Sound" often denotes acoustic phenomena and aspects of production and reception that register outside the realm of "music" or displace its objects and cultural histories into an apparently broader rubric. But does the term "sound" always accurately frame the particularities of soundscapes, media circulations, techniques of listening and epistemologies of aurality, even when the practices in question are widely recognized as musical and the sounds consistently heard and described as music? The generalizability of sound, in its most imprecise uses, can sidestep the effects of institutional histories and the structuring influence of entrenched debates. While we are not endorsing doctrinaire approaches, the risk of ignoring the historical particularity of sonic categories is the misrecognition of sound's specific cultural formations.

In anthropology, the deeply coconstitutive relationship of sound and culture has long been apprehended—from Franz Boas's pioneering linguistic study of "sound-blindness" (1889) to the homology of myth and music that runs throughout Claude Levi-Strauss's *The Raw and the Cooked* (1973)—but not recognized as a distinct subject of study until the end of the twentieth century. Feld first described his work as an "anthropology of sound" in the 1980s through his fieldwork in the Bosavi rainforest, which launched and helped organize the field around methodologies that bring the phenomenological and environmental emplacements of sounding and listening into ethnographic research (Feld 1996, 2012 [1982]). Studies of language and voice, space and place, the body and the senses, music and expressive culture, and other topics now consistently put sound at the center of analysis. This turn is further reflected in recent institutional projects, including a critical overview in the *Annual Review of Anthropology* (Samuels et al. 2010), a pair of issues dedicated to sound in *Anthropology News* (vol. 51, issues

9 and 10), and the establishment of a Music and Sound Interest Group in the American Anthropological Association in 2009.

Anthropology's signal contribution is the application of ethnographic methodologies and theories in everyday experiences of sound and listening. Ethnography offers sound studies an ear into the expressive, embodied, and participatory relationships with sound as it unfolds into powerful articulations of particular selves, publics, and transcultural identities (Erlmann 2004). Fieldwork in multitrack recording studios, for example, has shown how technologies of sound production can reveal conflicting language ideologies among musicians and engineers (Porcello 2004), stage a sonic "Nativeness" in powwow recordings (Scales 2012), or represent "the sound of Africa" as a transformative mix of different "tracks" of cultural mediation (Meintjes 2003). Ethnographies have also begun to develop sound studies' potential to address comparative global perspectives of cultural difference. Contributors to this book bring an anthropological concern with social constructions of power and agency to bear on playback singers in Indian popular cinema, Islamic listening publics, Aboriginal radio broadcasters, and day laborers making noise in an Osakan tent city.

But despite the interdisciplinary breadth of sound studies, the field as a whole has remained deeply committed to Western intellectual lineages and histories. As one example, of the dozens of books about sound published by MIT Press—a leader in science and technology studies, philosophies of aesthetics, and cognition—none is principally invested in non-Western perspectives or subjects. Sound studies has often reinforced Western ideals of a normative subject, placed within a common context of hearing and listening. Presumptions of universality have also led scholars to treat sounds as stable objects that have predictable, often technologically determined, effects on a generalized perceptual consciousness, which might even be reduced to an entire "human condition." This bias is detectable in the work of sound studies' de facto founder, R. Murray Schafer (1977), who did not explicitly recognize the constitutive differences that participate in the "soundscape" as a multivalent field of sounds with divergent social identities, individual creativities and affordances, biodiversities and differing abilities.

However, increasing attention to sound in cultural studies, communication, literary criticism, and media studies has deepened understandings of the role sound plays in formations of social difference. A recent edition of *differences: A Journal of Feminist Cultural Studies* collected multiple perspectives on the poetics of sonic identity, as mediated through literature, film, and audio technologies, with the intention of questioning "(sonic) objectivity itself" (Chow and Steintrager 2011: 2). Also in 2011, *American Quarterly* divided the issue "Sound Clash: Listening to American Studies" (Keeling and Kun 2011) into three subsections relating to various forms of difference ("Sound Technologies and Subjectivities," "Sounding Race, Ethnicity, and Gender," and "Sound, Citizenship, and the Public Sphere"). The *Social Text* issue "The Politics of Recorded Sound" (Stadler 2010) gathered essays on topics ranging from ethnographic recordings of Nuyorican communities to audio reenactments of lynchings. Several contributors to these texts also participate in this book, where they and others address power relations that have subtended the possibilities of hearing and voicing, stigmatized disability, and subjugated different auralities.

While many keyword entries productively reference sonic identities linked to socially constructed categories of gender, race, ethnicity, religion, disability, citizenship, and personhood, our project does not explicitly foreground these modalities of social difference. Rather, in curating a conceptual lexicon for a particular field, we have kept sound at the center of analysis, arriving at other points from the terminologies of sound, and not the reverse. While we hope *Keywords in Sound* will become a critical reference for sound studies, it is not an encyclopedia that represents every sector of sound studies or includes every approach to the study of sound. Important and growing areas of sound research—such as archaeoacoustics, ecomusicology, and the rise of multinaturalism through interspecies studies of sound—are only gestured to at points. And while the physical sciences feature prominently in many of the keyword entries as points of cultural and historical inquiry, the fields of cognition, psychology, and brain science receive scant mention. No doubt this is partly due to the difficulty of bridging gaps between the physical and social sciences, but it is also a result of our admitted skepticism toward studies that assume a universal human subject without a full accounting of social, cultural, and historical context.

It goes without saying that many possible keywords are absent for more pragmatic reasons. Some, such as media, are folded into other terms (e.g. phonography) or addressed from multiple perspectives by individual contributors across different keyword entries. Others, such as senses, would have ideally been included and were not only because of practical limitations. We were not able to suitably address sound art, a field that has exploded in creative activity of every kind, from an efflorescence of theoretical and historical writing to the establishment of pedagogy in art schools such as the Department of Sound at the Art Institute of Chicago and to the sound installations that have become a norm at underground galleries and major museums, including MoMA and the Whitney.[3] Other possibilities will undoubtedly arise in "retuning the world" of sound studies; we hope that this project will play a generative role in the ongoing recognition of its conceptual categories.

Broadly speaking, our criteria for inclusion gave less weight to the specific words themselves than to their intellectual connections with the contributors who wrote about them. We invited each of the authors to take up a key concept that could serve as a nexus for multiple reference points in critical discourse. Going beyond summaries of existing thought, we encouraged them to push further in creative elaborations of their keywords from within their own work—often a focused analytical example, drawn from ethnographic, historical, or philosophical research that has the potential to challenge existing discourses and suggest possibilities for further inquiry.

Any intellectual engagement with sound will necessarily reshape its material significances and extend its metaphorical lives in particular ways. Just as Williams's writings about culture informed the critiques of "writing culture" that followed his publication, we submit these keywords as reflexive considerations of past writings about sound, as elaborations on the broad conceptualizations of sound in everyday life, and as entry points for future debate.

Notes

We thank all twenty authors for their patience in the back-and-forth (and sometimes round-and-round) loops of feedback in the editorial process. We also thank Ken Wissoker and the team at Duke University Press, as well as the anonymous reviewers who gave suggestions on the progress of the book. Finally, thanks to Peter Bloom, Steven Feld, and Jonathan Sterne for their helpful advice on earlier versions of this introduction.

1. Williams also laid the groundwork for more recent reference works that similarly inspired us, including *Words in Motion*, edited by Carol Gluck and Anna Tsing (2009), *Critical Terms for Media Studies*, edited by W. J. T. Mitchell and Mark Hansen (2010), and *Key Terms in Language and Culture*, edited by Alessandro Duranti (2001), along with Jean-Francois

Augoyarde's and Henry Torge's *Sonic Experience: A Guide to Everyday Sounds* (2006), which describes the experiential conditions and phenomenological effects of sound.

2. The chapters of this book are referred to throughout as "entries," and are cross-referenced throughout the book by title.

3. Recent studies of sound art include Cox and Warner (2004), Demers (2010), Kahn (1999, 2013), Kelley (2011), Kim-Cohen (2009), LaBelle (2006), Licht (2007), Lucier (2012), Rodgers (2010), and Voeglin (2010).

References

Augoyarde, Jean-Francois, and Henry Torge, eds. 2006. *Sonic Experience: A Guide to Everyday Sounds*. Montreal: McGill-Queens University Press.

Boas, Franz. 1889. "On Alternating Sounds." *American Anthropologist* 2(1): 47–54.

Born, Georgina, ed. 2013. *Music, Sound, and Space: Transformations of Public and Private Experience*. Cambridge: Cambridge University Press.

Bull, Michael, ed. 2013. *Sound Studies*. London: Routledge.

Chow, Rey, and James Steintrager, eds. "The Sense of Sound." Special issue, *differences* 22(2–3).

Cox, Christopher, and Daniel Warner, ed. 2004. *Audio Culture: Readings in Modern Music*. New York: Continuum.

Demers, Joanna. 2010. *Listening through the Noise: The Aesthetics of Experimental Electronic Music*. New York: Oxford University Press.

Duranti, Alessandro. 2001. *Key Terms in Language and Culture*. London: Wiley-Blackwell.

Erlmann, Veit. 2004. "But What of the Ethnographic Ear? Anthropology, Sound, and the Senses." In *Hearing Cultures: Essays on Sound, Listening and Modernity*, ed. Veit Erlmann, pp. 1–20. Oxford: Berg.

Feld, Steven. 1996. "Waterfalls of Song: An Acoustemology of Place Resounding in Bosavi, Papua New Guinea." In *Senses of Place*, ed. Steven Feld and Keith Basso, 91–136. Santa Fe: School of American Research Press.

Feld, Steven. 2012 [1982]. *Sound and Sentiment: Birds, Weeping, Poetics, and Song in Kaluli Expression*. 3rd ed. Durham: Duke University Press.

Gluck, Carol, and Anna Lowenhaupt Tsing, eds. 2009. *Words in Motion: Toward a Global Lexicon*. Durham: Duke University Press.

Gopinath, Sumanth, and Jason Stanyek, eds. 2014. *The Oxford Handbook of Mobile Music Studies*. Vols. 1 and 2. Oxford: Oxford University Press.

Kahn, Douglas. 2013. *Earth Sound, Earth Signal: Energies and Earth Magnitude in the Arts*. Berkeley: University of California Press.

Kahn, Douglas. 1999. *Noise Water Meat: A History of Sound in the Arts*. Cambridge, MA: MIT Press.

Katz, Mark. 2010. *Capturing Sound: How Technology Has Changed Music*. Rev. 2nd ed. Berkeley: University of California Press.

Keeling, Kara, and John Kun. 2011. "Sound Clash: Listening to American Studies." Special issue, *American Quarterly* 63(3).

Kelley, Caleb. 2009. *Cracked Media: The Sound of Malfunction*. Cambridge, MA: MIT Press.

Kim-Cohen, Seth. 2009. *In the Blink of an Ear: Toward a Non-cochlear Sonic Art*. New York: Continuum.

Labelle, Brandon. 2006. *Background Noise: Perspectives on Sound Art*. New York: Continuum.

Lakoff, George, and Mark Johnson. 1980. *Metaphors We Live By*. Chicago: University of Chicago Press.

Levi-Strauss, Claude. 1973. *The Raw and the Cooked*. Trans. John and Doreen Weightman. London: Jonathan Cape.

Licht, Alan. 2007. *Sound Art: Beyond Music, between Categories*. New York: Rizzoli.

Lucier, Alvin. 2012. *Music 109: Notes on Experimental Music*. Middletown: Wesleyan University Press.

Meintjes, Louise. *Sound of Africa!: Making Music Zulu in a South African Studio*. Durham: Duke University Press. 2003.

Mitchell, W. J. T., and Mark B. N. Hansen, eds. 2010. *Critical Terms for Media Studies*. Chicago: University of Chicago Press.

Pinch, Trevor, and Karin Bijsterveld, eds. 2011. *Oxford Handbook for Sound Studies*. New York: Oxford University Press.

Porcello, Thomas. 2004. "Speaking of Sound: Language and the Professionalization of Sound-Recording Engineers." *Social Studies of Science* 34: 733–758.

Rodgers, Tara. 2010. *Pink Noises: Women on Electronic Music and Sound*. Durham: Duke University Press.

Samuels, David, Louise Meintjes, Ana María Ochoa, and Thomas Porcello. 2010. "Soundscapes: Toward a Sounded Anthropology." *Annual Review of Anthropology* 39: 329–345.

Scales, Christopher A. 2012. *Recording Culture: Powwow Music and the Aboriginal Recording Industry on the Northern Plains*. Durham: Duke University Press.

Schafer, R. Murray. 1977. *The Tuning of the World*. New York: Knopf.

Stadler, Gustavus, ed. 2010. "The Politics of Recorded Sound." Special issue, *Social Text* 102.

Sterne, Jonathan. 2012. *MP3: The Meaning of a Format*. Durham: Duke University Press.

Suisman, David, and Susan Strasser, eds. 2009. *Sound in the Age of Mechanical Reproduction*. Philadelphia: University of Pennsylvania Press.

Voegelin, Salome. 2010. *Listening to Noise and Silence: Towards a Philosophy of Sound Art*. New York: Continuum.

Williams, Raymond. 1985. *Keywords: A Vocabulary of Culture and Society*, Rev. 2nd ed. New York: Oxford University Press.

[I] Steven Feld

acoustemology

Acoustemology conjoins "acoustics" and "epistemology" to theorize sound as a way of knowing. In doing so it inquires into what is knowable, and how it becomes known, through sounding and listening. Acoustemology begins with acoustics to ask how the dynamism of sound's physical energy indexes its social immediacy. It asks how the physicality of sound is so instantly and forcefully present to experience and experiencers, to interpreters and interpretations. Answers to such questions do not necessarily engage acoustics on the formal scientific plane that investigates the physical components of sound's materiality (Kinsler et al. 1999). Rather, acoustemology engages acoustics at the plane of the audible—akoustos—to inquire into sounding as simultaneously social and material, an experiential nexus of sonic sensation.

Acoustemology joins acoustics to epistemology to investigate sounding and listening as a knowing-in-action: a knowing-with and knowing-through the audible. Acoustemology thus does not invoke epistemology in the formal sense of an inquiry into metaphysical or transcendental assumptions surrounding claims to "truth" ("epistemology with a capital E," in the phrasing of Richard Rorty, 1981). Rather it engages the relationality of knowledge production, as what John Dewey called contextual and experiential knowing (Dewey and Bentley 1949).

I coined the term "acoustemology" in 1992 to situate the social study of sound within a key question driving contemporary social theory. Namely, is the world constituted by multiple essences, by primal substances with post facto categorical names like "human," "animal," "plant," "material," or "technology?" Or is it constituted relationally, by the acknowledgment of conjunctions, disjunctions, and entanglements among all copresent and historically accumulated forms? It was the latter answer that compelled a theorization of sounding and listening aligned with relational ontology; the conceptual term for the position that substantive existence never operates anterior to relationality.

Relational ontology can be traced across a number of discourses linking philosophy, sociology, and anthropology. Phrasings associated with both Ernst Cassirer (1957) and Alfred Schütz (1967) argue that "actors plus locations" are produced by "relations-in-action." Cassirer's formal antisubstantialism argued that being was never independent of relating. Schütz's lifeworld philosophy focused on the character of sharing time and space with consociates, compared to sharing or not sharing time with contemporaries and predecessors. Relationality as "inter-action" and "trans-action" appears in John Dewey's writings with the hyphen for emphasis on both across-ness and between-ness (Dewey 1960). Without the hyphen, these terms became sociological keywords anew in the 1960s and 1970s, always in the service of arguing against the reduction of agency to a set list of entities or essences (Goffman 1967; Emirbayer 1997).

British social anthropology, in its formative period, focused on the study of "relations of relations" (Kuper 1996). This idea echoed into new frontiers with the conjunction of the terms "social" and "ecology," "ecology" and "mind," and "cybernetic" and "epistemology" in the writings of Gregory Bateson (2000 [1972]). The notion that actors plus relationships shape networks both within and across species or materialities is part of how more contemporary theorists—such as Donna Haraway (2003), Marilyn Strathern (2005), and Bruno Latour (2005)—have schematized relationality's critical logic. These themes are likewise present in contemporary writings on interspecies and nature/culture relations by Philippe Descola (2013) and Eduardo Viveiros de Castro (2000), as well as in posthumanist theories refiguring human relational presence and action with all technological, animal, and environmental others (Wolfe 2009).

Acoustemology's logical point of connection to a relational ontology framework is here: existential relationality, a connectedness of being, is built on the between-ness of experience. Acoustemology, as relational ontology, thus takes sound and sounding as "situational" (Haraway 1988) among "related subjects" (Bird-David 1999); it explores the "mutual" (Buber 1923) and "ecological" (Bateson 1972) space of sonic knowing as "polyphonic," "dialogical," and "unfinalizable" (Bakhtin 1981, 1984). Knowing through relations insists that one does not simply "acquire" knowledge but, rather, that one knows through an ongoing cumulative and interactive process of participation and reflection. This is so whether knowledge is shaped by direct perception, memory, deduction, transmission, or problem solving. Perhaps this is why relational epistemology is also invoked regularly as a cornerstone of decolonized indigenous methodologies (Chilasa 2012).

Beyond an alignment with relational ontology, the acoustemology coinage was also meant to refine and expand what I had called, for the previous twenty years, the anthropology of sound. This approach had emerged in critical response to perceived limitations of the dominant anthropology of music paradigms of the 1960s and 1970s: Alan Merriam's theorization of "music in culture" (1964) and John Blacking's theorization of "humanly organized sound" (1973). The anthropology of sound idea advocated for an expanded terrain when engaging global musical diversity. That expansion acknowledged the critical importance of language, poetics, and voice; of species beyond the human; of acoustic environments; and of technological mediation and circulation.

While the idea of an anthropology of sound was meant to help decolonize ethnomusicology's disciplinary paradigms, the presence of "anthropology" still made it too human-centric; the prepositional "of" marked too much distance and separation, and the nominal "sound" seemingly made it more about propagation than perception, more about structure than process. It was a case of "the master's tools will never dismantle the master's house" (Lorde 1984). Other intellectual equipment was needed to address the sounding worlds of indigenous and emergent global geographies of difference across the divides of species and materials. For this reason, the relational ontology background shaped acoustemology as a way to inquire into knowing in and through sounding, with particular care to the reflexive feedback of sounding and listening. The kind of knowing that acoustemology tracks in and through sound and sounding is always experiential, contextual, fallible, changeable, contingent, emergent, opportune, subjective, constructed, selective.

Acoustemology writes with but against "acoustic ecology" (Schafer 1977). It is neither a measurement system for acoustic niche dynamics nor a study of sound as an "indicator" of how humans live in environments. R. Murray Schafer's World Soundscape Project associated acoustic ecology with activities like evaluating sound environments for their high or low fidelity according to volume or density, and cataloging place-based sounds and soundmaking objects through physical space and historical time. Acoustemological approaches, while equally concerned with place-based space-time dynamics, concentrate on relational listening histories—on methods of listening to histories of listening—always with an ear to agency and positionalities. Unlike acoustic ecology, acoustemology is about the experience and agency of listening histories, understood as relational and contingent, situated and reflexive.

Acoustemology likewise writes with but against "soundscape," the key legacy term associated with Schafer and particularly his debt to the theories of Marshall McLuhan (Kelman 2010). Against "soundscapes," acoustemology refuses to sonically analogize or appropriate "landscape," with all its physical distance from agency and perception. Likewise it refuses to replace visualist ocularcentrism with sonocentrism as any sort of determining force of essentialist sensory master plans. Acoustemology joins critiques and alternatives offered by Tim Ingold (2007) and Stefan Helmreich (2010) in recent essays deconstructing "soundscape." Along with their proposals, acoustemology favors inquiry that centralizes situated listening in engagements with place and space-time. Acoustemology prioritizes histories of listening and attunement through the relational practices of listening and sounding and their reflexive productions of feedback.

Acoustemology, then, is grounded in the basic assumption that life is shared with others-in-relation, with numerous sources of action (*actant* in Bruno Latour's terminology; 2005) that are variously human, nonhuman, living, nonliving, organic, or technological. This relationality is both a routine condition of dwelling and one that produces consciousness of modes of acoustic attending, of ways of listening for and resounding to presence. "Companion species rest on contingent foundations," Donna Haraway tells us (2003: 7). Making otherness into "significant" forms of otherness is key here. Acoustemology figures in stories of sounding as heterogeneous contingent relating; stories of sounding as cohabiting; stories where sound figures the ground of difference—radical or otherwise—and what it means to attend and attune; to live with listening to that.

Acoustemology did not arrive conceptually as a result of pure theory or from direct abstraction. Its emergence was deeply stimulated by my ethnographic studies of the sociality of sound in the Bosavi rainforest region of Papua New Guinea. Indeed, the relational linkage of "significant" to "otherness" was in many ways the key challenge when I went to Papua New Guinea for the first time in 1976 and set in motion the twenty-five years of research that recast an anthropology of sound into acoustemology.

I initially imagined that Bosavi songs were an acoustic adaptation to a rainforest environment. I had no idea that "adaptation" was an inadequate framework for understanding relationality in a forest of plurality. And I had no idea that I would need an equal amount of skill in ornithology and natural history to add to my training in music, sound recording, and linguistics. I had no idea that Bosavi songs would be vocalized mappings of the rainforest, that they were sung from a bird's point of view, and that I would have to understand poetics as flight paths through forest waterways; that is, from a bodily perspective rather different from perceiving with feet on the ground. And I had no idea that Bosavi women's funerary weeping turned into song and that men's ceremonial song turned into weeping: in other words, that apprehending Bosavi soundmaking would require a gendered psychology of emotion in addition to a dialogic approach to vocality.

So there were many surprises, and after more than fifteen years of them I felt that I had exhausted the conceptual repertoire of an anthropology of sound, particularly those approaches deriving from theoretical linguistics, semiotics, communications, and more formal theorizations in symbolic anthropology. This was when I realized the necessity to reground and revise all of my recording and writing work through a deeper engagement with the phenomenology of perception, body, place, and voice (Feld 2001, 2012 [1982]).

This realization became especially powerful for me in trying to develop the mental equipment to understand human/avian relationality in Bosavi, with all that implied about transformative interplays of nature/culture, and life/death. To Bosavi ears and eyes, birds are not just "birds" in the sense of totalized avian beings. They are *ane mama*, meaning "gone reflections" or "gone reverberations." Birds are absences turned into presence, and a presence that always makes absence audible and visible. Birds are what humans become by achieving death.

Given this transformative potency, it is not surprising that bird sounds are understood not just as audible communications that tell time, season, environmental conditions, forest height and depth but also as communications from dead to living, as materializations reflecting absence in and through reverberation. Bird sounds are the voice of memory and the resonance of ancestry. Bosavi people transform the acoustic materials of bird soundmaking—their intervals, sound shapes, timbres, and rhythms—into weeping and song. In the process, they create a poetry that imagines how birds feel and speak as absented presences and present absences. They become like birds by sounding the emotion of absence into newborn presence. Human weeping turns into song, and song turns into crying because sound always becomes and embodies sentiment; sonic materiality is the transformed reverberation of emotional depth. To paraphrase Donna Haraway (riffing on Claude Lévi-Strauss), birds here are more than "good to think"; they are good to live with, as a companion species. For Bosavi people, birds are the other that one becomes, as one becomes another.

What can it mean that Bosavi ears and voices sensuously absorb and reverberate by vocalizing daily with, to, and about birds in the rain-soaked and sun-dried *longue durée* of rainforest cohabitation? This question led me to the idea that listening to the rainforest as a coinhabited world of plural sounding and knowing presences was, most deeply, a listening to histories of listening. And it shaped the dialogic methodology of recording and composing the CDs *Voices of the Rainforest* and *Rainforest Soundwalks* (Feld 2011a, b), which transformed an anthropology of sound into an anthropology in sound (Feld 1996).

After years of privileging symbolic and semiotic representations of modes of knowing (particularly ritual expression), acoustemology pushed me to think more through recording and playback, to conjoin practice with experiment. I returned to the basic questions that had intrigued me from my earliest times in Bosavi. How to hear through the trees? How to hear the relationship of forest height to depth? Where is sound located when you can't see more than three feet ahead? Why does looking up into the forest simply take one's senses into the impenetrable density of the canopy? How to inquire into the sounding-as and sounding-through knowing that shaped the mundane everyday world of rainforest emplacement: the everyday world that in turn shaped the poesis of song maps, and of vocalities linking local singers with the soundings of birds, insects, and water?

Passing by the village longhouse as I headed to the forest to listen and record, I'd invariably encounter groups of children who would join and guide my forest walks. We'd play a simple game. I'd attach a parabolic microphone to my recorder and enclose my ears in isolating headphones. Standing together in the forest, I'd point the parabola in the direction of unseeable forest birds. That would be the signal for the children to jump up, take my forearm, readjust its angle, and anchor it. Sure enough, as they made their move, a bird was in all-of-a-sudden sharp acoustic focus in my headphones. Then the kids would burst out laughing, meaning it was time for me to come up with something more challenging.

This was a daily lesson in listening as habitus, a forceful demonstration of routinized, emplaced hearing as an embodied mastery of locality. It is only a matter of seconds before a twelve-year-old Bosavi kid can identify a bird by sound, describe its location in the forest density, and tell a good bit more about the location of its food, nests, and partners. How does this knowledge happen? The lesson was bodily, powerful, and gripping. Acoustically coinhabiting the rainforest ecosystem, Bosavi life is relationally built through all-species listening as co-living, as intertwined presence. Could this be the acoustemological foundation of how and why Bosavi songs are machines for cohabitation, or, in today's more radical philosophical parlance, interspecies cosmopolitanism (Mendieta 2012)?

In addition to my younger teachers, some exceptional Bosavi adults also guided my introspection into such questions. One was Yubi (Feld 2012: 44–85). For years, every encounter with him made me wonder, why were Bosavi's most prolific composers also its most accomplished ornithologists? Yubi taught me to hear acoustic knowing as coaesthetic recognition. He taught me how each natural historical detail had symbolic value-added. He taught me how knowing the world through sound was inseparable from living in the world sonically and musically.

Ulahi was another guide to how songs sung in a bird's voice linked the living and dead, present and past, human and avian, ground and treetops, village and forest. She explained that songs don't sing the world as experienced by travel on foot but move through watercourses, following the flight paths of forest birds (Feld 1996). Ulahi taught me how water moves through land as voice moves through the body. She taught me how songs are the collective and connective flow of individual lives and community histories. Just one creek and its flow from her local home and to the gardens and land beyond mapped dozens of poeticized names of birds, plants, shrubs, trees, sounds, intersecting waters, and all of the activities that magnetize them to the biographies of lives and spirits in her local social world.

Over twenty-five years, with the help of Yubi, Ulahi, and many other singers, I recorded, transcribed, and translated about one thousand Bosavi bird-voiced forest path songs. They contain almost seven thousand lexical descriptors, names of places, of flora, fauna, and topography as well as sensuous phonaesthetic evocations of light, wind, motion, and sound qualities. These songs constitute a poetic cartography of the forest, mapping the layered biographies of social relationships within and across communities. The chronotopic historicity of sounding these songs is thus inseparable from the environmental consciousness they have produced. This is why, as knowledge productions—as listenings to histories of listenings—Bosavi songs are an archive of ecological and aesthetic coevolution.

This realization takes me back to Maurice Merleau-Ponty's sensory phenomenology, which posits perception as the relationality of bodies dimensional to a milieu (1968). *Dabuwɔ?* ("Did you hear *that?*") Could it be that when Bosavi people utter just this one word they are acknowledging audibility and perceptibility as simultaneously materializing past, present, and future social relations? Could they, in that sparse gesture, be theorizing that every sound is equally immediate to human experience and to the perceptual faculties of others, of perceivers who may even be absent, nonhuman, or dead?

For Donna Haraway, companion species tell "a story of co-habitation, co-evolution, and embodied cross-species sociality" (2003: 4–5). In the context of her work with dogs she asks: "how might an ethics and politics committed to the flourishing of significant otherness be learned from taking dog-human relationships seriously?" (3) Bosavi acoustemology likewise asks what's to be learned from taking seriously the sonic relationality of human voices to the sounding otherness of presences and subjectivities like water, birds, and insects. It asks what it means to acoustically participate in a rainforest world understood as plural (Brunois 2008). It asks if what are more typically theorized as subject-object relations are in fact more deeply known, experienced, imagined, enacted, and embodied as subject-subject relations. It asks how Bosavi life is a being-in-the-world-with numerous "wild" or "non-domesticated" others, others who may be sources of food, trouble, or danger, others whose soundings may readily announce caution or nervous copresence, as well as something like Haraway's "cross-species sociality."

This was where and how the conceptual term "acoustemology" was born: in years of listening to how sounding-as- and sounding-through-knowing is an audible archive of long-lived relational attunements and antagonisms that have come to be naturalized as place and voice.

References

Bakhtin, M. M. 1981. *The Dialogic Imagination*. Ed. Michael Holquist and translated by Caryl Emerson and Michael Holquist. Austin: University of Texas Press.

Bakhtin, M. M. 1984. *Problems of Dostoevsky's Poetics*. Edited and translated by Caryl Emerson. Minneapolis: University of Minnesota Press.

Bateson, Gregory. 2000 [1972]. *Steps to An Ecology of Mind*. With a new foreword by Mary Catherine Bateson. Chicago: University of Chicago Press.

Bird-David, Nurit. 1999. " 'Animism' Revisited: Personhood, Environment, and Relational Epistemology." *Current Anthropology* 40: S67–S91.

Blacking, John. 1973. *How Musical Is Man?* Seattle: University of Washington Press.

Brunois, Florence. 2008. *Le jardin du casoar, la forêt des Kasua: Epistémologie des savoir-être et savoir-faire écologiques, Papouasie-Nouvelle-Guinée*. Paris: Maison des Sciences de l'Homme.

Buber, Martin. 1923. *I and Thou*. New York: Scribner.

Cassirer, Ernst. 1957. *The Philosophy of Symbolic Forms*. Vol. 3. *The Phenomenology of Knowledge*. Trans. Ralph Manheim. New Haven: Yale University Press.

Chilasa, Bagele. 2012. *Indigenous Research Methodologies*. New York: Sage.

Descola, Philippe. 2013. *Beyond Nature and Culture*. Trans. Janet Lloyd. Chicago: University of Chicago Press.

Dewey, John. 1960. *On Experience, Nature and Freedom*. New York: Bobbs Merrill.

Dewey, John, and Arthur Bentley. 1949. *Knowing and the Known*. Boston: Beacon Press.

Emirbayer, Mustafa. 1997. "Manifesto for a Relational Sociology." *American Journal of Sociology* 103 (2): 281–317.

Feld, Steven. 1994. "From Ethnomusicology to Echo-muse-ecology: Re-reading R. Murray Schafer in the Papua New Guinea Rainforest." *Soundscape Newsletter* 8: 9–13.

Feld, Steven. 1996. "Waterfalls of Song: An Acoustemology of Place Resounding in Bosavi, Papua New Guinea." In *Senses of Place*, ed. Steven Feld and Keith Basso, 91–135. Santa Fe: School of American Research Press.

Feld, Steven. 2001. *Bosavi: Rainforest Music from Papua New Guinea*. Washington, DC: Smithsonian Folkways Recordings. CD and booklet.

Feld, Steven. 2011a [2001]. *Rainforest Soundwalks*. CD. Santa Fe: Voxlox.

Feld, Steven. 2011b [1991]. *Voices of the Rainforest*. CD. Washington, DC: Smithsonian Folkways Recordings.

Feld, Steven. 2012 [1982]. *Sound and Sentiment: Birds, Weeping, Poetics, and Song in Kaluli Expression*. 3rd ed. Durham: Duke University Press.

Goffman, Erving. 1967. *Interaction Ritual: Studies in Face to Face Behavior*. New York: Anchor Books.

Haraway, Donna. 1988. "Situated Knowledges: The Science Question in Feminism and the Privilege of Partial Perspective." *Feminist Studies* 14(3): 575–599.

Haraway, Donna. 2003. *The Companion Species Manifesto: Dogs, People, and Significant Otherness*. Chicago: Prickly Paradigm.

Helmreich, Stefan. 2010. "Listening against Soundscapes." *Anthropology News* 51(9): 10.

Ingold, Tim. 2007. "Against Soundscape." In *Autumn Leaves: Sound and the Environment in Artistic Practice*, ed. Angus Carlyle, 10–13. Paris: Double Entendre.

Kelman, Ari Y. 2010. "Rethinking the Soundscape: A Critical Genealogy of a Key Term in Sound Studies." *The Senses and Society* 5(2): 212–234.

Kinsler, Lawrence E., Austin R. Frey, Alan B. Coppens, and James V. Sanders. 1999. *Fundamentals of Acoustics*. 4th ed. New York: Wiley.

Kuper, Adam. 1996. *Anthropology and Anthropologists: The Modern British School*. 3rd ed. New York: Routledge.

Latour, Bruno. 2005. *Reassembling the Social: An Introduction to Actor–Network Theory*. Oxford: Oxford University Press.

Lorde, Audre. 1984. *Sister Outsider: Essays and Speeches*. New York: Crossing Press.

Mendieta, Eduardo. 2012. "Interspecies Cosmopolitanism." In *Routledge Handbook of Cosmopolitan Studies*, ed. Gerard Delanty, 276–288. New York: Routledge.

Merleau-Ponty, Maurice. 1968. *The Visible and the Invisible*. Trans. Alphonso Lingis. Evanston: Northwestern University Press.

Merriam, Alan P. 1964. *The Anthropology of Music*. Evanston: Northwestern University Press.

Rorty, Richard. 1981. *Philosophy and the Mirror of Nature*. Princeton: Princeton University Press.

Schafer, R. Murray. 1977. *The Tuning of the World*. New York: Knopf.

Shütz, Alfred. 1967. *The Phenomenology of the Social World*. Trans. George Walsh. Evanston: Northwestern University Press.

Strathern, Marilyn. 2005 [1991]. *Partial Connections*. 2nd ed. Lanham, MD: AltaMira Press.

Viveiros de Castro, Eduardo. 2000. "Cosmological Deixis and AmerIndian Perspectivism." *Journal of the Royal Anthropological Institute* (NS): 4: 469–488.

Wolfe, Cary. 2009. *What Is Posthumanism?* Minneapolis: University of Minnesota Press.

acoustics

An Irony of Definition

Acoustics conventionally designates the branch of physics concerned with sound. Like physics in general, acoustics is not simply a subject matter or body of knowledge. Just as "physics" is not synonymous with "the physical" (as in "the physical world"), "acoustics" is not synonymous with "the acoustical" (as in "acoustical phenomena"). Physics is probably best described rather as a *mode* of knowledge, a way of knowing about the world, one that brings into focus quantifiable aspects of matter, force, and motion. So we might say that acoustics, by extension, is a way of knowing about sound, one that brings into focus quantifiable aspects of matter, force, and motion involved with it.

But this intuitive distinction opens up onto a more surprising margin between acoustics and its nominal object. In a strange turn of historical events, it has become possible, perhaps even common, to define acoustics in almost completely nonaural terms. As one representative textbook has it, "acoustics as a science may be defined as the generation, transmission, and reception of energy as vibrational waves in matter"—a pithy yet broad formulation that says precisely nothing about sound-as-heard. Acoustics here is simply the physics of vibration, with hearing reduced to the bet-hedging "reception," which could just as easily refer to a microphone or recording device as to an ear. We read further that the form of energy in question involves "tensile force when a spring is stretched, the increase in pressure produced when a fluid is compressed, and the restoring force produced when a point on a stretched wire is displaced to its length." Sensory experience, finally, is adduced only as a special case (albeit a particularly well-known one) of such patterns of movement: "the most familiar acoustic phenomenon is that associated with the sensation of sound" (Kinsler et al. 2000: 1).

In short, acoustics has come to be understood in such a way that it both exceeds and falls short of sound. It exceeds it in the sense that the physical phenomena constituting heard sound appear to belong only to a particular species within the genus of "acoustics." And it falls short of it in the sense that the sonic arrives as a kind of belated, culminating step in the unfolding of the physical-acoustical field, a moment at which the energy of oscillating matter suddenly leaps into a new form, which is no longer just a figure of vibration but has become something beyond, apprehended via an altogether different modality—the aural. It is true that "acoustics" may be cajoled into a more immediately aural encounter through such specifications as "physiological acoustics" (the study of the bodily and nervous mechanisms enabling aural sensation), "psychoacoustics" (the concern with aural perception along parameters other than the corporeal), or "musical acoustics" (a preoccupation with the physical materials engaged in musical practices, often traditionally emphasizing certain beliefs concerning the "nature" of European harmonic materials). But none of these qualifications neutralizes the peculiar paradox that has come to attach itself to the root term. For all the implicit promise of an immediate encounter with "the real" borne by such enunciations as "this room has good acoustics"—let alone the tangentially related appeal to authenticity implicit in statements such as "I prefer acoustic instruments"—acoustical knowledge remains set slightly apart from the sonic. It is neither straightforwardly "about sound" in any phenomenologically purified sense nor "of sound" in the sense of involving a mode of knowledge that is itself "acoustical." This is not to deny that there might be other acoustical knowledges, only that such a notion would not name what we familiarly mean when we talk about acoustics.[1] The following discussion observes some of the historical circumstances that have contributed to the paradoxical separation of acoustics from the heard qualities of sound.

Early Modernity to Twentieth Century

The earliest uses of the English word "acoustics" coincided with Francis Bacon's watershed articulation of a new scientific method that would subsist in manipulating and interacting with the matter of the world, rather than primarily in calculation or speculation.[2] Particularly in contrast to the classical tradition of "harmonics," a legacy of numerological abstraction and cosmological ambition associated with the ancient Greek mystic Pythagoras, the nascent field of acoustics was situated within a relatively local economy of use values. For one writer in the Baconian tradition, "the *Excellency* and *Us[e]fulness of Acousticks*"—"this (yet very imperfect, though noble) Science"—would be proven in three achievements: (1) "*to make the least Sound* (by help of Instruments) *as loud as the greatest; a whisper to become as loud as the shot of a Canon*"; (2) "*to propagate any* (the least) *Sound to the greatest distance*"; and (3) "*that a Sound may be convey'd from one extreme to the other* (or from one distant place to another) *So as not to be heard in the middle*" (Marsh 1684: 487–488). In short, a preoccupation with pragmatic, communicative values—with emplacing and transmitting sound—set the agenda for the early modern discipline.

This mode of knowledge did not persist in quite the same form into the slightly later acoustics introduced by the French mathematician Joseph Sauveur around 1700. In his report for the Académie Royale des Sciences of that year, Sauveur coopted the umbrella notion of *acoustique* (while falsely claiming to coin it) but aligned it more directly than had his English predecessors with a concern that had already emerged as central to physicalist research in sound a century earlier: vibration (1984: 68–77). In the intervening generations, a redoubled and fastidious attention to the vibrational frequency of strings—and in particular to the messy relations between frequency and string tension, density, and other variables—had enabled a critical shift from the late Pythagoreanism of Renaissance music theory (e.g., Gioseffo Zarlino) to the "modern" physicalism characteristic of the early scientific revolution (e.g., Vincenzo Galilei; see Cohen 1984). With the rational perfections of ancient "harmonics" dismantled, it was left to Sauveur to initiate a crucial but often overlooked shift from what we might think of as a classical preoccupation with rationalization to a modern preoccupation with standardization. For example, he transformed the topic of acoustic "beats" (*battemens*) from its expected role in an account of the phenomenon of musical dissonance into a simple, translatable method for establishing a fixed pitch, which could be used in any location whatsoever without transporting some material standard of measure from one place to another.[3] Sauveur maintained that by carefully tuning any two organ pipes to a frequency ratio of 24:25 in such a way that they produced four beats per second, one could be reasonably sure of the frequency of the upper pipe:

Just as the tone of the Paris Opera may be determined in relation to a fixed Sound, one may be certain of doing it precisely in China. And it matters not at all whether the two pipes one uses for the beating experiment in China are of the same length, the same thickness, the same material as those in Paris. It suffices that, with the two pipes, whatever they are, one finds a sound that would make 100 vibrations per Second. This sound is always the same, independent of the Instruments that produce it, and its entire nature consists in the determinate number of vibrations per Second. (Sauveur 1984: 73)

This acoustics is no longer a matter of matching sound to number for the sake of sheer magical, metaphysical, or physical correspondence.[4] Nor is it immediately a matter of improving or extending the senses, or of either imagining or enacting the transmission of some particular sound several miles down the road, across the fields, or over the water. Rather, Sauveur began to envision transmitting the conditions for knowledge itself, leveraging a few basic elements of mechanical and acoustical know-how into a theoretical assemblage that would, in principle, transcend place. While he did not pursue this vision much further himself—and indeed, the conditions of political economy necessary for such a pursuit were not yet at hand—the underlying impulse toward what we might call the "disemplacement" of vibration through standardization would become increasingly manifest over the subsequent century and a half.

The link between vibration and standardization has emerged in some historiography as a running leitmotif. As post-Napoleonic Europe saw increasing cross-border trade, the push to ensure consistency in standards and measures drew interested parties from many fields spanning science and industry. It is perhaps unsurprising that it was a German silk industrialist, Johann Heinrich Scheibler, who provided the most robust methods of refining and standardizing intonation techniques beginning in the 1830s (see Jackson 2006: 151–181). But vibration's role in a historical pattern of standardization went beyond the decades-long negotiations over the prospects for an international concert tuning (so crucial for instrument manufacturers interested in nonlocal markets). In fact, periodic oscillation figured centrally in the imagination of an increasingly calibrated world. To take one illustrative example, the modest tuning fork was readily refunctioned from a pitch-measurement device to a time-measurement device. A century before the advent of the atomic clock, sinusoidal traces of an oscillating fork prong etched on a rotating roll of sooted paper could provide a visual scale for determining the duration of infinitesimal events, including human reaction times and other processes of interest to experimental psychophysiology (see Schmidgen 2005, 2009; Jackson 2012). In short, tone, the original "object" of investigation, was occluded in deference to a new set of concerns. Yet the central phenomenon of vibration, whether aurally or visually at hand, nevertheless seemed to point toward the possibility of a freshly stabilized and regulated image of the physical world. To the extent that acoustics came to form a bridge among such a wide range of nonsonic knowledges and practices, it assumed a unique mediating function, turning its increasingly loose bond with heard sound to unexpected advantage.

The seeming incongruity of using an acoustical apparatus for nonacoustical ends has in fact been commonplace from at least the late eighteenth century. One of its most celebrated instances involves the physicist and instrument-builder E. F. F. Chladni (sometimes referred to as the founder of modern acoustics, though the epithet is vacuous in light of the prior roles played by Bacon, Sauveur, and others). Chladni attracted the curiosity of an emergent public (including Napoleon) by generating uncannily complex geometrical images in sand, which was strewn across a metal plate and vibrated with a violin bow while various circumferential nodes were stopped with the fingers (Chladni 1787: 78; Jackson 2006: 13–44). In an irony characteristic of the history of acoustics, accounts of these *Klangfiguren*, or "sound figures," all but ignore their sonic aspect, focusing instead on the seemingly magical ways in which an otherwise banal acoustic happenstance afforded visual displays of unusual grace.

Such enigmas called out for interpretation—the acoustical occasioning the legible. The Romantic response was to deem such phenomena natural signs of a transcendental language.[5] But that now largely unfamiliar attitude also shades into the more general observation that, where experimental technique estranged acoustical phenomena from their nominal character as sound, some counterbalancing form of thought would be required to paper over the gap. The elaboration of a sophisticated mathematical discourse for modeling acoustics belongs, of course, to the wider history of the emergence of the modern physical disciplines and was accordingly accompanied by the increasingly formalized training regimens required to *interpret* acoustical signs (and, from a Romantic point of view, safeguard the continuity of nature's "legibility"). For at least one physicist, the relationship between math and sound had obtained a peculiar tension or complication by 1830: "I have always been of the opinion that acoustics belongs to those parts of mathematical physics where the most radiant progress is to be made. Indeed, acoustics is merely a matter of spatial and time relations, and the object should be capable of being made subservient to mathematics. And yet how little, how extremely little we still know!" (quoted in Wiederkehr 1967: 36; see also Jackson 2006: 132–133). The angst infusing this sort of statement might be said to stem not just from the clichéd desire to dominate nature but also from the perception of a widening rift between phenomenon and discourse.

The major texts of late nineteenth-century acoustics generally display two divergent responses to this anxiety: on the one hand an impulse toward popularization through the sustained, methodical conversion of everyday aural experience into an assortment of isolable sensations and concepts; on the other hand an impulse toward professionalization, which essentially jettisoned any pretense at engaging everyday phenomena and instead coaxed the reader-practitioner into an expanding flow of specialist mathematical reasoning. The popularizing impulse was enacted by the physiologist and physicist Hermann von Helmholtz, whose book *On the Sensations of Tone as a Physiological Basis for the Theory of Music* (1863) became an instant classic, due in no small part to its adept presentation of acoustical complexity in terms accessible to musicians and amateurs, as well as to specialists in more remote academic fields. But whatever Helmholtz's wider cultural-historical significance, it was the professionalizing impulse, as exemplified by the Cambridge University mathematician Lord Rayleigh, that became typical of what is generally meant by "pure acoustics." Rayleigh's two-volume textbook, *The Theory of Sound* (Strutt 1877–78), which distilled the ascetic pedagogical culture of Victorian Cambridge while remaining authoritative for decades after its publication, exemplifies the kinds of discursive mechanisms required for the propagation of ideational skill and discipline even in present-day natural science training.[6] Only in the text's twenty-third and final chapter, after roughly nine hundred pages analyzing in minute detail what is generically referred to as "vibration," does the student encounter material pertaining to "audition"—that is, to "sound" as an aspect of familiar experience. Though no doubt extreme in this regard, Rayleigh's course serves as a vivid reminder of the perhaps obvious, but nonetheless easily forgotten, fact that there is no "acoustics" without a dense background and dissemination of techniques of study, speech, and writing, well outside the states of affairs of empirical experience.

Contemporary Implications

So far, this discussion has revolved around the seemingly contrarian goal of drawing out the irony of the historical inaudibility of acoustics. Yet it would not be difficult to demonstrate how, after Rayleigh, the twentieth century witnessed a dramatic reversal of his flight from emplacedness and from the empirically heard.[7] The burgeoning of architectural acoustics after around 1900, as well as the professionalization of phonetics and phonology—representing a return of the communicative values that had characterized early modern acoustics—testify to such a development.[8] It would be misleading, then, to suggest that the abstraction of the figure of vibration from sonic experience irreversibly diverted acoustics from its aural orbit, but it is worth reflecting on a mostly unnoticed irony in the two overlapping strands of this history. In addition to the tendency of acoustics toward a separation of vibration from sound itself, there is also the corollary narrative of what we might call a "quiet acoustics"—in other words, the tacit background conditions for sonic knowledge. Where the latter strand is internal to the character of the discipline, the former thematizes the discipline's potential to reach outward beyond itself, enabling the figures of calibrated regulation noted above.

But there is equally a sense in which a heightened attention to the non-sonic conditions and implications of the sonic is of a piece with a recent tendency in sound studies more broadly. If early sound studies—"sound studies" *avant la lettre*, in the manner of R. Murray Schafer—can be said to have been preoccupied with the cordoning off, naturalization, or intensive policing of a specific difference of the aural, it would seem that contemporary work has productively softened this defensive attitude by exploring phenomenologies or epistemologies of the subaquatic, of deafness, and indeed of silence itself.[9] It may come as little surprise that the history of acoustics turns out to be tethered to aurality so nonmonoga-mously. Yet these circumstances may in turn require us to reconsider our historiography. Returning to Helmholtz, an especially prominent case, we might wonder how his brand of experimentalism fits with the notion of a "quiet acoustics." Surely, if anyone stood for a "noisy acoustics," it was the figure whose popular impulse led him to segregate his text into two sections, with mathematical theory—"discourse," and the particular skills it entails—confined to a series of highly specialized appendices, while the main body staged a virtuoso display of empirical observation, choreographing sound as a direct aural knowledge (Steege 2012). Elsewhere, Helmholtz went so far as to characterize the muting of "mere" discourse as an emancipatory gesture, particularly with regard to what he considered the undue institutional power of an antiquated humanism that maintained a monopoly on educational, clerical, and state networks of power. Institutional leaders "must be emboldened or compelled by the public opinion of the judgment-capable classes of the entire people, of men as well as women," to embrace the empiricist values of what he variously calls "observation," the "actual source of knowledge," and "new truth," as opposed to self-perpetuating dogmas (Helmholtz 1971: 365–378).

Having briefly observed some of the peculiarities of the history of acoustics, we are now in a position to ask what strategies lie behind the kind of rhetoric Helmholtz uses. His bold and politically charged stance against humanist linguocentrism makes it all too easy to adopt someone like him as a kind of hero figure for sound studies—even perhaps for the recent posthumanisms, speculative realisms, and new materialisms that might at moments promise to nourish the still-nascent agendas of the field—however philosophically distant his work ultimately remains from these projects.[10] But given his sleight of hand in concealing what I have been calling discursive skill behind a veil of popularizing empiricism, we might wish to think twice about how a Helmholtzian enthusiasm for a "new truth" of sonic experience in fact squares with the agendas of sound studies. Acoustical knowledge turns out to be constitutively porous, impure, and only casually committed to the ear. Our historiographies of acoustics ought to remain attentive to this peculiarity, and if not correspondingly casual in their commitments to the aural, then at least deliberative in coming to terms with the implications of such ironies.

Notes

1. When, for example, Jonathan Sterne writes that "particular ways of knowing sound have been integral to the development of key modern sonic practices" (2012: 8), the prospect of some form of knowledge other than "acoustics" is presumably at hand. Similarly, a panel of papers titled "Acoustics and Experiences of the Limit," at the 2012 meeting of the Society for Ethnomusicology, suggests a desire to think an acoustical knowledge in terms more amenable to emerging music-anthropological projects.

2. See Gouk (1999: 157–192). The phrase "Acoustique Art," often quoted as if it appeared in a 1605 treatise by Bacon himself, is in fact a posthumous English translation of Bacon's original Latinized Greek "acoustica" (1640: 135). In any case, the notion of acoustics goes relatively undeveloped in its immediate context there, though Bacon wrote extensively about experiments in sound elsewhere. See Gouk (2000).

3. To be sure, his *mémoire* for the Royal Academy from the following year turned to a more conventional theory of harmony. See Sauveur (1984: 99–166).

4. And yet Roger Mathew Grant (2013) rightly points out that, contrary to most accounts, the physicalization of music-theoretical knowledge between 1600 and 1700 cannot be said to have led to an uncomplicated demystification of number, since the mathematics of this period often remained linked to magical and metaphysical commitments much longer than the traditional historiography of the first "scientific revolution" would suggest.

5. Valuable recent commentary appears in Welsh (2003: 185–216). The trope endured at least as late as 1934, when Theodor W. Adorno singled out the Chladni figures as precursors to what he considered the mystifying reifications of modern recording technology. See Adorno (1990).

6. See Strutt 1877–78. On Rayleigh in the context of Cambridge mathematical physics, see Warwick (2003: 18–24, 276–277).

7. And it is only fair to note that Rayleigh himself pursued watershed experiments on binaural sound localization—a direct engagement with acoustical emplacement if there ever was one. See Strutt (1907).

8. See Thompson (2002). For a sense of the flourishing study of speech and vocalization, a glance at any recent issue of the *Journal of the Acoustical Society of America* will suffice.

9. See, for example, the recent reflections of Stefan Helmreich (2012) and Mara Mills (2010) (see also SILENCE).

10. Even in terms of Friedrich Kittler's older work, for example, Helmholtz (in an unholy alliance with Richard Wagner) would fit the persona of the iconoclastic proto-theorist of media, heralding a dissolution of the "republic of letters" that had helped to sustain the so-called discourse network of 1800 (Kittler 1990).

References

Adorno, Theodor W. 1990. "The Form of the Phonograph Record." Trans. Thomas Y. Levin. *October* 55 (winter): 56–61.

Bacon, Francis. 1640. *Of the Advancement and Proficience of Learning, or the Partitions of Science*. Oxford: Young and Forrest.

Chladni, E. F. F. 1787. *Entdeckungen über die Theorie des Klanges*. Leipzig: Weidmanns Erben und Reich.

Cohen, H. F. 1984. *Quantifying Music: The Science of Music at the First Stage of the Scientific Revolution, 1580–1650*. Dordrecht: Reidel.

Erlmann, Veit. 2010. *Reason and Resonance: A History of Modern Aurality*. New York: Zone Books.

Friedner, Michele, and Stefan Helmreich. 2012. "Sound Studies Meets Deaf Studies." *Senses and Society* 7(1): 72–86.

Gouk, Penelope. 1999. *Music, Science and Natural Magic in Seventeenth-Century England*. New Haven: Yale University Press.

Gouk, Penelope. 2000. "Music in Francis Bacon's Natural Philosophy." In *Number to Sound: The Musical Way to the Scientific Revolution*, ed. Paolo Gozza, 135–153. Dordrecht: Kluwer Academic.

Grant, Roger Mathew. 2013. "Ad Infinitum: Numbers and Series in Early Modern Music Theory." *Music Theory Spectrum* 35(1) (spring): 62–76.

Helmholtz, Hermann von. 1863. *Die Lehre von den Tonempfindungen als physiologische Grundlage für die Theorie der Musik*. Braunschweig: Vieweg und Sohn. Published in English as *On the Sensations of Tone as a Physiological Basis for the Theory of Harmony*. 1885. Trans. Alexander J. Ellis (from 3rd ed.) London: Longman.

Helmholtz, Hermann von. 1971. "Über das Streben nach Popularisierung der Wissenschaft" (1874). In *Philosophische Vorträge und Aufsätze*, ed. Herbert Hörz and Siegfried Wollgast, 365–378. Berlin: Akademie-Verlag.

Helmreich, Stefan. 2012. "Underwater Music: Tuning Composition to the Sounds of Science." In *The Oxford Handbook of Sound Studies*, ed. Trevor Pinch and Karin Bijsterveld, 151–175. New York: Oxford University Press.

Jackson, Myles W. 2006. *Harmonious Triads: Physicists, Musicians, and Instrument Makers in Nineteenth-Century Germany*. Cambridge, MA: MIT Press.

Jackson, Myles W. 2012. "From Scientific Instruments to Musical Instruments: The Tuning Fork, the Metronome, and the Siren." In *The Oxford Handbook of Sound Studies*, ed. Trevor Pinch and Karin Bijsterveld, 201–223. New York: Oxford University Press.

Kinsler, Lawrence E., Austin R. Frey, Alan B. Coppens, and James V. Sanders. 2000. *Fundamentals of Acoustics*. 4th ed. New York: Wiley.

Kittler, Friedrich. 1990. *Discourse Networks 1800/1900*. Stanford: Stanford University Press.

Marsh, Narcissus. 1684, January 1. "An introductory Essay to the doctrine of Sounds, containing some proposals for the improvement of Acousticks." *Philosophical Transactions of the Royal Society* 14 (155–166): 472–488.

Mills, Mara. 2010. "Deaf Jam: From Inscriptions to Reproduction to Information." *Social Text* 28(1) (spring): 35–58.

Sauveur, Joseph. 1984. *Collected Writings on Musical Acoustics (Paris 1700–1713)*. Ed. Rudolf Rasch. Utrecht: Diapason Press.

Schmidgen, Henning. 2005. "The Donders Machine: Matter, Signs, and Time in a Physiological Experiment, ca. 1865." *Configurations* 13(2) (spring): 211–256.

Schmidgen, Henning. 2009. *Die Helmholtz-Kurven: Auf der Spur der verlorenen Zeit*. Berlin: Merve Verlag.

Steege, Benjamin. 2012. *Helmholtz and the Modern Listener*. Cambridge: Cambridge University Press.

Sterne, Jonathan. 2012. "Sonic Imaginations." In *The Sound Studies Reader*, ed. Jonathan Sterne, 1–17. London: Routledge Press. 2012.

Strutt, John William, Lord Rayleigh. 1877–78. *The Theory of Sound*. 2 vols. London: Macmillan.

Strutt, John William, Lord Rayleigh. 1907. "On Our Perception of Sound Direction." *London, Edinburgh, and Dublin Philosophical Magazine and Journal of Science*, ser. 6, 13(74) (February): 214–232.

Thompson, Emily. 2002. *The Soundscape of Modernity: Architectural Acoustics and the Culture of Listening in America, 1900–1933*. Cambridge, MA: MIT Press.

Warwick, Andrew. 2003. *Masters of Theory: Cambridge and the Rise of Mathematical Physics*. Chicago: University of Chicago Press.

Welsh, Caroline. 2003. Hirnhöhlenpoetiken: Theorien zur Wahrnehmung in Wissenschaft, Ästhetik und Literatur um 1800. Freiburg: Rombach.

Wiederkehr, K. H. 1967. Wilhelm Eduard Weber: Erforscher der Wellenbewegung und der Elektrizität, 1804–1891. Stuttgart: Wissenschaftliche Verlagsgesellschaft.

body

Sound Effects

The first sounds: whosh hiss thump thump thump.
The body wakes to the sounds of the body. Blood and heart rhythms in an ocean of amniotic fluid. It is another's body—the body of the mother—but it is the same body. The body of the mother and the child, a symbiosis of sound.
Whoosh hiss whoosh krrrrrrr. The roar of a tidal wave. The cervix opens, a passage is crossed, an entry broached. The limens are sounded. Whosh
The child emerges, separate but connected in sound and sensation.

The coursing of blood repeats its drone as it passes in and out of the heart, finding its ostinato beat in the tributaries of the body; but a new sound is heard—the sound of air sweeping the cavities of the nose, hair follicles in a damp wind, and then through the trachea, the bronchi, the cilia vibrating, the alveoli pulsing like small accordions. Breath. The ether connecting inner and outer.

The sound of the muscles, intercostal, stretching.
The sound of the joints releasing air, pop, crack.

And then the voice as air passes through the vocal chords, a sounded gasp, a cry, a coo, a wail.

The body begins with sound, in sound. The sound of the body is the sound of the other but it is also the sound of the same. From the beginning, subjectivity emerges from intersubjectivity, the one is born from the many. We resound together. Psychoanalyst Julia Kristeva calls this the "chora"— the space of continuity where sound, shapes, sensations do not belong to anyone, they simply are; the mother's voice, the child's sonic home

(Kristeva 1982, 1984; see Anzieu 1987). For twentieth-century philosopher Emmanuel Lévinas, our mutual humanity passes through the recognition afforded by the eye, which affirms both our particularity and our commonality, but in fact sound and sensation precede the visual in human interaction; they are the first passages, and the philosophical standing of the body finds no ground without this acknowledgment. Jean-Luc Nancy says that the self knows itself first as an echo—a sound repeated, the voice returned to itself (renvoi). A cry. A re-sonance.

The body: "the complete physical form of a person or animal" (OED), and yet the body is never "complete," only transforming. The body: "an assemblage of parts, organs, and tissues that constitutes the whole material organism" (OED). Yet this is just the physical body (korper). There is also the lived body (lieb), a perfusion of hormones, chemicals, synapses, nerves; a plethora of molecules shedding and spreading beyond the skin, a substance that responds to the rhythms of its environment. The body: a site of recognition, an evanescent materiality, a pliant ambiguity.

"When I think of my body and ask what it does to deserve that name," notes theorist Brian Massumi, "two things stand out. It moves. It feels" (Massumi 2002). We can also say, it sounds. Every movement is in fact a vibration, and every vibration has a sound, however inaudible to the human ear. What we cannot hear, we can sense. Intuition is this: awareness of the body perceiving, the senses moving (Bergson 2007). And sound knowledge—a nondiscursive form of affective transmission resulting from acts of listening—is the fruit of this perception (Kapchan forthcoming). What I call here the sound body emerges in the paradox of being a part of and yet distinct from the "sound affects" of being.

What are the material effects of the sound body? And how might attention to sound and affect produce a body unfettered by the dualisms of the Enlightenment—mind/body, nature/culture, man/woman, human/animal, spirit/material?

Sufi Sound Bodies

Here, no doubt, begins the human: I listen the way I read; i.e., according to certain codes.—Roland Barthes, "Listening" (1985 [1976]: 245)

Join me in a sumptuous garden in the north of Morocco behind tall adobe walls. In the midst of this garden stand a large house and several dependencies, with separate quarters for women and men. A thick green lawn spreads around the circumference of the property, with palm trees, rose bushes, and a large gazebo. This is the summer sanctuary of one of the largest Sufi orders in Morocco—the Qadirriyya Boutshishiyya—where the octogenarian shaykh of the order lives most of the year.

In the main room of the house women are singing Sufi poems, *qasaid*. Their fingers run over prayer beads like water on rocks. Their eyes are closed. I change into my djellaba, put a scarf around my head, and join them. A few open their eyes as they hear me sit down, making a place for me in the circle and raising their hands to their hearts in acknowledgment of my presence. We sing. Suddenly one woman begins to weep loudly. Then another seems to jump into the air from the floor, emitting a loud "Allah!" Eyes remain closed except for my own (which instinctively open and shut several times on registering the change in amplitude and rhythm in the circle). When women are taken up in this kind of bodily rapture, it is impolite to stare. And in any case, it is a common occurrence.

The strongest singer initiates a new song at intervals, creating a continuous chain of praise poems, punctuated by sudden movements and cries, the effects and affects of being in *al-hal*. Literally "the state," the term *al-hal* denotes a transition from (one of many) normal states of everyday existence to (one of many) spiritual states of rapture and communion. The realignment of bodily rhythms with sonic and spiritual ones causes the body to jerk, swoon, scream, and sway in unpredictable ways as it approaches the ineffable.

And then the voice as air passes through the vocal chords, a sounded gasp, a cry, a coo, a wail. Sound brings the body home. The body returns to the world as vibration.

For the Sufis in this order (as in many others), initiation has everything to do with listening. Indeed, they have a word for it: *sama'*—which is both the verb "to listen" and the genre of music listened to. Sama' contains both subject (listener) and object (sound) in its very meaning. Indeed, the performers of this music are not called "singers" (*mughaniyyin*) as in other musical genres but are called "listeners" (*musama'yyin*). It is not an ordinary listening, however, but a *genre of listening* informed by the intention (*niya*) of listening to find another way of being. If listening according to learned codes defines the human (as Barthes notes in the epigraph to this section), Sufis learn to listen beyond the quotidian, as angels or other nonhuman entities might). Sama' is an active listening; indeed it is a "listening act" of a very particular order, one that transforms the body (Kapchan forthcoming). Like J. L. Austin's (1962) "locutionary acts," listening acts *enact*—that is, they are "performative," they do not simply represent sound, as waves reach the ears and are relayed to the brain, but they *transduce* these sound waves, changing the waves, the body and the environment in the process (see TRANSDUCTION; Szendy 2007).

Insofar as listening invites vibrations and new rhythms into the body, it is always transformative. In Sufism, for example, one learns to listen to the prayers attentively, intoning them silently and aloud with others. Listening in this context is a method of initiation, a way of imbibing the liturgy. But there are many genres of listening, each with its own relation to time and space (Kapchan forthcoming, 2008, 2009, 2013). When listening to Sufi *dhikr* (chanting or ritual "remembrance") and song, for example, we are often in the present tense; indeed, listening creates presence:

My shaykh is like a white dove
shaykh-i ka hamama bayda
Living in my soul and satisfying me
sakina fi-ruh-i wa qna'-ni
My love is in Madagh
hubbi-i fi madagh
Let's go there and meet him
yalla bi-nah n-lqau-h

There is nothing particularly magical about this quatrain, yet when these lines are sung by the soloist and listened to in a particular way, the women devotees accede to another state. The soloist touches the listeners with her verse, sung in a call and response, and this vibration, this touch, makes the others break with the ostinato rhythms of the refrain to begin polyrhythmic and polyphonic harmonies. These are not pre-scripted. Rather the women listen closely to each other as they are taken up in the *hal*, responding to each other either in rhythmic and melodic imitation or counter-distinction. The effect is a richly textured soundscape of devotion, with close intervals sung in multiple meters. Listening to this often cacophonous fabric of voices makes the "veil" between different states of being fall away, permitting these women to inhabit another ontology, or *barzakh*.

Barzakh: The Sound Body as Ontology

Delineated by twelfth-century Sufi mystic and philosopher Ibn al-'Arabi, the realm of the barzakh is where material worlds are spiritualized and immaterial worlds are made corporeal. It is a realm of vibration, sometimes taking color and shape, sometimes sounded, sometimes ineffable but felt. We can think of a barzakh as a "change in ontological register" (Crapanzano 2004: 14), a way of superseding the merely human. Rocks vibrate at a different frequency than mountains or humans or symphonies, words or paintings (see Whitehead 1929). All sentient beings experience only the world their senses reveal. The difference in these worlds lies as much in the instruments or technologies of perception (in this case bodies), as in the things themselves. A barzakh itself is an isthmus, a passage between, in which divine knowledge is apprehended in the only way humans can understand—through symbols. These symbols—whether sonic, imagistic, or embodied—are not simulacra, but materializations of divine knowledge in the realm of human perception. In other words, a barzakh is not a representation but a material reality: "there are only barzakhs," says Ibn al-'Arabi (Chittick 1989). What exists is a function of our ability to perceive it. For the Sufi, this means acceding to levels of gnosis that consequently open onto other, more subtle worlds. Listening is a port of entry as well as a method for the realization of the sound body. Indeed, while sonic religious practices are often thought to be conservative, Sufi listening may be said to "queer" conventional listening practices in order to exceed the limits of human experience (Brett and Wood 1994).

As one Sufi soloist said to me recently, "I am going to stop singing sama' soon." "Why?" I asked, surprised. "I listen differently now than I did before," she answered. "Before I used to hear the songs. I heard their tempo, their rhythm. I liked some songs a lot. But now," she continued, "I hear vibration. It may be selfish to want to just listen, but you have to be selfish sometimes. If a plate of food passes before you and you don't take anything from it, you'll be hungry." For this Sufi, listening is more important than singing. Despite the fact that she is a respected, renown, and recorded singer of Sufi song, she would rather listen to vibrations.

Such sonic rapture through listening is not unique to Sufis of course. Indeed, listening as a mode or method of gnosis exists in many traditions. Tanya Luhrmann discusses how Pentecostal Christians in the United

States hear what they describe as the voice of God through "learning to listen" (Luhrmann 2012; also see Kapchan 2009; Henriques 2011: 88–122). Drawing on the theories of Donald Winnicott, Luhrmann attributes this to the ability of humans to develop a "theory of mind" that is porous to its social environment. But this listening is also a deep identification with the sound body, a body attuned to and transformed by the vibrations of its environment—in this case, one in which the presence of an invisible intelligence (God) is felt. Psychoanalyst Didier Anzieu would say that the ego skin of the sonorous body is thin and thus available to other influences (Anzieu 1995 [1987]). There are many examples of artists, mystics, and others possessed by spirits who develop, either willfully or accidently, a porosity between material and imaginal realms of sound (Friedson 1996; Masquelier 2001; Becker 2004; Oliveros 2005; Trower 2012). Such sublime experiences with sound are not confined to sacred traditions but can be found in popular forms such as Jamaican dancehall (Henriques 2011) or the genre of Noise in Japan (Novak 2013). In these contexts, participants create and submit themselves to experiences of such sensory intensity that the body's boundaries dissipate in the "ever-present now" (Bergson 2007). Sublimity is corporeal: sound knowledge circulates in the "feedback" between body and body, body and environment, body and machine (Racy 2003; Novak 2013).

Where Sufi practices differ from some of these practices is not necessarily in Sufis' faith or deism but in their belief that the human body itself contains technologies that remain hidden to the self, which are revealed at different maqam, or stations of initiation. Maqam is also the word for a musical scale, with each note as a progressive step, each stage holding its own secrets and methods. These are the technologies that take the Sufi into other worlds of perception in the same way the stethoscope takes us into rhythms not usually heard (Sterne 2003) or the telephone into spaces the physical body cannot transverse (Mills 2012). This is the sound body: a resonant body that is porous, that transforms according to the vibrations of its environment, and correspondingly transforms that environment.

Despite its cultural ubiquity, however, the sound body—a body able to transform by resonating at different frequencies—is the marked status of human beings, that is, a state socially designated as standing apart from the norm. Why is this the case?

Sound Affects

Against the legal body—the body defined by jurisprudence—the sound body is marked as unusual or extraordinary. Since at least the Enlightenment, the legal body has become second nature, the one Western subjects inhabit most unconsciously. The legal body is equated with property—and specifically with property-in-the-person. It is a sovereign (Rousseauian) body with inalienable rights—including the rights to own private property and to dispense of its property as it wishes. This quasi-Protestant body is a laboring body with a presumed agency: its boundaries are the edges of the skin. While this body has been defined against the abomination of slavery (and the free subject, who cannot by definition be owned by another), nonetheless historically it has had dominion over other bodies—notably women and children (Patemen 1988, 2002). In its current incarnation, this body is inextricable from a capitalist and neoliberal body: it acquires, it consumes, it owns, and in so doing it creates waste. For consumption and acquisition of necessity produce excess, and historically the extent of one's property has been demarcated by one's ability to pollute—sonically, radioactively, symbolically (Serres 2011).

The sound body, however, resists the property principle. Despite attempts of the market to harness and copyright sound, the sound body refuses to be owned. It inhabits but does not appropriate. It sounds and resounds but cannot be captured. It creates nests that disperse with the wind.

> My shaykh is like a white dove
> Living in my soul and satisfying me

If the twentieth-century legal body was defined largely by its *effects*— what it performed in the world, whether intentionally or unintentionally (rights, sovereignty, ownership)—the body in the twenty-first century is a body defined by its *affects*, its materialities of feeling.

The Sound Affective Body

The unmarked legal body is very different from the phenomenological body. For Merleau-Ponty, the perceiving body was the site of enmeshment with the world. Intentionality was located in the body-mind (*corps-sujet*). His unfinished work bequeaths the notion of "flesh," the sensate interface with the environment. "Flesh" (*chair*) is a living and transforming organ, permeable to its external environment, a fragile membrane in an even more fragile life system. Flesh breathes. It is porous, responsive, and connects the inner to the outer. It belongs to and encases the separate self but transmits sensation from other worlds. It is a form of fascia—connective tissue. He notes, "the thickness of the body, far from rivaling that of the world, is on the contrary the sole means I have to go unto the heart of the things, by making myself a world and by making them flesh" (Merleau-Ponty 1968: 259).

The fleshly sound body unfolds as a chiasm, a barzakh from self to world, an intertwining of world with self. It has a texture, a touch (Connor 2004). And touch always has a sonic dimension, as rhythms collide at different frequencies and oscillations. Touch is vibration, and vibration, sound. Sound affects: we feel it and it creates feeling.

Indeed, it is the affective dimension of the sound body that transforms. As Brennan and others have shown, not only ideas but also the actual chemistry of our bodies changes in the encounter with other bodies, sentient and non-. Our hormonal systems are in constant communication, affecting and modifying each other, and changing the environment as well (Brennan 2004: 73). The visual limits of our bodies—the soft interface of flesh—are exceeded by technological, hormonal, and prosthetic extensions that respond to and act upon our worlds, often in unexpected ways. Posthumanism is characterized by the impossibility of separating bodily consciousness from machine. If for Merleau-Ponty consciousness and (objective) reality are both located in the body, in a postphenomenological world "technologies can be the means by which 'consciousness itself' is mediated. Technologies," notes phenomenologist Don Ihde, "may occupy the 'of' and not just be some object domain" (Ihde 2009: 23, italics in original). This is evident in hearing disabilities where technology is clearly a means of perception—in cochlear implants, for example (Rapp and Ginsburg 2001, 2011). For feminist theorist Karen Barad, these technologies do not precede the body, nor are they created by the body; rather, bodies and technologies give rise to one another (Barad 2003: 815).

Among the prostheses and technologies that extend the body is music. "Music is more than an object," noted Jacques Attali in 1977, "it is a way of perceiving the world. A tool of understanding" (Attali 1985 [1977]: 4). Listening to ambient music like Brian Eno's *Music for Airports* conduces a different perception from that evoked by Sun Ra in his film *Space Is the Place*. Both reorient the listening body toward a virtual future, either explicitly

(Sun Ra) or by employing an aesthetic meant to unhinge the body from its known aesthetic parameters (Eno). As Sun Ra notes in the film, if the earth hasn't yet fallen, it's because of the music: "the music of the earth, the music of the sun and the stars, the music of your self vibrating—yes, you are all music too, you're all instruments" (Sun Ra 1974, minutes 19:11–19:34). And how do we know anything, save through the instruments that we are?

Contemporary subjects are moving from a paradigm of relationality (intertextuality, intersubjectivity, intersensoriality, intercorporeity) to an *intramodal ontology*, a paradigm of imbrication, cohabitation, and co-extension wherein the limits of the subject cannot be assumed. The way through is in, the way in (or out, or anywhere) is through. *The sound body is a material body that resonates (with) its environment, creating and conducting affect.*

When Sufis travel to the sanctuary they become imbued with an energy that continues to activate them. The body carries the songs and their vibrations in its cellular memory. This is why the notion of blessing or grace (*baraka*, in Arabic, not to be confused with *barzakh*) is understood to be contagious in North African Sufism; baraka is a material energy with its own force that, when transduced by the body, transforms all it touches. Grace, like sound, is vibration. It has an affective materiality and performativity. Nourished by the plate of food that passes by, the pilgrims return home with a different chemistry. Like food that affects the enteric nervous system in the gut, the sonic vibrations of the liturgy transform the body (Furness 2008). And a new body, like a new ear, is a new world.

Worlds are composed of territories, however, and territories are more likely than not claimed as property, whether in Sufi gardens in Morocco (where Sufism counters a rising Islamist influence) or Sufi music on the stages and in the living rooms of secular France (Kapchan 2013). While this kind of sonic affective territory does not need to be owned (it can be inhabited, used, rented), nonetheless territory-as-property is the main source of violence and war on the planet. Increasingly its designation as sacred or secular is cited as a cause of defense and aggression. What then is the political impact of the sound body? Can an unmarking of the sound body—that is, a public recognition of its social ubiquity—unweave the indexical threads that tie bodies to property and property to sacred and secular divisions of the same? As Barad notes, "the belief that nature is mute and immutable and that all prospects for significance and change reside in culture is a reinscription of the nature/culture dualism that feminists have actively contested. Nor, similarly, can a human/nonhuman distinction be hardwired into any theory that claims to take account of matter in the fullness of its historicity" (2003: 827). Sound, even when inaudible, is indelibly material. As vibration, it permeates everything, unloosening thereby the knotted dualisms of nature/culture, human/nonhuman, body/ mind. The promise of the sound body is a release from these confines. Indeed "inaudible sound" is a paradox that, like a Zen koan, or Ibn al-'Arabi's insistence that "God is and God isn't" (huwa laysa huwa), bypasses rationality to unlock a Bergsonian intuition, that is, an awareness of our sentient perception. This is sound knowledge—not a privileging of sound over other senses but a portal into necessarily intersensorial worlds and ways of conscious being (Porcello et al. 2010).

Acknowledging the porosity of the body is also recognizing its evanescence and impermanence, its perpetual transformation in and through time and space, such that any continuity of identity is a labor undertaken both alone and in common, a labor that may (or may not) be engaged in consciously and with intuition. Sound knowledge (a nondiscursive form of affective transmission resulting from acts of listening) becomes both a method and a state of being and awareness in this regard, a way to break free of the discourses (of capitalism, of culture and education, of neoliberal politics) that make and remake the body in their own images. Sound—as affect, as vibration—heralds a new body, and a new paradigm for the body: the resonant body, the intramodal body, the sonic-affective body, the postphenomenal body, the technobody, the transgendered body. Adjectives proliferate. The body persists.

References

Anzieu, Didier. 1995 [1987]. Le Moi Peau. Paris: Dunod.
Attali, Jacques. 1985 [1977]. Noise: The Political Economy of Music. Trans. Brian Massumi. Minneapolis: University of Minnesota Press.
Austin, J. L. 1962. How to Do Things with Words. Cambridge, MA: Harvard University Press.
Barad, Karen. 2003. "Posthumanist Performativity: Toward an Understanding of How Matter Comes to Matter." Signs: Journal of Women in Culture and Society 28(3): 801–831.
Barthes, Roland. 1985 [1976]. "Listening." In The Responsibility of Forms, 245–260. New York: Hill and Wang.
Becker, Judith. 2004. Deep Listeners: Music, Emotion and Trancing. Bloomington: Indiana University Press.
Bergson, Henri. 2007. Matter and Memory. New York: Cosimo Books.
Brennan, Teresa. 2004. Transmission of Affect. Ithaca: Cornell University Press.

Brett, Philip, and Elizabeth Wood. 1994. *Queering the Pitch: The New Gay and Lesbian Musicology*. New York: Routledge Books.

Chittick, William C. 1989. *The Sufi Path of Knowledge: Ibn al-'Arabi's Metaphysics of Imagination*. Albany: State University of New York Press.

Connor, Steven. 2004. "Edison's Teeth: Touching Hearing." In *Hearing Cultures: Essays on Sound, Listening and Modernity*, ed. Veit Erlmann, 153–172. Oxford: Berg.

Crapanzano, Vincent. 2004. *Imaginative Horizons: An Essay in Literary-Philosophical Anthropology*. Chicago: University of Chicago Press.

Friedson, Steven. 1996. *Dancing Prophets: Musical Experience in Tumbuka Healing*. Chicago: University of Chicago Press.

Furness, John Barton. 2008. *The Enteric Nervous System*. New York: Wiley.

Geurts, K. L. 2003. *Culture and the Senses: Bodily Ways of Knowing in an African Community*. Berkeley: University of California Press.

Henriques, Julian. 2011. *Sonic Bodies: Reggae Sound Systems, Performance Techniques and Ways of Knowing*. New York: Continuum Press.

Howes, David. 2003. *Sensual Relations: Engaging the Senses in Culture and Social Theory*. Ann Arbor: University of Michigan Press.

Ihde, Don. 2009. *Postphenomenology and Technoscience: The Peking University Lectures*. New York: State University of New York Press.

Jackson, M., ed. 1996. *Things as They Are: New Directions in Phenomenological Anthropology*. Bloomington: Indiana University Press.

Kapchan, Deborah. 2008. "The Promise of Sonic Translation: Performing the Festive Sacred in Morocco." *American Anthropologist* 110(4): 467–483.

Kapchan, Deborah. 2009. "Singing Community/Remembering in Common: Sufi Liturgy and North African Identity in Southern France." *International Journal of Community Music* 2(1): 9–23.

Kapchan, Deborah. 2009. "Learning to Listen: The Sound of Sufism in France." Special issue, *World of Music* 51 (2): 65–90.

Kapchan, Deborah. 2013. "The Aesthetics of the Invisible: Sacred Music in Secular (French) Places." *Drama Review* 57, 3 (T219): 132–147.

Kapchan, Deborah. forthcoming. "Introduction: Hearing the Splash of Icarus: Theorizing Sound Writing/Writing Sound Theory" and "Listening Acts: Hearing the Pain (and Praise) of Others." In *Theorizing Sound Writing*, ed. Deborah Kapchan.

Kristeva, Julia. 1982. *Powers of Horror: An Essay on Abjection*. Trans. Leon Roudiez. New York: Columbia University Press.

Kristeva, Julia. 1984. *Revolution in Poetic Language*. Trans. Margaret Waller. New York: Columbia University Press.

Lefebvre, Henri. 2004 [1992]. *Rhythmanalysis: Space, Time and Everyday Life*. New York: Continuum Books.

Lévinas, Emmanuel. 1969 [1961]. *Totality and Infinity: An Essay on Exteriority*. Pittsburgh: Duquesne University Press.

Luhrmann, Tanya M. 2012. *When God Talks Back: Understanding the American Evangelical Relationship with God*. New York: Knopf.

Masquelier, Adeline. 2001. *Prayer Has Spoiled Everything: Possession, Power, and Identity in an Islamic Town of Niger*. Durham: Duke University Press.

Massumi, B. 2002. *Parables for the Virtual: Movement, Affect, Sensation*. Durham: Duke University Press.

Merleau-Ponty, Maurice. 1968. *The Visible and the Invisible*. Evanston: Northwestern University Press.

Mills, Mara. 2012. "The Audiovisual Telephone: A Brief History." In *Handheld? Music Video Aesthetics for Portable Devices*, ed. Henry Keazor, 34–47. Heidelberg: ART-Dok.

Nancy, Jean-Luc. 2007. *Listening*. New York: Fordham University Press.

Novak, David. 2013. *Japanoise: Music at the Edge of Circulation*. Durham: Duke University Press.

Oliveros, Pauline. 2005. *Deep Listening: A Composer's Sound Practice*. New York: iUniverse, Inc.

Patemen, Carole. 1988. *The Sexual Contract*. Palo Alto: Stanford University Press.

Patemen, Carole. 2002. "Self-Ownership and Property in the Person: Democratization and a Tale of Two Concepts." *Journal of Political Philosophy* 10(1): 20–53.

Porcello, Thomas, Louise Meintjes, Ana María Ochoa, and David W. Samuels. 2010. "The Reorganization of the Sensory World." *Annual Review of Anthropology* 39: 51–66.

Racy, Jihad Ali. 2003. *Making Music in the Arab World: The Culture and Artistry of Tarab*. Cambridge: Cambridge University Press.

Rapp, Rayna, and Faye D. Ginsburg. 2011. "Reverberations: Disability and the New Kinship Imaginary." *Anthropological Quarterly* 84(2): 379–410.

Rapp, Rayna, and Faye D. Ginsburg. 2001. "Enabling Disability: Rewriting Kinship, Reimagining Citizenship." *Public Culture* 13(3): 533–556.

Serres, Michel. 2011. *Malfaisance: Appropriation through Pollution?* Palo Alto: Stanford University Press.

Sun Ra and Joshua Smith (writers). 1974. *Space Is the Place* (film). Directed by John Coney. Distributed by Outerspaceways: http://outerspacewaysinc.com

Sterne, Jonathan. 2003. *The Audible Past: Cultural Origins of Sound Reproduction*. Durham: Duke University Press.

Szendy, Peter. 2008. *Listen: A History of Our Ears*. With a foreword by Jean-Luc Nancy. New York: Fordham University Press.

Trower, Shelley. 2012. *Senses of Vibration: A History of the Pleasure and Pain of Sound*. New York: Continuum Press.

Whitehead, Alfred North. 1929. *Process and Reality. An Essay in Cosmology*. Gifford Lectures Delivered in the University of Edinburgh during the Session 1927–1928. Cambridge: Cambridge University Press.

deafness

A *deaf spectrum*—or "deafnesses"—has replaced the deaf/hearing binary in both the biomedical and cultural realms. At the same time, audiometric categories of hearing impairment do not map neatly onto deaf identities. Depending on technology use and community affiliation, individuals with audiograms that register similar types of impairment might identify quite differently as Deaf (a cultural group defined by sign language use), deaf, late-deafened, deaf-blind, hearing, or hard of hearing. *Deafness* may be used colloquially to designate any kind of hearing difference; however, members of Deaf culture often reject the term as itself pathologizing.

In addition, Deaf scholars have reconceived *hearing loss* as *deaf gain* to account for the new representations, communities, and forms of cognition afforded by bodily and communicative difference (Bauman and Murray 2009). These gains range from the neurodiversity that accompanies visual-gestural languages to aesthetic and technical innovations. With regard to technology, gains often occur because inaccessible media systems necessitate adaptations; examples include closed captioning (sound-to-text translation) and telephone relay services. Deaf communities also produce their own "minor" media. Deaf Space, for instance, refers to architecture designed specifically for inhabitants who sign and, to a lesser extent, use personal amplification devices.[1] For scientists and engineers, deafness has yielded insights into the elements of speech and hearing, as well as possibilities for their reconfiguration: new techniques for sound synthesis and visualization, for instance, or new modes of listening.

Definitions of deafness have varied across time and national context, the net trend being the expansion of the category and the diversification of allied identities. Deafness did not become an object of scientific investigation and pedagogical intervention in Europe until the early modern period. Before the 1500s, congenitally deaf individuals and families were highly isolated. In the absence of amplification devices and precise audiometric measurements, "deaf-mute" or "deaf and dumb" referred to those who—from an early age—could not hear the frequency range of the human voice.[2] It was widely believed that rational thought was dependent on speech. Prelingual deafness seemed inextricably linked to muteness; in turn, deaf people seemed incapable of intelligence and moral reason.

Early efforts at deaf education, motivated by the goal of religious instruction, yielded numerous visual and gestural modes of communication, including new methods for transcribing and analyzing speech. In 1620, the Spanish priest Juan Pablo Bonet published *Reduction de las letras y arte para enseñar a hablar los mudos*, the first treatise on deaf education, which discussed print reading, lip-reading, and the manual alphabet. Bonet advised "the reduction of letters" through the use of a phonetic alphabet as an aid for deaf students learning speak. Of Bonet, and the heirs to his system, Jonathan Reé comments, "the first inquirers to attempt an absolute notation for speech, tied down to invariant standards of sound, were the early oral educators of the deaf" (Rée 1999: 249).

The growth of the natural sciences and the general expansion of education encouraged further study of deafness in the 1600s. Anatomists had already begun to examine the outer and middle ear by the sixteenth century, but new instrumentation—microscopes and tiny surgical instruments—allowed the dissection of the cochlea and the auditory nerve beginning in the seventeenth. The mapping of anatomical structure provoked finer-grained theories of hearing and its impairment: loud sounds might damage the tympanum, for instance, or the bones might fuse in the middle ear. It had long been understood that human hearing was limited and declined with age, but now the boundaries of hearing capacity began to be charted. Using tuned organ pipes, physicist Joseph Sauveur offered an early estimate of the upper and lower thresholds of hearing around 1700.

Up to the sixteenth century, many anatomists believed hearing impairment to be untreatable, despite the prevalence of folk remedies. By the end of the 1500s, however, clinical examination became more elaborate, and the recesses of the ear began to be examined with a speculum. Artificial tympana and surgical treatments were proposed for middle-ear deafness. According to Georg von Békésy and Walter Rosenblith, "the new and more mechanical way of looking at the human body and the high development of mechanical art in the 16th and 17th centuries was responsible for the manufacture and use of prosthetic devices to replace parts of the body that had been injured" (1948: 745). Shells and animal horns had been used for amplification since ancient times; however, designs for ear trumpets and bone conduction devices began to proliferate alongside theories of acoustics and hearing.[3] Amplifying trumpets were imagined to have manifold uses; tin dealers and trumpeters offered their devices for the hard of hearing, for overhearing, and for loud-speaking. Still, the term deafness was applied to "a wide variety of experiences including hearing impairments such as tinnitus and age related hearing degeneration" (Cockayne 493).

With deafness seeming like a difference in degree rather than a difference in kind, philosophers began to see in it the answer to many puzzles of communication: the nature of speech (its physiology and its instinctiveness), the interchangeability of the senses, and the comparability of sign systems. Another preoccupation of the seventeenth century was the possibility of a "universal language"—for international communication (spurred by the growth of vernacular publications and global trade); for language rationalization; or for insight into the origins of speech. As a route to philosophical experiment with simplified alphabets and artificial languages, scholars from diverse fields were motivated to teach prelingually deaf children.

Tutoring and small schools for deaf pupils spread throughout Europe in the second half of the seventeenth century, along with new pedagogical strategies and technical aids. Lines began to be drawn between the "oral" and "manual" approaches to deaf communication, represented most famously—and in nationalist terms—by the rivalry between "the German method" of Samuel Heinicke and "the French method" of Charles-Michel de l'Épée. The oral method propelled studies of the material voice, alongside protocols for lip-reading and articulation, and devices for synthesizing speech. The speech versus sign debate provided the foundation for the modern distinction between two deaf identities: deaf and Deaf, respectively.

In the nineteenth century, European methods for deaf education were exported around the world, often as a result of missionary work. In 1817, Thomas Gallaudet brought the French model and a deaf student from l'Épée's school to the United States. Gallaudet and the student, Laurent Clerc, founded the American School for the Deaf in Hartford, Connecticut. An American Sign Language (ASL) emerged at this site through the mixing of French, local, and home signs (gestures developed for communication on an ad hoc basis within families without formal sign language). Most of the deaf schools founded in the United States immediately thereafter also offered instruction in sign language. These residential schools—

with their ASL communities, publications, and traditions—incubated what became known, in the following century, as American Deaf culture.

By the 1860s, however, oralism began to prevail in the school system, partly through misguided Darwinism. Sign language, previously believed to be a natural and even uncorrupted human language, suddenly seemed "primitive" (Baynton 1996: 42). Speech became the primary feature that distinguished humans from the other animals. At the same time, studies of speech and hearing multiplied with the rise of phonetics, the pedagogical sciences, and the medical specialties of otology and laryngology. In the post–Civil War era, sign language instruction also suffered as the result of widespread demands for a unified national language. In 1880, when the International Conference of Teachers of the Deaf met in Milan, those present—mostly oralists—voted to advance a "pure" oral method on a global scale. Sign language would not even be a supplement; it had been reconceived as detrimental to oral education and even to rationality.[4] Although the classification of students in U.S. oral schools had previously included such categories as deaf, semi-deaf, deaf-mute, and semi-mute, oralists increasingly rejected the term "mute."

The best-known advocate of oralism from this time period is surely Alexander Graham Bell—now a canonical figure in sound studies. In 1871, Bell moved to the United States from Canada (his family had previously emigrated from Britain) to teach at the Boston School for Deaf Mutes. At the outset, he taught lip-reading and articulation with the aid of the Visible Speech system created by his father, Alexander Melville Bell. A founder of modern phonetics, Melville Bell had followed his own father into the field of elocution, and his wife—Graham Bell's mother—was deaf. Melville Bell developed an iconic script, or "physiological alphabet," for representing the positions of the vocal organs during the production of speech sounds. He foresaw this Visible Speech as an aid for streamlining spelling, in any language, and for teaching articulation to deaf people.

Melville Bell also saw in the science of phonetics the key to the design of new sound technologies: "Scientific men . . . have elaborated theories of optics—and look at the result? Wonderful mechanical adaptations of optical principles, before undreamt of, and which, otherwise, would never have been discovered. Might not an analogous result attend the philosophical investigation of the faculty of speech; and acoustic and articulative principles be developed, which would lead to mechanical inventions no less wonderful and useful than those in optics?" (1916: 41). John

Durham Peters proposes that we think of modern technical media and psychotechnical interfaces as cases of "applied physiology" (Peters 2004). Indeed, the telephone eventually built by Graham Bell made use of the "tympanic principle" of the human middle ear to transfer speech vibrations to an electrical current (Sterne 2003). The telephone was preceded by Bell's work on an "ear phonoautograph," a second generation Visible Speech machine that used an actual eardrum, attached to a stylus, to inscribe speech waves on a plate of sooted glass. Graphic inscription was known as the "universal language of science" in the 1800s for its ability to visualize the waveforms of which all the world's motions and sensory phenomena seemingly consisted. Graham Bell had hoped the phonoautograph would assist his investigations into the nature of vowels, and also supply visual feedback to his students (one of whom he married) as they practiced their articulation. As Hans Günter Tillmann explains, regarding the new phonetics, "it was assumed, first, that speech could be exhaustively investigated as a purely mechanical process, and secondly that the listener could be replaced by a deaf observer" (Tillman 1995: 402).

Later in his career, Graham Bell would also play a formative role in the emerging biopolitical approach to deafness. He became interested in eugenics as a means of "positive" population management; after conducting genealogies of deaf families and surveys of deafness in schools, he advocated deafness prevention through measures such as hygiene and bans on intermarriage among those born deaf. Bell's eugenics is an extreme example of what Tom Humphries calls "audism": the privileging of speech and hearing to the point of discrimination against those who are deaf, and especially those who communicate via sign (Humphries 1977).

Beginning in the nineteenth century, occupational hearing loss—induced by noise—attracted increasing medical interest (Dembe 1996). The development of electronic audiometry in the 1920s facilitated the medicalization of deafness—the creation of a "normal curve" for hearing and a new set of physiological categories by which deafness was named. Medicalization gained broad momentum in this time period, as medical jurisdiction expanded over matters previously considered to be educational, legal, or religious. In the United States, the "medicalization" of deafness resulted from a collaboration between physicians, social workers, and the telephone company; the latter supplied the electronic equipment for school audiometry and for the first National Health Surveys of hearing in 1936. Although statistics emerged as a discipline in the nineteenth century—at a time when tuning fork tones and watch ticks were used to gauge impairment—the "parametrization" of hearing did not take place until electronic audiometers afforded precise control over the volume and frequency of sound. The National Health Survey established a preliminary "reference zero" for hearing; along with this norm came graded categories of hearing loss: that is, mild, moderate, severe, and profound impairment.[5] These categories were at once individualizing and relative; rather than evoke identity or collectivity, they defined the individual as a variant of a population.[6]

In the early 1900s, activists at the New York League for the Hard of Hearing began to insist on a distinction between those born deaf and raised in institutions, whether signing or oral, and those who were *deafened* later in life, whether in part or in full. Prior to the twentieth century, adults with late hearing loss tended to be described simply as deaf or semi-deaf. "Hardness of hearing" was a euphemism in both instances. League members argued that "the deafened" required medical and paramedical interventions—surgery, prosthesis, speech therapy—to correct their "adventitious" impairments, which they contrasted to innate "defects." The League petitioned for hearing loss to be recognized as a military disability in 1918. In turn, the rehabilitation policies of the Veterans' Bureau, aimed at returning people with disabilities to work, would spur the prosthetic and therapeutic fields.

Deafening became a vast—and vastly salient—concept in the early twentieth century, fueled by a parallel discourse on noise. Audio engineers and noise reformers alike became concerned with noise-related hearing loss, which might be situational (occurring over radio sets and telephone lines) or literal (caused by earsplitting factories, battlegrounds, and urban centers). No longer defined by silence and alienation, deafness became associated with noise, immersion, masking, and inefficiency. Disability per se was not universalized, however: physical impairment remained distinct from situational deafening, as did "normal limitations" from actual disabilities.

The shift of deafness from a state of dissimilarity or philosophical curiosity to one of quantifiable deficit from a norm dovetailed, around World War I, with the aims of the rehabilitation movement. Audiometry facilitated treatment as well as tracking in the school system. Childhood screenings identified as "hearing impaired" children who might otherwise be considered deaf and educated in sign language; with the advent of wearable vacuum tube hearing aids in the 1930s, those children were increasingly mainstreamed.

Taken together, the rise of oral institutions and the mainstreaming of students with "moderate impairments" worked against the formation of sign language communities in residential schools (Baynton 1996: 94).[7]

Many deaf people, of course, continued to use sign language outside the classroom. Moreover, as part of the civil rights movement in the latter half of the twentieth century, many members of the sign language community began to insist that their "disability" was socially constructed, the result of stigma and barriers in the built environment. James Woodward proposed the concept of Deaf culture in 1972, capitalizing the term to distinguish the linguistic minority definition from the audiological one (Woodward 1972). As Harlan Lane clarifies, "late deafening and moderate hearing loss tend to be associated with the disability construction of deafness while early and profound deafness involve an entire organization of the person's language, culture, and thought around vision and tend to be associated with the linguistic minority construction" (Lane 2006: 80). The linguistic approach expanded the category of deafness: hearing children of deaf adults (CODAs) might also be Deaf, if they used sign language and participated in this minority culture.

The following decade, FDA approval of the cochlear implant commenced the biomedicalization of deafness; this electronic device transduces and processes environmental sounds, transmitting corresponding signals directly to the auditory nerve. While cochlear implant users are technically deaf, their audiograms post-implant may be comparable to those who are hard of hearing. In general, the boundary between deafness and hearing is now impossible to pinpoint. As human longevity increases, and as individuals are exposed to amplified sounds for significant fractions of their lives, hearing loss has become the norm.

That many electronic and acoustic innovations since the late nineteenth century are indebted to deafness—for example, telephones, carbon microphones, subminiature vacuum tubes, sound spectrography, closed captioning—is an indication of the commonness of hearing impairment, especially in an increasingly complex media ecology where "good communication" is narrowly defined. Several well-known inventors of audio-related technologies have themselves identified as deaf or hard of hearing (e.g., Thomas Edison, Oliver Heaviside, John Ambrose Fleming). Deafness has afforded insights into otology, acoustics, and phonetics, and in turn given rise to new psychotechnical devices. "Assistive" technologies designed for deaf and hard of hearing people have been repurposed for broad use. In still other cases, deaf users have appropriated mainstream audio technology: telephones have been turned into hearing aids; radio receivers have become tactile interfaces; videophones have been employed for long-distance signing.

The prevalence of deafness in the invention and development of telegraph, telephone, radio, Internet, and microelectronic technology has led historians to see disability as one of the "conditions of possibility" for modern media. In Friedrich Kittler's words, "handicaps"—especially deafness and blindness—"stood at the beginning of all media technology" (2006: 45). Yet even when deafness is conjured in this hyperbolic manner, it rarely features as more than a metaphor or exemplar.

In 2003, Jonathan Sterne observed that the field of sound studies had largely failed to incorporate the insights of Deaf and disability theory: "scholars of speech, hearing, and sound seem largely ignorant of the cultural work on deafness" (2003: 346). At present, a few authors have centered deafness in their accounts. In "Sound Studies Meets Deaf Studies" (2012), Michele Friedner and Stefan Helmreich enumerate several Deaf practices that enlarge the standard definitions of sound and listening. Deaf people, for instance, "infer sound" through observations of hearing behaviors. The deaf and the hearing alike experience low-frequency sound in the tactile register. Parallel to this emerging scholarship, deaf sound artists have worked to denaturalize hearing and otherwise-invisible communication infrastructures. As one example, Christine Sun Kim manipulates sound as a tool to teach her audiences to "unlearn sound etiquette."[8] Likewise, Hillel Schwartz chastises scholars of sound who posit hearing as "an invariable physiology: the sounds people hear may change, and their reactions to those sounds do change, but how people hear remains the same" (Schwartz 2011: 22). In *Making Noise*, he enumerates the ways human hearing varies—among individuals and across time periods—as a result of disease and nutrition; medicine and education; architecture and fashion; occupation and recreation; manner and law.

The history of deaf communication makes clear that sound is always already multimodal. Sound waves transfer between media (air, water, solids), and can be experienced by sensory domains beyond the ear. Vibrations, visual recordings, and speech gestures are all possible components of an acoustic event. The ear itself is a composite organ, which hears by mechanical and electrical means. Although attention to hearing difference has yet to become a regular feature of sound studies, deaf and hard of hearing people have long testified to the heterogeneity of ear-listening.

Joseph Furnas, historian and hearing aid wearer, wrote about his experience of "forty percent hearing" in the mid-twentieth century: navigating echoes in rooms with hard surfaces; seeking good lighting for speechreading; missing words and lines; picking up clothing noise and the buzz of neon lights with a body-worn hearing aid (1957). More recently, cochlear implant users like Michael Chorost describe the experience of electrical hearing: learning to correlate electronic sounds to speech and environmental noises; listening to music imperfectly rendered through a speech processor; picking up noise from electrical fields; listening to sounds that never exist as airborne waves, by connecting an implant directly to another electronic device (2005). Deafness is thus a variety of hearing; alternately, it can be conceived as a precondition of hearing or as the resistance to hearing and audism.

Notes

1. See the Deaf Space page of the Gallaudet University website, www.gallaudet.edu /Campus_Design/DeafSpace.html.

2. In contrast, today those with a 56- to 70-decibel hearing loss in the speech frequency range are considered to have only "moderately severe impairment." Although they cannot hear speech unaided, electronic amplification enables oral communication; here technology has transformed the classification system.

3. Bone conduction hearing aids pass sound waves to the auditory nerve through the teeth or skull.

4. As the second resolution from the conference stated, "the simultaneous use of speech and signs has the disadvantage of injuring speech, lipreading and precision of ideas."

5. Deafnesses also varied in kind: one might have hearing loss in the high or low frequency ranges; the cause might be traced to the middle or the inner ear; tinnitus or ringing might be the primary symptom.

6. For a more detailed critique of audiometric classification systems, and their industrial and legal applications, see Clark.

7. In 1975, the Education for All Handicapped Children Act formally encouraged mainstream schooling, with accommodations, over deaf-only institutions.

8. See Sun Kim's website, www.christinesunkim.com.

References

Bauman, H-Dirksen L., and Joseph M. Murray. 2009. "Reframing: From Hearing Loss to Deaf Gain." *Deaf Studies Digital Journal* 1: 1–10.

Baynton, Douglas C. 1996. *Forbidden Signs: American Culture and the Campaign against Sign Language.* Chicago: University of Chicago Press.

Békésy, Georg von, and Walter Rosenblith. 1948. "The Early History of Hearing—Observations and Theories." *Journal of the Acoustical Society of America* 20(6): 727–748.

Bell, Alexander Melville. 1916. *Principles of Speech and Dictionary of Sounds, Including Directions and Exercises for the Cure of Stammering and Correction of All Faults of Articulation.* Washington, DC: Volta Bureau.

Bonet, Juan Pablo. 1620. *Reduction de las Letras y Arte para Enseñar a Hablar los Mudos.* Madrid: Biblioteca Nacional de España.

Chorost, Michael. 2005. *Rebuilt: How Becoming Part Computer Made Me More Human.* New York: Houghton Mifflin. Available at http://christinesunkim.com/, accessed January 28, 2014.

Clark, John Greer. 1981. "Uses and Abuses of Hearing Loss Classification." *ASHA: A Journal of the American Speech-Language-Hearing Association* 23 (7): 493–500.

Cockayne, Emily. 2003. "Experiences of the Deaf in Early Modern England." *The Historical Journal* 46 (3): 493–510.

Dembe, Allard. 1996. *Occupation and Disease: How Social Factors Affect the Conception of Work-Related Disorders.* New Haven: Yale University Press.

Friedner, Michele, and Stefan Helmreich. 2012. "Sound Studies Meets Deaf Studies." *Senses and Society* 7(1): 72–86.

Furnas, J. C. 1957, June 1. "My First Ten Years with a Hearing Aid." *Saturday Evening Post,* 32–33, 40, 43. Available at www.gallaudet.edu/Campus_Design/DeafSpace.html, accessed January 28, 2014.

Humphries, Tom. 1977. "Communicating across Cultures (Deaf-Hearing) and Language Learning." Ph.D. diss., Union Institute and University, Cincinnati.

Kittler, Friedrich. 2006. "Thinking Colours and/or Machines." *Theory, Culture, and Society* 23: 39–50.

Lane, Harlan. 2006. "Construction of Deafness." In *The Disability Studies Reader,* ed. Lennard J. Davis, 79–92. New York: Routledge.

Peters, John Durham. 2004. "Helmholtz, Edison, and Sound History." In *Memory Bytes: History, Technology, and Digital Culture,* ed. Lauren Rabinovitz and Abraham Geil, 177–198. Durham: Duke University Press.

Rée, Jonathan. 1999. *I See a Voice: Deafness, Language, and the Senses—A Philosophical History.* New York: Metropolitan Books.

Schwartz, Hillel. 2011. *Making Noise: From Babel to the Big Bang and Beyond.* New York: Zone Books.

Sterne, Jonathan. 2003. *The Audible Past: Cultural Origins of Sound Reproduction.* Durham: Duke University Press.

Tillman, Hans Günter. 1995. "Early Modern Instrumental Phonetics." In *Concise History of the Language Sciences: From Sumerians to the Cognitivists,* ed. E. F. K. Koerner and R. E. Asher, 401–415. Oxford: Pergamon.

Woodward, James. 1972. Implications for Sociolinguistic Research among the Deaf. *Sign Language Studies* 1(1):1–7.

[5] Mark M. Smith

echo

Writing Sound History

An echo is nothing if not historical. To varying degrees, it is a faded fac-simile of an original sound, a reflection of time passed. It invites a habit of listening that not only allows us to locate origin (temporally and spatially) but, more important, test authenticity: how illustrative the sound was of the historical moment in which it was produced. The acoustic world in which echoes are generated after the original ring, bang, vocal moment—sound generally—is, inherently, a historical world. For this reason, his-torians, either consciously or unwittingly, think and write about echoes when analyzing sounds of the past (M. Smith 2002).

To what extent the echo can, does, or should have fidelity to the original sound is a question preoccupying historians of any period. Put simply, how, if at all, do historians hear, say, the boom of cannon during the American Civil War, the clang of bells in the nineteenth-century French countryside, or urbanization in the twentieth century? Plainly, the sounds generated in the past—in the years, months, weeks, even moments removed from the present—*seem* ephemeral and, for most of human history, were not subject to electromagnetic recording. As Bruce Smith has written, "for an histo-rian interested in the sounds of the past, there would seem to be nothing *there* to study, at least until the advent of electromagnetic recording devices early in the twentieth century" (B. Smith 2002: 307). This assumption re-garding the ephemerality of sound and its tight tethering to technologies of recording has proven seductive. It has veined the very epistemology of some historical thinking. Several historians invite us to write about both the electromagnetically recorded and unrecorded sounds of the past either by exercising what they call the historical imagination or by trying to reex-perience the sound through a sort of performative reenactment.

This tendency courts a number of questions central to the epistemol-ogy and ontology of what we might think of as *historical acoustemology.*

Historical acoustemology, as Bruce R. Smith has argued, not only recognizes (à la Steven Feld) that cultures establish their identities aurally as well as visually but invites the historian "to investigate whether people heard things—and remembered what they heard—in ways different from today" (B. Smith 1999: 48; see also Feld 1996). Among the most important questions guiding historical acoustemology are: is print capable of recording sound? Or must we insist on trying to re-create that same sound—that same cannon boom using salvaged cannon and gunpowder from the period—to reproduce what some perceive as a wholly accurate echo, one that our listening ears can reliably hear and say, yes, that's the sound of the past? What are the implications of such a practice? Can we or should we profitably distinguish between the (re)production of a sound and our consumption of it? And does it matter if the sounds in which the historian is interested occurred in an age when sounds could not be recorded electromagnetically? Does the reproducibility of a sound, either on record, on tape, or electronically, make that sound more accessible for the historian? If so, is the historian of the pre-record era at an impossible disadvantage, unable to make sense at all of the acoustic past? What are the ethics of these inquiries?

Historians by no means agree on answers to these questions of how to identify, locate, evaluate, and interpret echoes. How historians interpret the meaning, value, and relevance of sound not only reflects their epistemological preferences but shapes in profound and meaningful ways how they interpret and write about the past. At base, thinking about echoes is a way to think about the retrievability or irretrievability of sonicity, the central importance of historical context to understanding sound as sense and as subject, and the ability of print to reliably capture what actors in the past thought about what they heard, and what they did not.

Debating Sound History

Scholarly histories of sound and listening are burgeoning. We now possess fine studies of sound in colonial America (Rath 2003), the history of noise (Schwartz 2011), listening and voice in colonial Australia (Carter 1992), and acoustemology in early modern England (B. Smith 1999), among many others. Major historical journals, including the *Journal of American History* and the *American Historical Review*, now take the history of sound seriously and have, in the past few years, published several articles on the topic (Rath 2008; Rosenfeld 2011). Historical acoustemology has also gained public relevance. Increasingly, museums and professionals in historic preservation call on historians to suggest how to introduce sound to the general public. Museums around the world are turning to sound installations in an effort to better "engage" the general public and educate their visitors, and historians of sound are often asked to comment on these efforts and, sometimes, to serve as consultants (M. Smith 2010).

In other words, there's quite a lot at stake in working with echoes.

The lines of disagreement among historians are fairly well delimited. On one side, there is a very tenuous claim that we can recapture and reexperience the sounds of the past. The most radical of these claims posits the recapturing of sounds—from any period of history—as undiluted and unmediated. According to this position, past sounds are directly exportable to the present through listening to recordings and the reenactment of sounds. The driving force behind this assumption seems to have a great deal to do with the desirability of "consuming" history by inviting students and the general public to experience the sounds of the past and thereby, somehow, to make the past more accessible and, perhaps critically, more commercially relevant. The alternative argument maintains that efforts along these lines are deeply misleading and insists that without sufficient appreciation of the context in which the sounds occurred, we warp our understanding of echoes to the point of intellectual desiccation. This line of inquiry also makes the case, either explicitly or implicitly, for the power of text to capture, with fidelity and authenticity, the meaning of sounds to the people who were doing the listening at the time of their production.

Producing and Consuming Sound

Many historians stress the need to historicize the senses, "to distinguish between the historicity of a physical experience (in this case sense perception) and the form in which it has been preserved or handed down" in order "to break with the aprioristic assumption of the 'naturalness' of sense perception" (Jütte 2005: 8, 9). In other words, we "should not merely describe the range of sounds and smells that existed at a particular time, as evocative as that might be, but should uncover the meanings those sounds and smells had for people" (Classen 2001: 357). Wise words, but ones not always heard, even by the most careful listeners of the past.

Take, for example, an important book on the history of American slavery by two gifted historians, Shane White and Graham White. In *The Sounds of Slavery: Discovering African American Thought through Songs, Sermons, and Speech* (2005), the Whites catalog some of slavery's sounds, mostly musical and linguistic, from the mid-eighteenth century to the period just after the Civil War. The book is accompanied by a CD with eighteen tracks of field calls, prayers, spirituals, and sermons uttered by ex-slaves that were recorded and collected by folklorists John and Alan Lomax in the 1930s. The authors include these recordings in an effort "to illustrate more clearly the nature and meaning of African American sounds" and, critically, to "bring us about as close as we are ever going to get to hearing" the sounds of slavery. Here, the Whites offer a very particular reading and understanding of echoes. While they acknowledge that we "cannot really recover the sounds" of slavery, they nevertheless invite us in their text to listen to particular tracks in an effort to "hear something similar" recorded in the 1930s, seventy or so years after slavery had been abolished in the United States.

Clearly, though, it is impossible to listen to the sounds of slavery: not just because they were never recorded but because of the radical differences between the contexts in which these sounds were produced and the contexts in which we currently listen. Moreover, the 1930s recordings themselves harbor the bias of ethnographic recording. As Jonathan Sterne has pointed out at length, the U.S. ethnographers who recorded the sounds and voices of African Americans and Native Americans in the early decades of the twentieth century used recording technology in a way that reflected core prejudices and conceits. As Sterne puts it: "the phonograph became a tool of embalming an already supposedly frozen native present for the future," rendering the recorded sound as "an artifact of an event, not simply as the event itself." Part of what we hear in such recordings, then, is an effort by those doing the recording to artifactualize a living culture: a sort of salvage ethnography that in its very act of production harbors an act of—and hope for—reproduction and consumption. For this reason, among others, the CD accompanying the Whites' book tells us more about the values of those producing the recording than it does about the meaning of sounds uttered and heard during slavery.

This perhaps explains why other historians have resisted the temptation to accompany their texts with recordings, even when their subject matter has been recorded and preserved to some degree. For example, we could easily imagine Karin Bijsterveld including a CD of recordings of traffic and aircraft noise in her study *Mechanical Sound: Technology, Culture, and Public Problems of Noise in the Twentieth Century*, to demonstrate to readers what noise supposedly sounded like in the 1940s, 1950s, and 1960s. But she did not because, as her study shows, sounds and noises can only be understood in their historical context. She explains, quite correctly: "listening to a recording of museum steam machines might give you the impression that these machines were not very 'loud' at all, forgetting that steam machines may not have been as well oiled when originally in use as in a museum decades later" (Bijsterveld 2009: 25). In other words, recordings are inherently ahistorical and, as such, not only fail to communicate which constituencies heard what and how and why; they also lull unwitting listeners into thinking that what they are hearing is freighted with the same meaning as the sound (or silence) in its original context.

Historicizing Sound

Efforts by professional historians and museum curators wrongly marry the production of the past to its present-day consumption, and strongly suggest that written evidence in print is not as effective in granting us access to the past as are the recreated, reproduced, and relived echoes of recordings. The problem with all of this has to do with our apparent need to consume—and therefore render consumable—something that is, in fact, beyond consumption. While it is perfectly possible to recreate the decibel level and tone of a hammer hitting an anvil from the nineteenth century, or a piece of music from 1600 (especially if we still have the score and original instruments), it is impossible to experience those sensations in the same way as those who heard these sounds in the past. What was loud or melodious or pleasing to the ear is not, in this way, recoverable (Ross 2001). This point emerges, albeit sometimes implicitly, in the study of archaeoacoustics. While a good deal of attention is paid to the question of intentionality—whether or not certain resonances and echoes were intended by the architects themselves—what seems most salient about archaeoacoustics is precisely the point being advanced here: that we can recreate even prehistorical architectural sounds, but in the absence of written sources explaining what those sounds, echoes, and resonances meant to people at the time, it is extremely difficult to fathom their meanings (Scarre and Lawson 2006). The same holds true for all historical evidence, visual included. For example, "we" do not "see" the engraving of a slave whipping from the 1830s in the same light, with the same meaning, as the abolitionist did at the time. That something as seemingly straightforward as a color was, as Michel Pastoureau's (2001) wonderful history of the color blue makes clear, subject to significant variation—not only in its meaning but in its very definition—suggests the danger in making easy, ahistorical claims for the senses.

The argument about echoes and the historicity of the senses, their reproducibility, and whether or not we can (or ought) to try to reexperience the auditory and sensate past is beginning to have currency; this is surprising because this debate is not especially new. In his seminal commentary on how to best approach a history of the senses, Alain Corbin worried about Guy Thuillier's efforts to trace the evolution of the sensory environment by cataloging and compiling "the relative intensity of the noises which might reach the ear of a villager in the Nivernais in the middle of the nineteenth century." Such an approach, said Corbin, "implies the non-historicity of the modalities of attention, thresholds of perception, significance of noises, and configuration of the tolerable and the intolerable" (Corbin 1995: 183). Without a dedicated and careful attempt to attach specific historical meanings, a catalog of historical noises is not only of very modest heuristic worth but, in fact, quite dangerous in its ability to inspire unwitting faith that these are the "real" sounds of the past.

Many of the most serious historians of sound have taken Corbin's counsel to heart. Take, for example, Emily Thompson's (2002) masterful investigation of the emergence of the soundscapes of modernity. Thompson is interested in how architectural acoustic design in pre–World War II America reconfigured the way people understood the sounds they heard. She details the emergence of building design, the scientific basis of acoustic architecture, and the increasing use of sound-shaping and sound-absorbing materials to chart the introduction of a modern soundscape in urban America. In examining the emergence of the business of sound control, Thompson does not attempt to recreate or reexperience the acoustic spaces of 1930s office buildings in U.S. cities but relies instead on careful readings of the printed sources that detail the ways people understood and interpreted their changing acoustic environments. Thompson's first point is that public policy efforts to quiet urban America were far less successful than private, business solutions to containing and shaping the sounds of inside spaces. The solutions to combating modern urban din resided, suggests Thompson, not in regulating outside noise—as various municipal urban noise abatement societies had been trying to do for years—but in taking advantage of sound-suppressing materials used in offices and rooms. This, in turn, allows Thompson to make the important point that these materials did not simply eliminate noise; rather, they reconfigured and created new sounds that, because they lacked reverberation, came to be defined by listeners as new and, critically, as modern. Reverberated sound was consigned as noise, reflecting and inspiring the belief that cacophonic and reverberant environments were inefficient and sapped workers' productive capacity. This ability to deploy architectural material in new ways had a profound effect on the ways people understood their relationship to space. When reverberation—which had historically been a key mode of understanding space—was reconceived as noise, "a connection as old as architecture itself" (172) was severed.

Thompson makes all of these points by paying close attention to what people said and wrote about what they heard; what they said and wrote about reverberation, quietude, and the kinds of sounds produced by acoustic materiality. Her argument does not depend on recordings of city streets or offices from the era or attempt to reproduce the sounds she describes but relies exclusively on printed and written sources to make her case. To understand and explain how and why urban American workers came to hear in different, modern ways, Thompson necessarily has to pay close attention to the various meanings of hearing and listening prior to the adoption of noise-absorbing materials at the turn of the century, and from this, explain the ways people started to mediate and understand the new sounds they heard and the ones they now heard less often.

On the Value of Print

I will conclude by arguing that printed evidence offers a far more robust way to access the ways sounds and silences were understood in the past, regardless of whether those sounds were recorded electronically. In some instances, as Patrick Feaster shows in his keyword entry (see PHONOGRAPHY), writers could use, quite deliberately, the printed word to convey and even reproduce the sounds of words and events, at least for contemporaries reading their work. Beyond the examples offered by Feaster, print itself can do much to capture the spoken word and inscribe the meanings individuals and groups attach (or supposedly attach—for there were and are stereotypes about who made noise and who was a careful listener) to sounds and habits of listening. Aural metaphors, similes, onomatopoeia, and everyday descriptions did the work of recorded sound admirably and, used with care, used with an attention to context, can tell us a great deal about the meaning of sounds in the past (M. Smith 2001, 2014; Hibbitts 1994). For example, soldiers during the American Civil War elected to describe the sounds of bullets on the battlefield using prevailing metaphors that made sense to them. Soldiers described the sounds of bullets using comparisons from their world, not ours. This is why bullets sounded like buzzing bees and swarms of insects to many, comparisons that in turn, help remind historians of the largely agricultural background of many soldiers, a fact sometimes lost sight of when historians talk about the Civil War as a thoroughly industrialized or modern war (M. Smith 2014). In fact, so powerful are these echoes in print that even if we did have access to the unrecordable sounds of the past—even if we did magically manage to listen to electromagnetically reproduced sounds from slavery in the 1850s or the whizz of bullets and the boom of cannon from the American Civil War—we would be better off eschewing this evidence in favor of written and printed descriptions of what these sounds meant to the various constituencies of the time.

If the print revolution did, in fact, elevate the eye and denigrate the nose, ear, tongue, and skin (and of that claim I am not convinced), printed evidence and the sensory perceptions recorded by contemporaries nevertheless constitute the principal medium through which we can access the sounds of the past and their meanings. Historians and the general public deserve something better than an easily digestible, palatable auditory past. In offering an appropriately historicized one, we treat our subject matter and subjects with greater respect and also do something to dilute consumerist values that threaten to warp the teaching, understanding, and presentation of the past.

References

Bijsterveld, Karin. 2009. *Mechanical Sound: Technology, Culture, and Public Problems of Noise in the Twentieth Century*. Cambridge, MA: MIT Press.

Carp, Richard M. 1997. "Perception and Material Culture: Historical and Cross-cultural Perspectives." *Historical Reflections/Réflexions Historiques* 23: 260–300.

Carter, Paul. 1992. *The Sound In-Between: Voice, Space, Performance*. Sydney: New South Wales University Press.

Classen, Constance. 2001. "The Senses." In *Encyclopedia of European Social History from 1350–2000*, ed. Peter N. Stearns, 355–364. New York: Gale.

Classen, Constance. 2007. "Museum Manners: The Sensory Life of the Early Museum." *Journal of Social History* 40: 895–914.

Corbin, Alain. 1995. *Time, Desire, Horror: Towards a History of the Senses.* Trans. Jean Birrell. Cambridge: Polity Press.

Feld, Steven. 1996. "Waterfalls of Song: An Acoustemology of Place Resounding on Bosavi, Papua New Guinea." In *Senses of Place*, ed. Steven Feld and Keith H. Basso, 91–135. Santa Fe: School of American Research Press.

Hibbitts, Bernard J. 1994. "Making Sense of Metaphors: Visuality, Aurality, and the Reconfiguration of American Legal Discourse." *Cardozo Law Review* 16: 229.

Hoffer, Peter Charles. 2004. *Sensory Worlds of Early America.* Baltimore: Johns Hopkins University Press.

Jütte, Robert. 2005. *A History of the Senses: From Antiquity to Cyberspace.* Oxford: Polity Press.

Parr, Joy. 2001. "Notes for a More Sensuous History of Twentieth-Century Canada: The Timely, the Tacit, and the Material Body." *Canadian Historical Review* 82: 720–745.

Pastoureau, Michel. 2001. *Blue: The History of a Color.* Princeton: Princeton University Press.

Rath, Richard Cullen. 2003. *How Early America Sounded.* Ithaca: Cornell University Press.

Rath, Richard Cullen. 2008. "Hearing American History." *Journal of American History* 95: 417–431.

Rosenfeld, Sophia. 2011. "On Being Heard: A Case for Paying Attention to the Historical Ear." *American Historical Review* 116: 316–334.

Ross, Charles D. 2001. *Civil War Acoustic Shadows.* Shippensburg, PA: White Mane.

Scarre, Chris, and Graeme Lawson. 2006. *Archaeoacoustics.* Cambridge: McDonald Institute for Archaeological Research.

Schwartz, Hillel. 2011. *Making Noise: From Babel to the Big Bang and Beyond.* New York: Zone Books.

Smith, Bruce. 1999. *The Acoustic World of Early Modern England: Attending to the O-Factor.* Chicago: University of Chicago Press.

Smith, Bruce. 2002. "How Sound Is Sound History? A Response to Mark Smith." *Journal of The Historical Society* 2: 307–315.

Smith, Mark M. 2001. *Listening to Nineteenth-Century America.* Chapel Hill: University of North Carolina Press.

Smith, Mark M. 2002. "Echoes in Print: Method and Causation in Aural History." *Journal of The Historical Society* 2: 317–336.

Smith, Mark M. 2007. "Producing Sense, Consuming Sense, Making Sense: Perils and Prospects for Sensory History." *Journal of Social History* 40: 841–858.

Smith, Mark M. 2010, May 24. "Looking to Make Sense: Perils and Prospects in Applied Sensory History." Keynote address, Historic House Luncheon, Annual Meeting of the American Association of Museums, Los Angeles.

Smith, Mark M. 2014. *The Smell of Battle, the Taste of Siege: A Sensory History of the Civil War.* New York: Oxford University Press.

Sterne, Jonathan. 2003. *The Audible Past: Cultural Origins of Sound Reproduction.* Durham: Duke University Press.

Thompson, Emily. 2002. *The Soundscape of Modernity: Architectural Acoustics and the Culture of Listening in America, 1900–1933.* Cambridge, MA: MIT Press.

White, Shane, and Graham White. 2005. *The Sounds of Slavery: Discovering African American History through Songs, Sermons, and Speech.* Boston: Beacon Press.

hearing

I

The simple act of hearing implies a medium for sound, a body with ears to hear, a frame of mind to do the same, and a dynamic relation between hearer and heard that allows for the possibility of mutual effects. Hearing is all these things: it is human nature and human history, deeply personal and irreducibly intersubjective, environmentally grounded and stretched toward transcendence. When we study hearing, we hold its elements in tension with one another.

Before there was a field known as sound studies, there were rich traditions of thought about hearing in philosophy, theology, music, acoustics, psychology, physiology, education, interpersonal communication, ecology, anatomy, astronomy, sociology, history, poetry, art history, and many other fields. In this keyword entry, I sketch out one possible history of the idea of hearing, focusing on constructs that remain powerful and persuasive down to the present day.

In English, "hear" and "hearing" are very old words. Emerging from Germanic roots, constructs of "hear" as connoting the perception of sound or to be aware of something by means of the ear date back to the year 950; as "predicated of the ear" to 825. "Hearing" as an adjective to describe something or someone that hears dates to 1300, and as an act of perception or audience, to 1225 (OED, s.v. "hear," "hearing"). Of course, the concept is considerably older, and ancient and medieval notions of hearing are still very much with us in contemporary thought. A few brief lines at the beginning of Aristotle's "On Sense and the Sensible" have set the terms for centuries of subsequent discussion: "seeing, regarded as a supply for the primary wants of life, and in its direct effects, is the superior sense; but for developing intelligence, and in its indirect consequences, hearing takes the precedence. . . . For rational discourse is a cause of instruction in virtue of its being audible, which it is, not directly, but indirectly; since it is composed of words, and each word is a thought-symbol. Accordingly, of persons destitute from birth of either sense, the blind are more intelligent than the deaf and dumb" (Aristotle 1931, para. 8).[1] Here we have two founding binary oppositions in Western thought about hearing encapsulated in a few frequently cited lines: the distinction between hearing and Deafness, and the distinction between hearing and seeing, and the concomitant privilege of sight over hearing, the so-called hegemony of vision. I will consider each in turn.

The legacy of hearing as the basis of intelligence, and indeed the soul, can be found in classic and contemporary writings on hearing and listening. For Jean-Luc Nancy (2007: 6), hearing operates as the seat of subjectivity and intersubjectivity: "to be listening will always, then, be to be straining toward or in an approach to the self." Good enough, except for those who do not or cannot hear and must approach their selves by other means, without the benefit of the openness to others that is the basis of his theory of intersubjectivity. Against the presupposition of a hearing subject with full access to its own faculties, Mara Mills (2010) shows that the Deaf and hard of hearing are everywhere in sound history, both as objects and subjects. To understand the faculty of audition is, then, simultaneously to understand its possibilities and its limits, its status as embedded in real social relations, and its power as a figurative and imaginative metaphor for other registers of human action.

The binary division of hearing and seeing also carries a weighty legacy, especially as carried forward by Christian spiritualism, and its secular guise as "orality" and "secondary orality" in the writings of so-called Toronto School writers like Walter Ong, Marshall McLuhan, and Eric Havelock. Elsewhere I have characterized this legacy in terms of a litany of differences between hearing and seeing that are called forth as unquestioned warrants to support a host of arguments, the *audiovisual litany*. It proposes the following differences:

— hearing is spherical, vision is directional
— hearing immerses its subject, vision offers a perspective
— sounds come to us, but vision travels to its object
— hearing is concerned with interiors, vision is concerned with
surfaces

— hearing involves physical contact with the outside world, vision requires distance from it
— hearing places you inside an event, seeing gives you a perspective on the event
— hearing tends toward subjectivity, vision tends toward objectivity
— hearing brings us into the living world, sight moves us toward atrophy and death
— hearing is about affect, vision is about intellect
— hearing is a primarily temporal sense, vision is a primarily spatial sense
— hearing is a sense that immerses us in the world, while vision removes us from it (Sterne 2003: 15)

Not only did writers in the spiritualist tradition claim to account for the difference between hearing and seeing; they claimed that the hallmarks of the modern era—reason, rationalism, the subject/object split, science, and capitalism—all emerged from the privilege of sight over audition (McLuhan 1960, 1962; Ong 1967, 1982; Havelock 1988). As Don Ihde (2007) has shown in his classic phenomenological study of hearing, many of the aspects of auditory perception that writers attribute to the audiovisual litany do not actually hold up when we closely examine auditory experience. More recently, historians and anthropologists of sound have chronicled organizations of sonic culture that call into question the assumptions about sound, culture, and consciousness that would be implied from the audiovisual litany.[2] Yet in the cultural theory and history that it subtends, the oral-literate dyad (often joined by a third term, "electronic") continues to exert a surprising degree of influence. It often still frames the ways many scholars characterize the long history of communication in the West and is used heuristically to differentiate dominant Western constructs of communication from those of imaginary Others. The dreams of intersubjectivity based in hearing also animate romantic talk of listening publics in discussions of national radio. Going forward, our challenge will be to construct alternate narratives of world sensory history, ones that do not presuppose fixed sense-characteristics or ratios, while attending sensitively to the ideological persistence of these older senses of hearing.

II

The changing fortunes of hearing in the modern era can best be illustrated by the careers of two adjectives associated with the ear in the English language. The term *aural* began its history in 1847 meaning "of or pertaining to the organ of hearing"; it did not appear in print denoting something "received or perceived by the ear" until 1860. Until then, the term *auricular* was used to describe something "of or pertaining to the ear" or perceived by the ear. This was not a mere semantic difference: *auricular* carried with it connotations of oral tradition and hearsay as well as the external features of the ear visible to the naked eye (the folded mass of skin that is often referred to as the ear is technically either the *auricle*, the *pinna*, or the *outer ear*). *Aural*, meanwhile, carried with it no connotations of oral tradition and referred specifically to the middle ear, the inner ear, and the nerves that turn vibrations into what the brain perceives as sound (as in *aural surgery*) (OED, s.v. "aural," "auricular"). The idea of the aural and its decidedly medical inflection is a part of the larger historical transformations of sound over the last four hundred years. *Aural* implies ears that are objects and tools of scientific exploration, part of bodily and media systems, and able to receive sound which itself came to be understood as a form of transmission (Sterne 2003). While the idea of hearing as the basis of intersubjectivity would persist in various strands of humanistic thought, it could be argued that since the mid-nineteenth century, dominant ideas of hearing in science, technology, and medicine retreated further and further into the head, the inner ear, and the brain.

Modern physiology, acoustics, medicine, engineering, and psychoacoustics animate a construct of the hearing ear as something operational, quantifiable, and separable from subjective experience. Many branches of psychoacoustics—the study of auditory perception—explicitly separate the faculty of hearing from the meaning of what is heard. When psychoacousticians or audiologists use sound technologies to test and describe the mechanism of human hearing, they ask questions of the auditor that allow them to establish "just-noticeable differences," or the least perceptible unit of audible change in a sound ("raise your hand when you hear a tone"). Our modern measures of sound, like the decibel and normal frequency response of human hearing, arose from a body of research created by scientists who were intent on dividing hearing from listening, and who used listening to give access to hearing. When writers in sound studies ascribe to hearing the quality of pure physical capability and to listening subjective intention, they mobilize the same epistemic history. *When we talk about hearing in the state of nature, separate from any particular person or cultural scene, we animate this contradiction.*

The problem of overcoming subjectivity was perhaps best expressed in what is now called the Weber-Fechner law in psychophysics. The law says that changes in physical intensities (for instance, the loudness of a sound), do not automatically result in a change of perceived intensities. This is incredibly important: it posits instruments outside the body as more accurate auditors than human ears themselves, even as it also seeks to establish universal regularities in human hearing, the normal, and the pathological. As Alexandra Hui has shown, perhaps the greatest irony is that this supremely rationalist conception of hearing emerged from a German scientific field in the nineteenth century that was thoroughly intermixed with and infused by the contemporaneous Romanticism of the German musical field. While the psychophysicists came to know hearing through music, Hermann Helmholtz—whose famous 1863 *On the Sensations of Tone* still influences discussions of hearing—came to know hearing through tuning forks and resonators (Peters 2004; Kursell 2008; Pantalony 2009; Hui 2012). Something similar happened in the twentieth century when hearing tests conducted on children and on the hard of hearing with equipment from the telephone company led to the establishment of both modern understandings of the hearing subject and the acoustic parameters of the telephone system as we know it.

In many fields, the discursive rules of psychoacoustics and psychophysics condition the kinds of questions that can be asked about human hearing, how those questions can be investigated, and how they can be applied in research on sound technology. Our present psychoacoustic construct of *hearing in itself* is only accessible through sonic equipment, and through users who are comfortable working with it. Everything that is known about hearing in its natural state is a result of the interactions between ears and sound technologies.

These new kinds of hearing subjects came with a group of technocultural stand-ins: microphones, decibel meters, and reverberation equations. The ear itself became one particular iteration of a whole field of *hearing equipment*. While this might seem like a purely technological development, it must be stressed that hearing equipment was always tied to particular *ways of hearing* and institutional contexts that defined hearing, as well as what was heard. Microphones showed up in acoustics, telephony, and radio, and later public speech. Decibel meters migrated out from telephony into architectural acoustics and urban social policy; and so forth. While it may be tempting to think of technical and cultural innovations in hearing as separate things, they were inextricably intertwined; indeed, so much so that decades later prevailing cultural definitions of hearing would restate technical conceptions, and vice-versa. Emily Thompson (2002) shows how as architectural acousticians turned to microphones, decibel meters and other hearing delegates that allowed them to quantify sound, the definition and perception of noise grew—in everyday life, in science, and in aesthetics. At the same time, the same architectural acousticians redefined the acoustic signatures of physical spaces—their reverberant qualities—as a kind of noise and worked to construct an echoless "one best" modern sound. As Karin Bijsterveld (2008) argues, these ways of hearing would become the basis not only of scientific and technical knowledge, but of social policy and the construction of sound and noise as public problems. In both cases, a hearing subject is at the center of expert and public discussions of noise and sonic space, but that subject is represented through ensembles of hearing equipment. Its inner experience is rendered comparable and knowable through measurements, numbers, and professional expressions.

Where microphones, speakers, meters, and signal processing devices came together in various forms as "instruments" for scientists, engineers, and technicians, they came together as "media" in the everyday experience of nonprofessional listeners. Telephones and radios were made of much of the same material "stuff" as the instruments used by professionals, but because their institutional and cultural forms were different, they raised a slightly different set of questions about the status of hearing in modern life. In telephony, for instance, microphones heard for people at one end of the phone line and speakers spoke for them at the other, all enabled by a vast technical and industrial infrastructure that could connect speech and hearing at great distances. Thus, early sound media did not so much "extend" or "transform" a natural state of hearing as call it into question through the act of technical and institutional delegation.

These media also made use of the focused, quantified hearing subject of science, acoustics, and engineering, but that tendency was juxtaposed with distraction, an equally intense and important formation of hearing. One of the most durable forms of evidence for distraction as a cultural form is background music—music that was meant to be heard, but not listened to. Various forms of background or "middle music" had existed throughout the nineteenth century in bars and other public spaces. French composer Eric Satie famously proposed a "furniture music," explicitly composed to be heard and not listened to, which later became a business strategy of British war plants and the Muzak corporation (Jones and Schumacher 1992; Lanza 1994; Baade 2011), and even later the basis of ambient genres of electronic music. In *Being and Time* (1962: 140–141), Martin Heidegger worried over radio and telephone technologies producing excess familiarity through their "de-severing" tendencies, where distance and remoteness no longer had a necessary relationship. For Heidegger, the world heard through the phone was somehow closer to the subject than the receiver itself. Here distraction manifests a kind of alienation from the proper ratios of experience. Distraction was also a central theme in Frankfurt School writings: while Walter Benjamin (1968: 221) wondered after the choral performance that resounded in the drawing room, Theodor Adorno (2002: 257–258) wondered what would become of audiences who let their attention wander from the great works of the Western symphonic tradition.

Although these writers considered distraction an exceptional condition, alongside the tradition of background music, radio has come to be understood as a site for institutionalized, routine, and managed distraction (which is to say, everyday distraction). Recent radio historiography has shown that distraction was actually a constitutive feature of media audiencing, a fact well-known to the media industries themselves. The basic assumption that audiences might be listening in a state of distraction structured everything from TV dramas' backing music to the vocal inflections of broadcast sports announcers; television soundtracks were built around the idea of a domestic audience that might hear the program in another room and need to come in to see what was happening if something sounded interesting (Dinsdale 1932; Altman 1992; Goodman 2009; Russo 2010). Such programing techniques emerged from years' worth of experience with radio audiences. The hearing subject of sound media was thus an amalgam of the different modalities of hearing I have considered thus far. The hearing subject might be a person whose ears might be part of an ensemble of hearing equipment; it might be part of a listening public, animating collectivity through the intersubjective and imaginative powers of hearing; and it might *also* be hearing in a state of distraction, bound up in the rapid and shifting flows of modern experience.

III

People have no direct intellectual or experiential access to the faculty of hearing in its supposed state of nature. We can posit that the interiority of experience exists and try to describe it, but that access is always mediated. We can't even hear ourselves hearing, or not hearing. The only way a hearing researcher has access to hearing as pure faculty is through the subject's highly cultured act of listening. In a way, this is nothing more than Charles Sanders Peirce's proposition that we can only access actuality through relations: "as long as things do not act upon one another there is no sense or meaning in saying that they have any being" (1955: 76). The primary category of experience available to people is what he calls secondness, a knowledge of the world through things acting on other things, "a mode of being of one thing which consists in how a second object is": in a hearing test, my hearing is measured when my hand goes up, which is a reaction to my felt perception of a tone. Scholars may attribute a firstness to hearing, a being-in-itself, but "we can know nothing of such possibilities [except] so far as they are actualized" (76). Both listening and technology are prior to hearing, and investigating the scene of audibility always reveals power relations that subtend its most basic sonic possibilities. Every configuration of hearing and sounding implies people, power, and placement.

There are many approaches that assert the primacy of difference in the study of hearing. Ever since Franz Boas (1889) criticized his colleagues' assumptions that they understood how to hear native languages, anthropologists have had a rich tradition of cultural relativism to draw on. In the scientific field, psychoacousticians, especially working in the ecological psychology tradition, have emphasized the importance of culture and context for the analysis of hearing as a human faculty (Plomp 2002; Clarke 2005). The intellectual and cultural historians cited above have used terms like "aurality" and "soundscape" to similar effect. But these remain minority positions in the broader discourses around hearing, where writers in sound studies can intervene by offering a broader range of accounts of hearing in the service of promoting a plurality of sonic cultures. In this keyword entry, I have given several histories of hearing, but these are not just histories of hearing cultures. They are also histories of hearing natures.

Historicism and constructivism are usually considered to be on the epistemological side of relativism. But hearing and its limits can be at once an empirical, material, and sometimes brutal reality *and also* subject to historical and personal transformation. As Eduardo Viveiros de Castro has written, "we need not be surprised by a way of thinking which posits bodies as the great differentiators yet at the same time states their transformability" (1998: 481; see also Hage 2011, 2012). Just as the technological scene of a hearing test has a history, so too does the work of listening. Subjects of hearing tests are presumed to know a whole set of techniques—such as distinguishing tones in the headphones from other sounds, or for that matter, from the ringing of tinnitus. But tinnitus—and hearing damage in general—shows the limits of a purely culturalist (or symbolic) historicism. Hearing bodies are radically transformed by the worlds in which they dwell. As scholars we can isolate contexts like film sound, telephony, or concert hall acoustics. For hearing subjects who live in the modern world, and perhaps have sufficient experience of earbuds, jackhammers, airplanes, and dance clubs, film sound, telephony, and concert halls will be heard quite differently. Of course this falls somewhat short of Viveiros de Castro's propositions of coexistent competing natures (a multinaturalism more radical than multiculturalism). But it has the virtue of simplicity. Historicist and culturalist accounts of hearing have been a central thread in sound studies work to date. Expanding on the promise of these two approaches through multinaturalism would be a welcome challenge, as well as broadening the global scope of the field's objects and histories. The West is still the epistemic center for much work in sound studies, and a truly transnational, translational, or global sound studies will need to recover or produce a proliferating set of natures and histories to work with.[3]

Tinnitus and hearing damage point us in other critical directions as well. Sound studies has a creeping *normalism* to it—that is, an epistemological and political bias toward an idealized, normal, nondisabled hearing subject (see Davis 1995; Siebers 2008). If we are to believe Nancy and his fellow Romantics, the Deaf, the hard of hearing, and all of us hardening-of-hearing (one might say *those of us who continue to live*) are doomed to receding relations to authenticity and intersubjectivity. We should hold onto the idea that the ways people can hear, the limits of that hearing, and the conditions of possibility for hearing all provide points of entry into what it means to be a person at a given time or place (Erlmann 2010: 17–18). To study hearing is to study the making of subjects, which means it is also to study the denigration and unmaking of subjects. Work informed by disability studies, like Siebers's or Mills's, is immensely helpful here, because it shows how environments condition and transform bodies and subjectivities. Environments are ableing or disabling for hearing subjects—those qualities do not inhere in the subjects themselves, even if there are very real, material differences in hearing among people.

Without ears to hear it, there is no sound. All our definitions of sound and sonic phenomena tend toward anthropomorphism—as when geophones "hear" vibrations in the earth that are inaudible to the naked ear—or bioacoustics, as when sounds are defined as sounds with reference to the hearing of animals instead of people. But this too requires interrogation, since animals become referents for people, sometimes violently, as in laboratories. Microphones and animals do important work as our delegates (as more hearing equipment), but they too need to be accounted for, and not simply imagined as reflections of ourselves.

We ought to reflexively subject our own hearing to the critiques to which we subject the hearing of others. What would sound studies become if we began without the automatic assumptions that we have direct, full access to our own hearing, or through our hearing, direct access to the sonic world, or through the sonic world, intersubjectivity with others? Such a project is a little difficult to imagine, but it would at least substitute a new set of problems for the ones that come from idealizing hearing and idealizing ourselves as perfect auditors. If no sound is possible without hearing, then sound studies—but also many forms of politics—begins with hearing the hearing of others.

Notes

1. Aristotle is not the last or only word on hearing among the Greeks, but his position on hearing and Deafness is repeatedly invoked to argue both for the superiority of the hearing over the hard-of-hearing, and for the nobility of hearing. We can find examples in nineteenth-century tracts on hearing and Deafness (see Davis 1995, especially his discussion of nationalism and deafness), and also twentieth-century tracts on sound and culture (e.g., Berendt 1992).

2. Much of the work cited in my bibliography explicitly carries out this project. In addition to authors discussed in this essay, for other constructs of modern sonic culture, see also Feld (1986, 1996); Born (1995, 2013); Meintjes (2003); Rath (2003); Hirschkind (2006); Birdsall (2012); Taylor (2012); Novak (2013); Ochoa Gautier (2014).

3. Alas, as shown once again by this keyword entry, that Eurocentrism continues. Though that particular fault may also simply be an indication of the current limits of the author's ongoing education.

References

Adorno, Theodor. 2002. "The Radio Symphony." In *Adorno: Essays on Music*, ed. Richard Leppert. 251–270. Berkeley: University of California Press.

Altman, Rick. 1986. "Television/Sound." In *Studies in Entertainment*, ed. Tania Modleski, 39–54. Bloomington: Indiana University Press.

Aristotle. [1931]. *On Sense and the Sensible*. Trans. J. I. Beare. Adelaide: Univerisity of Adelaide Press. Reprint: e-book.

Baade, Christina. 2011. *Victory through Harmony: The BBC and Popular Music in World War II*. Oxford: Oxford University Press.

Barbour, J. Murray. 1951.*Tuning and Temperament*. East Lansing: Michigan State College Press.

Barker, Andrew. 1984. *Greek Musical Writings*. Cambridge: Cambridge University Press

Benjamin, Walter. 1968. *Illuminations*. Trans. Harry Zohn. New York: Schocken.

Berendt, Hans-Joachim. 1992. *The Third Ear: On Listening to the World*. Trans. Tim Nevill. New York: Holt

Bijsterveld, Karin. 2008. *Mechanical Sound: Technology, Culture, and Public Problems of Noise in the Twentieth Century*. Cambridge, MA: MIT Press.

Birdsall, Caroline. 2012. *Nazi Soundscapes: Sound, Technology and Urban Space in Germany, 1933–1945*. Amsterdam: Amsterdam University Press.

Boas, Franz. 1889. "On Alternating Sounds." *American Anthropologist* 2(1): 47–54.

Born, Georgina, ed. 1995. *Rationalizing Culture: Ircam, Boulez and the Institutionalization of the Musical Avant-Garde*. Berkeley: University of California Press.

Born, Georgina, ed. 2013. *Music, Sound, and Space: Transformations of Public and Private Experience*. Cambridge: Cambridge University Press.

Butler, Judith. 1990. *Gender Trouble*. New York: Routledge.

Clarke, Eric. 2005. *Ways of Listening: An Ecological Approach to the Perception of Musical Meaning*. New York: Oxford University Press.

Davis, Lennard. 1995. *Enforcing Normalcy*. New York: Verso.

Dinsdale, Alfred. 1932. *First Principles of Television*. London: Chapman and Hall.

Erlmann, Veit. 2010. *Reason and Resonance: A History of Modern Aurality*. Cambridge: Zone Books.

Feld, Steven. 1986. "Orality and Consciousness." In *The Oral and the Literate in Music*, ed. Yoshiko Tokumaru and Osamu Yamaguti. Tokyo: Academia Music.

Feld, Steven. 1996. "Aesthetics as Iconicity of Style (Uptown Title) or (Downtown Title) 'Lift-up-over-Sounding': Getting into the Kaluli Groove." In *Music Grooves*, Charles Keil and Steven Feld. Chicago: University of Chicago Press.

Fletcher, Harvey. 1929. *Speech and Hearing*. With an introduction by H. D. Arnold. New York: Van Nostrand.

Fletcher, Harvey, and R. L. Wegel. 1922. "The Frequency-Sensitivity of Normal Ears." *Physical Review* 19(6): 553–566.

Goodman, David. 2009. "Distracted Listening: On Not Making Sound Choices in the 1930s." In *Sound in the Age of Mechanical Reproduction*, ed. David Suisman and Susan Strasser, 15–46. Philadelphia: University of Pennsylvania Press.

Hage, Ghassan. 2011. "Dwelling in the Reality of Utopia." *Traditional Dwellings and Settlements Review* 23(1): 7–12.

Hage, Ghassan. 2012. "Critical Anthropological Thought and the Radical Political Imaginary." *Critique of Anthropology* 32(3): 285–308.

Havelock, Eric. 1988. *The Muse Learns to Write: Reflections on Orality and Literacy from Antiquity to the Present.* New Haven: Yale University Press.

Heidegger, Martin. 1962. *Being and Time.* New York: Harper and Row.

Helmreich, Stefan. 2009. *Alien Ocean: Anthropological Voyages on Microbial Seas.* Berkeley: University of California Press.

Hirschkind, Charles. 2006. *The Ethical Soundscape: Cassette Sermons and Islamic Counterpublics.* New York: Columbia University Press.

Hui, Alexandra. 2012. *The Psychophysical Ear: Musical Experiments, Experimental Sounds, 1840–1910.* Cambridge, MA: MIT Press.

Ihde, Don. 2007. *Listening and Voice: Phenomenologies of Sound.* 2nd ed. Albany: State University of New York Press.

Jones, Simon, and Thomas Schumacher. 1992. "Muzak: On Functional Music and Power." *Critical Studies in Mass Communication* 9: 156–169.

Kursell, Julia. 2008. "Sound Objects." In *Sounds of Science*, ed. Julia Kursell. MPI Preprints, 29–38. Berlin: Max Planck Institute for the History of Science.

Lanza, Joseph. 1994. *Elevator Music: A Surreal History of Muzak, Easy Listening, and Other Moodsong.* New York: St. Martin's Press.

McLuhan, Marshall. 1960. "Five Sovereign Fingers Taxed the Breath." In *Explorations in Communication, an Anthology*, ed. Marshall McLuhan and Edmund Snow Carpenter. Boston: Beacon Press.

McLuhan, Marshall. 1962. *The Gutenberg Galaxy: The Making of Typographic Man.* Toronto: University of Toronto Press.

Meintjes, Louise. 2003. *Sound of Africa! Making Music Zulu in a South African Studio.* Durham: Duke University Press.

Mills, Mara. 2010. "Deaf Jam: From Inscription to Reproduction to Information." *Social Text* 28(1) (summer): 35–58.

Mills, Mara. 2011. "Deafening: Noise and the Engineering of Communication in the Telephone System." *Grey Room* 43 (spring): 118–143.

Moore, Brian C. J. 2003. *An Introduction to the Psychology of Hearing.* New York: Academic Press.

Nancy, Jean-Luc. 2007. *Listening.* Trans. Charlotte Mandell. New York: Fordham University Press.

Novak, David. 2013. *Japanoise: Music at the Edge of Circulation.* Durham: Duke University Press.

Ochoa Gautier, Ana María. 2014. *Aurality: Listening and Knowledge in Nineteenth-Century Colombia.* Durham: Duke University Press.

Ong, Walter J. 1967. *The Presence of the Word: Some Prolegomena for Cultural and Religious History.* New Haven: Yale University Press.

Ong, Walter J. 1982. *Orality and Literacy: The Technologization of the Word.* New York: Routledge.

Pantalony, David. 2009. *Altered Sensations: Rudolph Koenig's Acoustical Workshop in Nineteenth-Century Paris.* New York: Springer.

Peirce, Charles S. 1955. *Philosophical Writings of Peirce.* New York: Dover.

Peters, John Durham. 2004. "Helmholtz, Edison and Sound History." In *Memory Bytes: History, Technology, and Digital Culture*, ed. Lauren Rabinovitz and Abraham Geil, 177–198. Durham: Duke University Press.

Plomp, Reinier. 2002. *The Intelligent Ear: On the Nature of Sound Perception*. Mahwah, NJ: Erlbaum.

Pohlmann, Ken C. 2005. *Principles of Digital Audio*. 5th ed. New York: McGraw-Hill.

Rath, Richard Cullen. 2003. *How Early America Sounded*. Ithaca: Cornell University Press.

Russo, Alexander. 2010. *Points on the Dial: Golden Age Radio beyond the Networks*. Durham: Duke University Press.

Schubert, Earl D. 1978. "History of Research on Hearing." In *Handbook of Perception*, vol. 4, *Hearing*, ed. Edward C. Carterette and Morton P. Friedman, 41–80. New York: Academic Press.

Schwartz, Hillel. 2011. *Making Noise: From Babel to the Big Bang and Beyond*. New York: Zone Books.

Siebers, Tobin. 2008. *Disability Theory*. Ann Arbor: University of Michigan Press.

Spigel, Lynn. 1992. *Make Room for TV: Television and the Family Ideal in Postwar America*. Chicago: University of Chicago Press.

Sterne, Jonathan. 2003. *The Audible Past: Cultural Origins of Sound Reproduction*. Durham: Duke University Press.

Sterne, Jonathan. 2012. MP3: *The Meaning of a Format*. Sign, Storage, Transmission. Durham: Duke University Press.

Streeter, Thomas. 1996. *Selling the Air: A Critique of the Policy of Commercial Broadcasting in the United States*. Chicago: University of Chicago Press.

Taylor, Timothy Dean. 2012. *The Sounds of Capitalism*. Chicago: University of Chicago Press.

Thompson, Emily. 2002. *The Soundscape of Modernity: Architectural Acoustics and the Culture of Listening in America 1900–1930*. Cambridge, MA: MIT Press.

Viveiros de Castro, Eduardo. 1998. "Cosmological Deixis and Amerindian Perspectivalism." *Journal of the Royal Anthropological Institutie* 4(3): 469–88.

Zwicker, Eberhard, and Richard Feldtkeller. 1999 [1967]. *The Ear as Communication Receiver*. Trans. Hans Müsch, Søren Buus, and Mary Florentine. Woodbury, NY: Acoustical Society of America.

image

Image? Surely there is some mistake. Why would sound studies have necessary recourse to a concept more typically to be found in the disciplines of art history or literary studies? Although one might respond by invoking the key role played by the "image" in Amiri Baraka's controversial essay "The Changing Same," in which the image designates music that points clearly to the source of its energy (Jones 1967), this invocation merely illustrates what it is invoked to explain. Instead, let me propose that if the image belongs fundamentally to the problematic of sound studies, it is because it designates a problem. This problem has been taken up directly in the phenomenological research of Don Ihde. He calls it "visualism."

Ihde develops this concept in his text *Listening and Voice*, where it is defined thus:

> This visualism may be taken as a symptomatology of the history of thought. The use and often metaphorical development of vision becomes a variable which can be traced through various periods and high points of intellectual history to show how thinking under this variable takes shape. . . . The visualism which has dominated our thinking about reality and experience is not something intrinsically simple. As a tradition it contains at least two interwoven factors. The first is more ancient and may be understood as an implicit *reduction to vision* whose roots stem from the classical period of Greek philosophical thought. . . . The roots of the second reduction lie almost indiscernibly intertwined with those arising from the preference for vision; the reduction *of* vision is one which ultimately separates sense from significance, which arises out of doubt over perception itself. Its retrospective result is to diminish the richness of every sense. (1976: 6, 9)

What Ihde foregrounds here is the role Western philosophy has played in generating a discourse about the perception of reality that establishes a grammar (Ihde's appeal to "metaphor" notwithstanding) of perception in which vision collaborates in the epistemological derogation of the senses. Whether one accepts Ihde's conclusions or not—and what of "phonocentrism" for example?—he invites one to consider how the faculty of vision, as an epistemological motif, operates to mediate our encounter with and thinking about sound.

As Ihde stresses, visualism is not "intrinsically simple." Indeed. So much so that one finds rigorous critics of Western philosophy, such as Theodor Adorno and Hanns Eisler, saying the following about the relation between the sound and the image in their writings on film music: "ordinary listening, as compared to seeing, is 'archaic'; it has not kept pace with technological progress. One might say that to react with the ear, which is fundamentally a passive organ in contrast to the swift and actively selective eye, is in a sense not in keeping with the present advanced industrial age and its cultural anthropology" (1994: 20). Strictly speaking, of course, they are speaking here of the faculties of seeing and hearing, and doing so in order to implicate capitalist modernity in the differentiation between them, but when they cash out this difference in political terms, sonic signifying—for them "music"—can lead to "deliberate misuse for ideological purposes" (21). What justifies such propositions is their sense that sound lacks the "unambiguous distinctness of the concept" (21), thus facilitating the pursuit of irrationality in the context of rationality. This is a perspective that implicitly aligns vision with reason, thereby undercutting, even denigrating, the epistemological authority of sound. Even though it is clear that Eisler and Adorno are keen to tease out the radical potential of the dialectic between looking and listening, it is no less clear that visualism has formed the terms of their discussion.

Within sound studies these issues have been taken up by, among others, Jonathan Sterne, who forged the expression "audiovisual litany" to capture what is at stake. With a nod to the performative character of theory, Sterne justifies his use of the term "litany" by underscoring the aural and auratic (that is, cultic) character of Western ways of mixing hearing and seeing, or listening and watching. In both The Audible Past and in his introduction to The Sound Studies Reader he drops into his text a list of no fewer than eleven assumptions about the articulation of hearing and seeing, meant in both contexts to draw out how these assumptions shape our ways of knowing, especially as they are brought to bear on the scholarly work of knowing sound. In this, Sterne and Ihde share a certain problematic, a certain configuration of problems and solutions. Indeed, a chapter from Ihde's study is the lead entry in Sterne's reader. What separates their projects, other than three decades, is that Sterne is more concerned to trace the disciplinary assimilation of a set of assumptions. Ihde is spared this responsibility but is also free to deploy visualism as a politico-theoretical construct whose relation to the very conception of a litany (an entreaty) invites attention.

Both Sterne and Ihde are concerned with knowledge, whether broadly disciplinary or strictly philosophical. This is important. But visualism has even found expression in linguistic theories of the verbal sign and thus might be said to be active within the very medium of knowledge. Consider, for example, what Saussure's students believed him to have said about the object of linguistics, the sign. "The linguistic sign unites, not a thing and a name, but a concept and a sound-image (*image acoustique*). The latter is the material sound, a purely physical thing, the psychological imprint of the sound, the impression that it makes on our senses. The sound-image is sensory, and if I happen to call it "material" it is only in that sense, and by way of opposing it to the other terms of the association, the concept, which is generally more abstract" (2011: 66). Here Saussure famously differentiates reference (the idea that a word "refers" to a thing whether psychical or physical) from signification (the idea that a word is composed of phonemes and the meaning they signify). Indeed, in the *Course* Saussure associates signification with the identification of a properly scientific object of linguistics, urging readers to take seriously the rigor of his analytical vocabulary: the "signified" as designating the meaning of a word; the "signifier" as designating the sounds composing the word; and, the "sign" as the relation—famously "arbitrary"—between them.

But "sound-image"? Given Saussure's well-known antipathy toward writing, why the visual phenomenon of the image? Aware that such a formulation buzzes with connotative complexity, the editors of the *Course* append here an explanatory footnote that attempts to mute the buzz by evoking the fundamental passivity of the speaking subject. "Image" is thought to evoke the imprint of sound made on the speaker/listener. Roy Harris, in his controversial translation of the *Course*, simply avoids the difficulties by rendering "sound-image" as "sound-pattern." Either way, what seems clear is that for Saussure, recourse to the image is warranted, if not compelled, by his contention that the sign—when grasped scientifically—is a rigorously *psychological* phenomenon. Indeed, in the introduction to the *Course* he is at pains to differentiate between the physiological and the psychological aspects of the "speech circuit," a difference that reiterates the tie between the scientific object of linguistics and the repudiation of referential models of language, while adding the body (the physiological dimension) to the list of things that language need not "refer" to in order to mean.

The distinction between the physiological and the psychological carries over to the acoustic image. Saussure argues that the sign's acoustic character is not "physical" (actual sounds—he is thinking here of the "sound" of one's inner voice) but "material," that is, psychological. Thus, despite the structural separation of the signifier and the signified, it is their distinctly psychological character that allows them to communicate. Somehow, the psyche is an organ where the sound cats and the image cats are all, as is said, gray, without, for that reason, undercutting Saussure's urgent appeal to the image.

Saussure's warrant for this argument is an old one. When, in "On Interpretation," Aristotle insists that "all men have not the same speech sounds, but the mental experiences . . . are the same for all, as also are those things of which our experiences are the images" (1941: 40), he frames the template for the theory of language that Saussure labors to rehabilitate. What this contributes to Ihde's account of "visualism" is the delicate and disturbing point that *any* effort to think the "meaning" or "sense" of sound (to experience it as some sort of "signifying" event) imports willy-nilly into the sound in question the status of sound within language as grasped within the discourse of "visualism." Derrida, of course, was among the first to recognize the contours of this dilemma as it arose in the gray matter at the heart of Saussure's psychology (1976: 27–73). Perversely, what Derrida teased out there was the counterintuitive favoring of speech in Saussure; not as a figure for sound (recall the critique of "physicality") but as a figure for the effacement of difference in the relation between thought and language. In effect, Derrida showed how insistently Saussure was concerned to ground meaning in psychic immediacy, thereby prompting us to visualize the image as the atemporal form of meaning. This is the voice that in keeping silent shows us how meaning is presumed to mean. One might reasonably speculate that such assumptions are precisely what drove Kristeva (1984), in her appropriation of Saussure, to situate the sign opposite the semiotic *chora*.[1]

Similar challenges in thinking the meaning of sound are discussed in Jonathan Rée's I See a Voice (1999), his engaging and thorough philosophical consideration of deafness (see DEAFNESS). In important ways Rée's study is a counterweight to Ihde's concept of visualism, although it is clear Rée is impressed with Ihde's account of auditory attention. This is so because Rée reminds us not to forget the assumption of "able-bodiedness" that drifts through and undergirds much philosophizing about meaning, perception, and the senses. To throw the bone of contention directly before us: if one cannot hear either well or at all, the use of "visual" signs to supplement this lack is not a matter of ideological partisanship, it is a matter of a certain communicative necessity. Put in more directly disciplinary terms: sound studies can ill afford the presumptions now roundly criticized by disability studies, even if, in the end, one wants to argue that sound has only a partial, tenuous link to the faculty of hearing. Literary studies might, of course, be issued the same warning as when Donald Gibson, in his introduction to W. E. B. Du Bois's Souls of Black Folk, glosses the "enigmatic" bits of musical notation that introduce each chapter as "mute ciphers" (1996: xvi). The "sounds of blackness" are, like the chora, far more keen.

In 1902 a seventy-five-second film was made in which a professor from Gallaudet College illustrated the power of "signing" by singing, in signs, the national anthem of the United States, whose first line—as many will recall—is, "Oh say can you see, by the dawn's early light." Significantly, this recording, made twenty-five years before the advent of the "talkies" (in Spanish, silent film is referred to as cine mudo: "mute film"), illustrates the rapidity with which the cinematic apparatus was recognized to have an oddly intimate relation not only to what Samuel Heinicke called a Sprachmaschine (1999: 162–165) but also to language acquisition, or what Lacan would later call the subject's entry into language (2006: 413). Despite this, and despite decades of attentive thinking about diction, dialogue, dubbing, and so on, it took someone with the tenacity of Michel Chion to embark on a systematic inquiry into the status of sound in cinema. As if conscious of his "responsibilities," Chion, in his first sole-authored study of film, The Voice in the Cinema (1982), took up directly the Sprachmaschine problem in an early section titled "When the Cinema was 'Deaf.'" As the quotation marks imply, Chion was concerned not simply to probe the retronym of "silent cinema," but to broach a debate about the concept of sound within film studies. The point was to question whether the conflation of voice and sound was not merely a symptom, but a symptom that had exhausted its analytical power. Although in this early study Chion does not take up visualism directly, it is clear that the trajectory of the argument is designed to underscore the necessity of delinking the voice and the face, that is, the image of the source of the voice and its sounds, while simultaneously mixing the voice into the "soundscape" of the film as one element among others.

In his more recent work, say *Audio-Vision*, Chion has followed through on his impulse, verging on the paradoxical, to abandon the concept of the soundtrack (that is, to take seriously the notion that sounds are relentlessly "magnetized" by the images and are thus never isolated in a separate "track") by taking up two crucial projects. One involves elaborating the logic of listening, a project sketched out for him by Roland Barthes and Roland Havas. In *Audio-Vision* this takes the form of elaborating three modes of listening, including so-called reduced listening. This term appears in Pierre Schaeffer's 1966 *Traité des objets musicaux*, where, through a moody reflection on the prominence of music in our thinking about listening (as if music were the only acoustic phenomenon worthy of listening), reduced listening is situated precisely between a listening that attends to indices (sounds with causes) and a listening that attends to signs (sounds with senses). Reduced listening thus is subtractive, and what it takes out or off of sounds is the traces of what Chion means by "magnetization," the predations of the image track on sound. What Schaeffer does not quite formulate, Chion adds namely, that reduced listening is a calculated self-conscious listening, that is, a listening to listening that attempts to render available to analysis the very assumptions about sounds that shape our perception of them.

A second project, indeed one that executes this discursive turn even more emphatically, is being conspicuously elaborated on Chion's website (www.michelchion.com), where one will find a "glossary" that runs for scores of entries, each dedicated to formulating terms and concepts meant to facilitate the audiovisual analysis of the cinema. A print version of the then (2009) current inventory appears at the end of Chion's book *Film, a Sound Art*. Each entry in the glossary gives a bit of history, but then essays to render "operational" relevant analytical tools. One such entry, "acousmêtre," invites comment because of the way it amplifies the image/sound matrix. Defined as "an invisible character," the *acousmêtre* embodies—if that is the right word—a rather particular challenge to visualism, in that it establishes through a repeated voicing (Chion invokes the famous example of Norman Bates's mother in Alfred Hitchcock's film *Psycho*) a character we expect to be visualized at any moment. This is not a "voice over" or even a "voice off" but potential for visualization that hovers around and behind the frame. Clearly, what Chion is attending to here is the dual need to recognize how powerfully and insistently the image establishes its right to appear, while showing that it is precisely through the Pythagorean staging of the veiled voice, the sound from the beyond (in *Psycho*, the maternal chora), that this right, this demand, is held in stasis.

Surely, it would not be much of a stretch to suggest that precisely what Chion is attempting to do here is to pressure what Foucault once called the "law of the difference," which defines, in this case, the discourse of cinema studies in the West. He wants to diagram how a certain disciplinary consensus about meaningful listening not only rules out the discernments captured in Schaeffer's distinctions between listening, hearing, attuning, and understanding but also in doing so risks losing the distinctly audiovisual medium of the cinema. The point is not that Chion is carrying out some form of theoretical heroism, but that his work testifies to a situation. One might argue, for example, that Jacques Rancière's book *The Emancipated Spectator* (2009), with its probing of the distinction between activity and passivity in the event of film reception, belongs to the same situation. But in Chion's case one is prompted to propose that he is stubbornly drawing attention—and I say this attuned to the necessary and essential precautions—not to the "deafness" of the cinema but to the "deafness" of cinema studies, to its grammar and its logic, both of which interfere so tenaciously in *thinking* sound, both there and elsewhere. If Barthes, in his late essay "The Image" (1985), felt prompted to express his disquiet about the becoming image of the name, *his* name, might we not recognize here his fear about the revenge of the image, its desire to silence the inventor of the "rhetoric of the image," the image's shared vocation with speech? About this fear we should conclude that it is a sign that visualism will not, as is said, go quietly.

Note

1. Kristeva introduces this term in *Revolution in Poetic Language*, specifically the chapter titled "The Semiotic Chora [sic], Ordering the Drives." Later defining it as "the place where the signifying process, rejecting stasis, unfolds" (1984: 182), Kristeva deploys

the chora to theorize the processes whereby matter assumes form, thus tying semiosis to productivity rather than signification. This prompts her to risk the formulation that the chora designates a space of maternality, precisely in giving expression to the rhythms, the starts and stops, that gestate form. Derrida, who was lecturing on the relevant Platonic source material (the *Timaeus*) around the same time, famously criticized this view as ontological, although in his own later essay "Khora" (1995) he conceded the irreducible "femininity" of the concept. For him, *khora* operates as a woman's name. It becomes a she, but as such a third/non person. Regardless, I deploy the term here as an intricate but ultimately stenographic evocation of the marking whose precarious effacement produces the unmarked subject: the white, middle-class, heterosexual male.

References

Adorno, Theodor, and Hanns Eisler. 1994. *Composing for the Films*. Translator unnamed. London: Athlone Press.

Aristotle. 1941. "On Interpretation." In *The Basic Works of Aristotle*, ed. Richard McKeon, trans. E. M. Edghill. New York: Random House.

Barthes, Roland. 1985. "The Image." In *The Grain of the Voice*. Trans. Richard Howard. New York: Hill and Wang.

Chion, Michel. 1994. *Audio-Vision: Sound on Screen*. Trans. and ed. Claudia Gorbman. New York: Columbia University Press.

Chion, Michel. 1999 [1982]. *The Voice in the Cinema*. New York: Columbia University Press.

Chion, Michel. 2009. *Film, a Sound Art*. Trans. Claudia Gorbman. New York: Columbia University Press.

Derrida, Jacques. 1976. *Of Grammatology*. Trans. Gayatri Spivak. Baltimore: Johns Hopkins University Press.

Derrida, Jacques. 1995. "Khora." In *On the Name*, 89–127. Stanford: Stanford University Press.

Foucault, Michel. 1996. *Foucault Live: Collected Interviews, 1961–1984*. Ed. Sylvère Lotringer. Trans. Lysa Hochroth and John Johnston. New York: Semiotext(e).

Gibson, Donald. 1996. Introduction to *The Souls of Black Folk*, by W. E. B. Du Bois. New York: Penguin.

Ihde, Donald. 1976. *Listening and Voice: A Phenomenology of Sound*. Athens: Ohio University Press.

Jones, LeRoi. "The Changing Same." In *Black Music*. New York: Morrow Paperbacks, 1967.

Kristeva, Julia. 1984. *Revolution in Poetic Language*. Trans. and ed. Leon Roudiez. New York: Columbia University Press.

Lacan, Jacques. 2006. *Ecrits*. Trans. Bruce Fink. New York: Norton.

Rancière, Jacques. 2009. *The Emancipated Spectator*. New York: Verso.

Rée, Jonathan. 1999. *I See a Voice: Deafness, Language and the Senses—a Philosophical History*. New York: Metropolitan Books.

Saussure, Ferdinand de. 2011. *Course in General Linguistics*. Ed. Perry Meisel and Haun Saussy. Trans. Wade Baskin. New York: Columbia University Press.

Schaeffer, Pierre. 1966. *La Traité des objets musicaux*. Paris: Editions du Seuil.

Sterne, Jonathan. 2003. *The Audible Past: Cultural Origins of Sound Reproduction*. Durham: Duke University Press.

Sterne, Jonathan, ed. 2012. *The Sound Studies Reader*. London: Routledge.

language

A Sense of Language for Sound Studies

That the English term "language" has accumulated a number of ambiguous meanings should surprise no one. Its etymological origins trace to the Old French spoken by Normans invading Britain in 1066. Despite its derivation from the French word for "tongue" (*langue*), however, "language" never eradicated older Anglo-Saxon terms in the English lexicon related to verbal communication such as "tongue" and "speech." One result of this history is that "language" has often been considered as a conceptual entity, divorced from the mechanisms of its material embodiment as socially circulating sound.[1] Recent scholarship has discovered and argued instead that there are significant areas of overlap between what had formerly been taken as separate domains. These include the sonic features of everyday speech acts, the ways in which sound is coupled with all forms of human symbolic and communicative practice, and the shared indexical and iconic associations of all forms of sounded expression.

Much discourse about language alternates between universalizing and exclusionary claims about its status in relation to other expressive systems. On the one hand is the claim, closely associated with structuralism, that everything is a language (or, to be safer, *like* a language). On the other are caveats to universality—that art is like a language except that its referents are vaguer, or that music is like a language in having something akin to syntax, but which does not refer to objects in the world. These reinforce the exclusionary claim that, in fact, nothing is like a language.

By acknowledging that language is one case (perhaps special, perhaps not) that overlaps with other sounded modes of signification, sound studies can enter into critical dialogue with an intellectual history that has largely emphasized language's cognitive properties at the expense of its sonic enactments. If language is framed purely as a conceptual system of reference and syntax—and all other forms of expression are judged in terms of how well they fit those default categories—the game is already conceded. For instance, onomatopoeia, a linguistic universal, has usually been treated as essentially secondary to the nature of language. Saussure, in his *Cours de linguistique generale*, lectured that the French word *pigeon* had descended from an onomatopoeic form for the bird's call in Vulgar Latin (*pipio*). But his point here was to show how the word had moved *out* of the sonic world and into its symbolic maturity as an arbitrary linguistic signifier. In other words, he acknowledged the sonic resemblance only in order to demonstrate the centrality of the free, unmotivated signifier as the basic unit of *langue*. Lost in these excisions of sound from language are considerations of voice and performance, speech play and verbal art, the phenomenological, affective and poetic dimensions of language, and the coordination of language and other sonorous expressive forms in ritual and ceremony.

This binary separation of internal cognition from external vibration is (like so many other lingering and robust binaries) a child of the Enlightenment. The uncoupling of language from rhetoric noted by Bakhtin (1981) was marked by a growing philosophical distinction between, for example, language and music as sounded modes of human expression. In essays on the role of language in rational human communication, music was often invoked as an alternate form of sonic expression, similar but inferior to the rationality of language. Locke, in his *Essay Concerning Human Understanding*, briefly used music in this way, contrasting the precise referentiality of words to the more diffuse sensations of pleasure or pain that a melody might bring to a listener. Rousseau, in his *On the Origin of Languages*, more extensively contrasted the primordial emotional power of music to a chronologically later and rationally more evolved state of linguistic development.[2]

Two Kinds of Symbols?

Arguments that used music as a foil for the superior rationalism of language hinged on language's potential for creating referential and semantic value. Faced with an abundance of expressive modalities, however, many of which employ sound and the voice, it is a short step from these hierarchies to the idea that there may be, in fact, two kinds of symbols. This view was most closely associated with Suzanne Langer's 1942 *Philosophy in a New Key* and the influential distinction she made therein between *discursive* and *presentational* symbols. Langer rejected a simple binary distinction that placed language in the camp of the rational and other symbolic forms in that of the emotional. All symbols, in Langer's argument, are vehicles of logical conceptualization. Influenced in part by the insights of Gestalt psychology, she grappled with the suspicion that some symbolic forms lend themselves to the precise conceptualizations of spoken or written language, while others appear more holistic. The former she called *discursive*, the latter *presentational*.

As welcome and important as Langer's struggle with symbolic inclusiveness was, her distinction between discursive and presentational forms was founded on a crabbed and limiting concept of what language might be. From the perspective of sound studies, there is arguably little that she wrote of presentational symbols that cannot be said of discursive symbols (Tedlock and Mannheim 1995; Welsh 1955). Consider, for example, Langer's discussion of the presentational nature of poetry. The "material" of poetry, she asserted, "is verbal," but "its import is not the literal assertion made in the words, but *the way the assertion is made*, and this involves the sound, the tempo, the aura of associations of words, the long or short sequence of ideas, the wealth or poverty of transient imagery that contains them, the sudden arrest of fantasy by pure fact, or of familiar fact by sudden fantasy, the suspense of literal meaning by a sustained ambiguity resolved in a long-awaited key-word, and the unifying, all-embracing artifice of rhythm" (1942: 261, emphasis in the original). In other words, by Langer's argument, poetry possesses sound, tempo, association, imagery, mixtures of fact and fantasy, ambiguity, and rhythm, but discursive language offers only the literal assertion made in the words. From the perspective of sound studies, a distinction between discourse and materiality is not tenable: the pertinent issue is to understand how language circulates socially in a world of sound.

Next, we explore four broad areas of inquiry into expression and communication that show how language is joined with, rather than separated from, other sonorous practices: Peirce's semiotic explorations; Jakobson's foundational work on linguistics and poetics; the turn toward verbal art as performance in anthropology; and Austin's tracing a class of verbs, known as *performatives*, that are constitutive rather than descriptive in scope.

Peircean Semiotics

C. S. Peirce's semiotic theory constitutes language as one particular expression of a unitary collection of nested sign types. Rather than propose language as a separate system of expression and communication, Peirce's semiotic approach demonstrates the ways language is encompassed within a larger universe of signs. All signs in this sense are interposed between the objects they stand for and the socially produced effects they have for those who encounter them. The most commonly used Peircean sign relationships are icon, index, and symbol. The first denotes a relationship of resemblance, such as onomatopoeia and sound symbolism in language. Fox discusses how country singers create icons of crying—through pharyngealization, chest pulses, breaks to the falsetto range, and vibrato—to perform "the upwelling of bodily processes in the sound-stream of texted song" (2004: 281). Iconicity is a feature of all forms of signification, however, and not unique to language. A typical digital amp modeler, for example, comes with presets that iconically represent the "sounds" of world-famous guitarists. The index, on the other hand, refers to a relationship of co-occurrence: for example, an echo is indexical of a large acoustic space with hard reflective surfaces, while in language, dialect often indexes various forms of social distinction, such as class or place of birth. Symbols denote an abstract, conventional link between an object and its socially produced effect on a mind, such as the referential relationship between a noun and its meaning: the sound-shape of "tree" bears no relationship to the physical object to which it refers. This last relationship—the symbolic—is close to Saussure's influential conception of language as abstracted from the material world.

We note three implications of the Peircean sign-type formulation for sound studies. First, the sign types are sequentially nested. Indexes are also already icons. One important reason why an emulating amplifier can give the guitarist a sound that is *indexical of* "Stevie Ray Vaughan," for example, is because the sound produced is at the same time materially similar to—that is, *iconic of*—the sound produced by a '59 Strat played through a Fender Super Reverb amp with Vaughan's various stomp boxes and signal processors. Similarly, symbols are also already both icons and indexes. For example, funeral bands are *symbolic of* (conventionally associated with) New Orleans, in part, because the sound of funeral bands *indexes* something one hears in that city and because funeral processions through contested public spaces are *iconic of* the city's racial and spatial boundaries.[3]

The semiotic features of sound, then, vary from sign to sign or from context to context. Think, for example, of the global circulation of cell phone ringtones as "musical *madeleines*" (de Vries and van Elferen 2010): the ringing sound of the brass dome bells in Western Electric P-type telephones—once heard as "the phone" but now as "old phone"—clearly has differently weighted iconic, indexical, and symbolic properties depending on the context in which it is heard. In an old Humphrey Bogart film, this sound indexes the urgency of a phone call. As a ringtone on a cell phone, its iconicity with the way phones used to sound adds indexical and symbolic layers that could be interpreted as irony, nostalgia, or personal aesthetics; assigned to a specific contact, it can index "my daughter is calling." The wide circulation of a sound clip known popularly as the "Universal telephone ring" reveals Peircean processes at work. Numerous television programs and films produced by Universal Studios feature the identical telephone sound, recognizable as iconic in part by a distinctive irregularity in intonational steadiness known as "tape wow" that occurred during transfer. With the passage of time, uses of the Universal telephone ring as a convention became more reflexive, indexical of a sound editor's attitude as much as of the sound of a telephone.[4]

A particularly rich example of the shifting values of icon, index, and symbol is found in the global circulation of the ringtone known as the "Crazy Frog." Gopinath (2013) offers a richly detailed history of the Crazy Frog ringtone, but dismisses its verbal content in a way that reveals what may be missed as a result of inattention to the overlap between domains of language and sound. The ringtone began as a recorded vocal representation of the sound of a two-stroke engine made by Swedish teen Daniel Malmedahl. His vocal performance makes use of linguistic resources—phonology and phonotactics, for example—to create a speech act in which iconic features of linguistic practice are highly salient. The iconicity of the performance can be heard in the way its vowels and consonants change as the sound of the engine's revolutions rises and falls: at moments of high rpm, the chosen vowel (/i/) and consonant (/d/) are higher in frequency than at low rpm (/ɔ/ and /b/, respectively). After becoming associated with a doe-eyed amphibian straddling an invisible motorcycle—the Crazy Frog—the recording was used in a song that became a top single in many global music markets.[5] How the sound of a two-stroke engine became associated with frogs, crazy or not, demonstrates shifting iconic, indexical, and symbolic associations at work in the circulation of this sound object.

Jakobsonian Poetics

Roman Jakobson's work (1960) in the poetics of language further developed understandings of the iconicity and indexicality of verbal forms by showing how every utterance serves multiple functions simultaneously, many of which are dependent on sound and the context of speech acts. Arguing against naïve sender-receiver models of communication, Jakobson proposed six functions that any utterance fulfills in varying degrees: the referential, the emotive, the conative, the poetic, the phatic, and the metalinguistic. Of these, Jakobson was most interested in exploring the poetic function, which focuses on the form of a message and the ways a message might be crafted to manifest such a focus.

Attention to the poetic function has led directly to a recalibration of the role of the voice in the connection between language and sound. By examining language as a temporally sequenced performance that uses the social and physical resources of the human body to produce its effects, new overlapping relationships between the technical minutiae of phonetics and phonology and the social efficacy of embodied sonorous performance have been uncovered. For example, more weight has been given to examining individuals' socialization into performance: that is, how members of a community learn to coordinate multiple layers of organization, beyond that of propositional content, to create and to recognize aesthetically or rhetorically effective uses of language. In the realm of oratory, Booth, for example, shows how the repetition of the open mid-back vowel /ɔ/ ("four," "score," "brought," "forth") and the repetition of the word "that" in its sundry grammatical functions help to make so memorable the cultural work that is Lincoln's Gettysburg Address, apart from any of the propositional content contained in its text (1998). In a discussion of singing as a particular indexically and iconically embedded form of sounded performance, Feld and colleagues (2004) discuss the differences in training and socialization that result in the buttery, "covered" sound of a *coloratura* soprano and the "twangy" vocal sound of a country singer.

Jakobson's approach to poetics extends Peircean insights by showing the many ways languages, in addition to being systems of reference and syntax, are systems of potential sonic iconicities. In Jakobson's model, individual languages offer their speakers varying arrays of sonic features that can be activated to create rhythmic patterns, rhyme schemes, alliteration, and assonances that operate at every level of sounded communication, from the most mundane to the most sophisticated. His book with Linda Waugh, *The Sound Shape of Language* (1979), still stands as a touchstone work in arguing for the life of language in its performed sonorousness, rather than resting solely in its semantic and syntactic rules, and his insights have contributed strongly to subsequent work on sound symbolism (e.g. Ohala, Hinton, and Nuckolls 1994).

Verbal Art

Influenced in part by Jakobson's focus on the poetic function of language, several scholars in anthropology, linguistics, sociology, and folklore turned toward the analysis of speech in performance (and indeed in everyday contexts) with a particular emphasis on the sonic materiality of performed utterances. This work demonstrated how social relations are simultaneously constituted by and constitutive of particular "units of speaking," whether more formal (e.g., framed storytelling) or less so (e.g., greetings, conversations) (Bauman and Sherzer 1974: 9).[6] Much of this work is characterized by its acute attention to the nonreferential dimensions of speech in nonsegmentable linguistic features such as pitch, intonation, metric patterns, and voice quality. There is a concrete attention to sonic detail, the "sonic resources" of individual speakers, and the social, interpersonal, and affective ends for which these resources are used.

There is also a body of scholarship on the links between sound, language, and performance in technological media. Jakobson (1981 [1933]) contributed an early and important essay on the emergence of film sound, and more recently, researchers have turned to the role of audio recording in the emergence of modern ethnographic methodologies (Brady 1999), and the ways sound technology influences linguistic recontextualization and remediation (Bauman 2010).

Austin and Performatives

The links between sound studies and verbal art also extend back to the foundational work of philosopher J. L. Austin, particularly his elaboration of a class of first person verbs he called *performatives* ("I *find* you guilty," "I now *pronounce* you husband and wife," "I hereby *declare* this bridge open"). In distinction to "constative" language, which described the world, Austin argued that these "phonic acts" or "utterances" (now more commonly called "speech acts") brought the world into being. Further, unlike constative utterances, which are judged as true or false, Austin argued that performative speech acts are subject to "felicity conditions" that can only be interpreted contextually. Anyone can say "I sentence you to three years imprisonment," but the utterance is only felicitous if spoken by a judge to a guilty party in the context of a criminal court proceeding.

Austin's explorations of performativity resulted in the publication of his most enduring work, *How to Do Things with Words* (1962), in which he proposed three different functions for speech acts that have consequences for sound studies. The first is the *locutionary*, which is the actual content of an utterance. The second is the *illocutionary*, which is what a speaker intends to achieve in forming the sounds of an utterance. The third is the *perlocutionary*, which refers to the effect that an utterance has on the hearer. The simultaneous interrelation of these three functions demonstrates how sounded communication resists simple reduction to written text, and that its performance as sound is crucial to the interpretation of its meaning. As John Haiman (1998) has argued in his exploration of the role of sarcasm in the evolution of language, one may say "It's a beautiful day outside" and, through control of sonic features such as intonation and stress patterns, give the statement the illocutionary force of its opposite. Thus the sonic material of speech has reality-producing effects in the world, and does not simply describe that world in a rational system of reference bound by the form of the syllogistic proposition. Austin's work demonstrates the impossibility of context-independent speech, and thus the saturated nature of sound patterns, semantics, and pragmatics in thinking about linguistic interaction.

Conclusion

That these four areas of inquiry are yoked to one another within the hybrid space of language as sonorous practice is exemplified by Porcello's work on discourse in recording studios. For example, in a simple question posed to a record producer—"What do you want the drums to sound like?"—one can readily see how language in fact circulates socially in a world of like and unlike sounds (2004). The resulting conversation demonstrates, for example, the multiple iconic and indexical representations of an imagined drum sound, through the use of imitation (e.g., sung cymbal patterns), onomatopoeic words (e.g., "ring"), and references to other performers and recordings (e.g., "a John Bonham sound"). This sounded conversation about sound demonstrates multiple Jakobsonian functions as well, notably the metalinguistic (in multiple comments about how one might best conduct a conversation about a yet-unheard drum sound), the poetic (via patterns of movement between onomatopoeic and indexical strategies for describing that imagined sound), and the emotive (in asides that make clear the interlocutors' frustration with impasses in their ability to communicate the desired sound clearly to the other).

The emphasis on the sonic materiality of speech is on display in this conversation too. While much analysis of verbal art is directed toward ritualized or marked genres of speech, everyday speech is replete with the same kinds of techniques deployed in more formally performed genres. In the drum sound conversation, the producer repeatedly vocalizes sounds emanating from the different elements of the drum kit, such as the snare or tom-toms or the cymbals, in a manner that complexly entwines singing and speaking while fully embodying neither. He also destabilizes the boundaries between phonemic English (and thus resists conducting the conversation "inside" of language per se) and vocal tract noisemaking— that is, between using language as a vehicle for imitation and using his body's nonlinguistic sounding abilities for that purpose as well. And finally, one can gloss the entire conversation as a lengthy example of a performative, not just in the sense of involving performance (which it clearly does), but specifically in Austin's sense of being a kind of utterance that brings about a changed state of affairs or generates something new. Prior to the conversation, there is, quite literally, no drum sound to be heard or recorded, and the goal (i.e., the illocutionary function) of the entire exchange is to bring a particular sound into existence in the world. While that sound is not ultimately reducible to the conversation that initially generated an understanding of its character (for in the context of a studio recording, multiple technologies and recording practices sit between the conversation and the recorded drum sound itself), neither can the eventual, acoustically realized drum sound be entirely divorced from its initial conception—and inception—in language.

Although the four streams of influence outlined here suggest significant territory shared by language and sound studies, they by no means exhaust their overlap. Ever more precise digital audio technologies increasingly hone our understanding of the sonic dimensions of language and open up new analytic, investigative, and creative spaces. At the crossroads of language and sound studies, for example, sit emerging practices and technologies of voice analysis (often used to diagnose incipient medical conditions, or to assess a speaker's emotional state or degree of stress), forensic audio (whether used in the service of enhancing intelligibility or of identity verification), and creative voice manipulation (such as the use of Auto-Tune on the singing voice). These fertile areas for future scholarship at the intersection of sound studies, linguistics, and anthropology reaffirm the important role that sound studies plays in foregrounding the material embodiment of language as socially circulating sound.

Notes

1. Sign languages are of course fully linguistic in the sense that they are composed of syntactic systems of nested noun phrase and verb phrase trees, with applicable phrase structures.

2. A number of cognitive scientists have renewed a neo-Rousseauian exploration of the evolutionary basis for the relationship between language and music. Elizabeth Tolbert (2001, 2002) has critiqued at some length the implications of the continued dedication to the primordial nature of nonlinguistic sound and the way it rehabilitates a number of animal/human, myth/science, body/mind, rational/emotional, immediate/mediated, feminine/masculine distinctions.

3. Peirce's insights thus overlap in interesting ways with the Bakhtinian chronotope (1981).

4. Film and television soundtracks are indeed prime examples of the complex layerings of iconic, indexical, and symbolic features accruing to particular sounds. Layered acousmatic iconicites of film sound contribute to the creating the indexicalites of known chronotopes: the hoot of the great horned owl as the sign of spooky woods at night, the sound of wolf howls and hawk screeches as signs of the open wilderness. The creation of these synecdoches blurs the line between diegetic and nondiegetic sound in film sound design (see Chion 1994; Kane 2014).

5. The song was a cover version of "Axel F," initially heard in *Beverly Hills Cop* as the music associated with Eddie Murphy's character Axel Foley, and was thus embedded in a separate chain of Peircean signification.

6. Urban (1991), for example, revealed the sociability of Shokleng myth narratives not in any structural oppositions within the text but rather in the alternating, syllable-by-syllable means by which the narratives were publicly performed.

References

Austin, John L. 1962. *How to Do Things with Words: The William James Lectures Delivered at Harvard University in 1955*. London: Oxford University Press.

Bakhtin, Mikhail M. 1981. *The Dialogic Imagination*. Ed. M. Holquist. Trans. C. Emerson and M. Holquist. Austin: University of Texas Press.

Bauman, Richard. 2010. "The Remediation of Storytelling: Narrative Performance on Early Commercial Sound Recordings." In *Telling Stories: Building Bridges among Language, Narrative, Identity, Interaction, Society and Culture*, ed. A. de Fina and D. Schiffrin, 23–43. Washington, DC: Georgetown University Press.

Bauman, Richard, and Joel Sherzer, eds. 1974. *Explorations in the Ethnography of Speaking*. New York: Cambridge University Press.

Blacking, John. 1973. *How Musical Is Man?* Seattle: University of Washington Press.

Booth, Stephen. 1998. *Precious Nonsense: The Gettysburg Address, Ben Jonson's Epitaphs on His Children, and Twelfth Night*. Berkeley: University of California Press.

Brady, Erika. 1999. *A Spiral Way: How the Phonograph Changed Ethnography*. Jackson: University Press of Mississippi.

Briggs, Charles. 1993. "Personal Sensations and Polyphonic Voices in Warao Women's Ritual Wailing: Music and Poetics in Critical Collective Discourse." *American Anthropologist* 95(4): 929–957.

Cavarero, Adriana. 2005. *For More Than One Voice: Toward a Philosophy of Vocal Expression*. Stanford: Stanford University Press.

Chion, Michel. 1994. *Audio-Vision: Sound on Screen*. Trans. and ed. Claudia Gorbman. New York: Columbia University Press.

Dolar, Mladen. 2006. *A Voice and Nothing More*. Cambridge, MA: MIT Press.

Donovan, J. 1891. "The Festal Origin of Human Speech." *Mind* 16(64):495–506.

Feld, Steven. 1996. "Waterfalls of Song: An Acoustemology of Place Resounding in Bosavi, Papua New Guinea." In *Senses of Place*, ed. S. Feld and K. H. Basso, 91–135. Santa Fe: School of American Research Press.

Feld, Steven. 2012 [1982]. *Sound and Sentiment: Birds, Weeping, Poetics, and Song in Kaluli Expression*. 3rd ed. Durham: Duke University Press.

Feld, Steven, and Keith Basso, eds. 1996. *Senses of Place*. Santa Fe: School of American Research Press.

Feld, Steven, and Donald Brenneis. 2004. "Doing Ethnography in Sound." *American Ethnologist* 31(4): 461–474.

Feld, Steven, et al. 2004. "Vocal Anthropology: From the Music of Language to the Language of Song." In *A Companion to Linguistic Anthropology*, ed. A. Duranti, 321–345. Malden: Blackwell.

Fox, Aaron. 2004. *Real Country: Music and Language in Working-Class Culture*. Durham: Duke University Press.

Gopinath, Sumanth. 2013. *The Ringtone Dialectic: Economy and Cultural Form*. Cambridge, MA: MIT Press.

Haiman, John. 1998. *Talk Is Cheap: Sarcasm, Alienation, and the Evolution of Language*. New York: Oxford University Press.

Harris, Roy. 1997. "From an Integrational Point of View." In *Linguistics Inside Out: Roy Harris and His Critics*, ed. G. Wolf and N. Love, 229–310. Amsterdam: John Benjamins.

Leanne Hinton, Johanna Nichols, and John J. Ohala. 1994. *Sound Symbolism*. Cambridge: Cambridge University Press.

Jakobson, Roman. 1981 [1933]. "Is the Film in Decline?" In *Roman Jakobson: Selected Writings*, vol. 3, *Poetry of Grammar and Grammar of Poetry*, ed. S. Rudy, 732–739. Berlin: de Gruyter.

Jakobson, Roman. 1960. "Closing Statement: Linguistics and Poetics." In *Style in Language*, ed. T. Sebeok. Cambridge, MA: MIT Press.

Jakobson, Roman, and Linda R. Waugh. 1979. *The Sound Shape of Language*. The Hague: Mouton de Gruyter.

Kane, Brian. 2014. *Sound Unseen: Acousmatic Sound in Theory and Practice*. New York: Oxford University Press.

Langer, Susanne. 1942. *Philosophy in a New Key: A Study in the Symbolism of Reason, Rite, and Art*. Cambridge, MA: Harvard University Press.

Lévi-Strauss, Claude. 1962. *La Pensée Sauvage*. Paris: Plon.

Porcello, Thomas. 2004. "Speaking of Sound: Language and the Professionalization of Sound-Recording Engineers." *Social Studies of Science* 34(5): 733–758.

Shannon, Claude E., and Warren Weaver. 1949. *The Mathematical Theory of Communication*. Urbana: University of Illinois Press.

Tedlock, Dennis, and Bruce Manheim. 1995. Introduction to *The Dialogic Emergence of Culture*. Urbana: University of Illinois Press.

Tolbert, Elizabeth. 2001. "The Enigma of Music, the Voice of Reason: "Music," "Language," and Becoming Human." *New Literary History* 32: 451–465.

Tolbert, Elizabeth. 2002. "Untying the Music/Language Knot." In *Music, Sensation, and Sensuality*, ed. Linda Phyllis Austern, 77–96. New York: Routledge.

Urban, Greg. 1988. "Ritual Wailing in Amerindian Brazil." *American Anthropologist* 90(2): 385–400.

Urban, Greg. 1991. *A Discourse-Centered Approach to Culture: Native South American Myths and Rituals*. Austin: University of Texas Press.

Vries, Imar de, and Isabella van Elferen. 2010. "The Musical Madeleine: Communication, Performance, and Identity in Musical Ringtones." *Popular Music and Society* 33(1): 61–74.

Webster, Anthony. 2009. "The Poetics and Politics of Navajo Ideophony in Contemporary Navajo Poetry." *Language and Communication* 29(2): 133–151.

Welsh, Paul. 1955. "Discursive and Presentational Symbols." *Mind* 64(254): 191–199.

listening

Meanings of "Listening"

The OED defines "listening" as "the action of the verb 'to listen,' meaning to hear attentively; to give ear to; to pay attention to (a person speaking or what is said)." Unlike hearing, then, listening is understood to involve a deliberate channeling of attention toward a sound. It is not so much that listening is somehow separate from or opposed to hearing; indeed, the distinction between listening and hearing is often unclear, and the two are frequently equated or conflated. Listening is generally considered to involve "making an effort to hear something" (to invoke obsolete terms, "hearkening" or "giving ear"), while hearing is generally considered a more passive mode of auditory perception (Truax 2001: 18). Hearing may also be regarded as a kind of sensory substrate in which listening is grounded: "listening requires hearing but is not simply reducible to hearing" (Sterne 2003: 19).

The term encompasses a wide variety of modes, qualities, or types of auditory attention. Thus, a person (I use a human listener as the default here, though nonhuman animals, objects, and technologies may also be said to listen) may be "listening for" or "listening out for" a particular sound, meaning that they are alert to and endeavoring to hear it. There is a sense here that sound is subtle, masked, easily missed or difficult to pick up, not necessarily declaring itself or imposing itself on a person's hearing, so that he or she must attend closely and carefully. The importance of effort and a conscious direction of auditory attention are foregrounded. "Listening to" a sound, however, implies that a person, having moved beyond the detection and/or location of the auditory stimulus, is attending to it with a degree of focus. Importantly, the intensity of that focus may vary considerably. A person may listen to something intently, absorbed in the sound, but distracted, indifferent, deconcentrated, or even unconscious listening are also possible (Goodman 2010).

Types of listening and terms for listening have developed in tandem with the creation of sound technologies (an idea that is at the heart of much sound studies research and that I explore in greater detail below). The expression "listen in," for instance, is thought to have become commonplace following the emergence of radio broadcasting and the attendance of radio hams and audiences to signals and programs (Douglas 1999). "Listening in" also came to refer to secret listening to telephone conversations that became possible following the creation of the telephone exchange and the party line. Indeed, listening often carries general connotations of secret or surreptitious activity, be it through clandestine eavesdropping on private conversations, military listening (in listening galleries or posts used to discern the position, movement, and communications of enemy forces), or the monitoring of telephone conversations and other communications by government or police as part of broader programs of surveillance.

"Listening to" a person may refer to paying close attention to what that person has to say and often describes a compassionate, sympathetic and/or empathetic mode of engagement (Back 2007). Numerous sources point to the importance of listening in therapeutic interactions in psychotherapy and psychoanalysis (e.g. Reik 1951; Freud 1958 [1912]; Schwaber 1983; Chessick 1989; Jackson 1992). However, there is a sense in which auditory attention may be demanded by a sound, or by an individual or group of people. Thus, to listen to a person may mean giving heed to that person: "Listen up!" is a commonplace imperative to pay attention, particularly to a set of instructions that are about to be issued. Listening to a person may also imply allowing oneself to be persuaded by another. Different senses of the term "listening," then, imply subtle shifts in acoustical agency, which reference nuanced varieties of active-receptive and passive-receptive auditory attention.

Listening involves the allocation of attention or awareness. However, in contemporary usage the term does not always refer to *auditory* attention. The meanings of "listening" have proliferated into nonauditory spheres. For instance, in contemporary popular discourse, "listening to your body" means attending to signals or signs that indicate the body's condition or needs. A company's claim that its representatives are "listening to their customers" might mean that the business is responding directly to vocalized complaints or comments made by patrons; however, this "listening" could also mean that the company is attending to written complaints or is taking into account customers' views as revealed in sales patterns. Notions of the "third ear" also refer to the possibility of listening to something that "has no actual aural existence," gesturing to listening as a mode of consciousness that reaches beyond the merely auditory (e.g. Reik 1951; Rozak 1993: 41; Kochhar-Lindgren 2004: 229).

The term "listening," then, carries a wide variety of associations. Next I will identify a (by no means comprehensive) set of broad analytical approaches to listening in sound studies, and suggest that each of these approaches has tended to emphasize certain aspects or qualities of listening, with particular consequences for the framing of listening practices and listening subjects.

Approaches to Listening

Considered from an evolutionary perspective, listening is a valuable survival skill. It facilitates the avoidance of danger and the seeking of food; it enables communication. In order to understand the physiological and cognitive mechanisms through which human listening is made possible, psychoacousticians have examined, for instance, how listeners stream auditory attention and information in order to recognize particular aspects of a complex sound or to assemble sonic elements into an integrated whole (e.g. Moore 2003). The psychoacoustical approach frames listening as a perceptual process that, broadly speaking, occurs in the same way for people everywhere. Sound studies research on the other hand typically emphasizes the role of social and cultural context in auditory attention. This literature, while recognizing listening as a general process of perception, situates it in specific practices strongly shaped by local culture, history, and environment.

Feld's (2012 [1982], 1991, 1996, 2003) canonical work on the Kaluli of Papua New Guinea shows how Kaluli listening is shaped and directed by a highly culturally particular set of interpretive practices, so that the cries and songs of certain birds in the rainforest are understood to be the voices of ancestors calling to their living relatives (see ACOUSTE-MOLOGY). In Feld's analysis, Kaluli ways of listening form part of the "everyday 'body hexis' (Bourdieu 1977: 8), the naturalized regime of 'body techniques' (Mauss 1979 [1935]) basic to routine Kaluli encounters in their world" (1996: 100). Here, then, rather than being a universal set of sensory aptitudes, ways of listening are an aspect of "habitus," a set of culturally informed bodily and sensory dispositions (Mauss 1979 [1935]; Bourdieu 1977). In a similar way, archaeologies and cultural histories of sound point out the historical particularity of listening practices and examine the ways communities in the past have attributed meaning to musical and sonic environments (e.g. Johnson 1995; Corbin 1998; B. R. Smith 1999, 2003, 2004; M. M. Smith 2001, 2004; Picker 2003). These approaches suggest that listening practices must be understood by reference to the broader cultural and historical context within which they are formed.

Practices of listening are also shaped by technologies and their interfaces and affordances, which have extended the reach of listening and multiplied its possibilities. Sound studies research has explored how, for instance, the telephone, gramophone, radio, personal stereo, and iPod have all generated new bodies of audible sound as well as related listening techniques (Gitelman 1999, 2006; Bull 2000, 2007; Sterne 2003; Katz 2010). Technology has also greatly increased the scope of what it is possible to listen to. To use a simple example provided by Ihde, "the ocean now resounds with whale songs and shrimp percussion made possible by the extension of listening through electronic amplification" (Ihde 2007: 4–5). Listening practices are generally not regarded as technologically determined but as malleable and capable of being developed, directed, and refined through engagements with technologies. At the same time, listening technologies are recognized as emerging within culturally and historically particular contexts, which carry accompanying sets of sensory priorities, possibilities, and predispositions.

Listening is often described and experienced as a solitary and individuated practice, sometimes deeply personal and private. However, musical listening in particular has also positioned the listener as involved, consciously or otherwise, in wider processes and communities of musical consumption, interpretation, circulation, and production (DeNora 2000; Tacchi 2003; Novak 2008; Bergh and DeNora 2009). Sociological perspectives have identified listening practices as markers of group membership and indexes of knowledge, taste, and social distinction. An archetypal example is the silent, reverent listening of classical music audiences, where obedience to a convention of stillness and the suppression of coughing, talk, and laughter are markers of cultivated musical sensibility and social respectability (Johnson 1995; DeNora 2003: 84). The public exhibition of dedication and discipline in the acquisition and application of listening skills is closely bound up with the performance of knowledge and virtuosity. Ostentatious performances of listening, linked to bodies of esoteric auditory knowledge, help negotiate in-group status and hierarchy in both amateur and professional circles of musicians, technologists, and medical professionals (Horning 2004; Porcello 2004; Krebs 2012; Rice 2013b).

Adorno (1991 [1972]) famously considered serious, concentrated listening (necessary, he believed, to an authentic engagement with music) to be under threat from a "regression of listening," which he associated with the radio. Writing on early radio use, Goodman relates how the overlistening (in terms of time) and underlistening (in terms of attention) that radio was perceived to make possible "stood in a clear moral contrast to the kind of deliberate, calm, rational, fully attentive and time-bounded listening that was always recommended by experts" (2010: 33). Listening practices, then, can serve as indicators of moral, social, civic, psychological, and even spiritual well-being or decline (Schafer 1977; Berendt 1983; Adorno 1991 [1972]; Hirshkind 2004; Oliveros 2005). However, sound studies research has moved beyond the sharp dichotomy between what Herbert (2012) calls "directed" listening ("in depth," "heavy," "profound") and undirected or "distracted" listening ("casual," "lightweight," "superficial"), creating scope both for a more subtle and nuanced categorization of listening modes and for a detailed appraisal of the possibilities, values, and moralities of forms of "ubiquitous listening" (Kassabian 2013).

Although listening might be regarded as a sensory process that involves the isolation and intensification of auditory attention and experience, several authors emphasize that listening involves a close interplay or collaboration with nonauditory senses (Leppert 1995; Bull 2000; McCartney 2004; Kochhar-Lindgren 2004; Lewis-King 2013). Indeed, listening can engage the whole of the listener's body, and in some listening contexts, such as dancing, it is the physicality of listening and the fullness of the body's response to sound (for instance, through rhythmic entrainment and corporeal vibration) that is foregrounded (see BODY; DeNora 2003; Henriques 2003). The sensory dimension of listening, however, might be understood as only one aspect of its wider cognitive and affective engagements. For instance, introducing his ecological approach to music listening, Clarke (2005) argues that the listener's prior musical knowledge—as well as his or her memory, imagination, mood, and relationship with the musical environment—is integral to the listening experience and the diverse opportunities for self-expression and exploration that music may afford the listener.

Numerous writers have sought to deconstruct listening as a single mode of sensory engagement by identifying a plurality of modes of listening or types of listener (e.g. Schaeffer 1968; Adorno 1976 [1962]; Chion 1994; Stockfelt 1997; Douglas 1999; Truax 2001; Huron 2002; Tuuri et al. 2007; Mailman 2012; Pinch and Bijsterveld 2012; Bijsterveld et al. forthcoming). In a famous instance of this approach, Chion distinguishes between three modes of listening: causal listening to a sound "in order to gather information about its cause (or source)" (1994: 25); semantic listening, which "refers to a code or a language to interpret a message"; and reduced listening, which "focuses on the traits of the sound itself, independent of its cause and of its meaning" (28, 29). Truax (2001) also proposes three listening modes, Mailman (2012) offers seven metaphors relevant to music listening, and Huron (2002) puts forward a nonexhaustive list of twenty-one listening styles and strategies for music. These taxonomies set out to express a diversity of modes and qualities of attention, while also specifying a range of distinct listening purposes, functions, and techniques (music listening, radio listening, listening to sonic displays, and so on). I would suggest, however, that these taxonomies of listening have also created what can feel like an infinite regress, where modes of listening continually proliferate without necessarily interlinking or building on one another in productive ways.

The approaches to listening (cultural/historical, technological, sociological, multisensory/corporeal, and so on) that I have outlined here represent particular orientations toward listening, all of which illuminate different aspects of listening as a sensory practice. I conclude by describing my own ethnographic research into ways of listening in a hospital setting, as a context in which a multiplicity of listening modes coexist. I point to the necessity of enlisting a variety of sound studies perspectives in order to reveal the density of meaning in medical listening practices.

Engaging with Hospital Listening

My research has focused on some of the different forms of listening practiced in hospitals, and has involved fieldwork in the Edinburgh Royal Infirmary in Edinburgh, Scotland, and St Thomas' Hospital in London, England (Rice 2003, 2008, 2010a, b, 2012, 2013a, b). The hospital is a space where several modes of listening are simultaneously in play and where multiple layers of auditory knowledge and experience may be found. In addition to patients' experiences of the sound environments that characterize hospital wards, there is also monitory listening practiced by nurses as they manage those patients, and diagnostic listening conducted by medical students and doctors. Indeed, stethoscopic listening or auscultation—the technique of listening to the body's internal sounds—became a particular focus of my research. I studied the different types of listening in the hospital setting in an attempt to reflect some of the sonic intricacy and diversity of a modern hospital, and to explore how listening practices can both underpin and undermine the production of medical knowledge. My research examined how sonic skills are taught to new medical students and hence how those skills are reproduced in new generations of doctors. I spent time on wards interacting with patients and nurses at St Thomas', but also took part in classes where medical students were given instruction in stethoscopic listening and shadowed doctors whose work required them to use auscultation.

Sterne argues that sound technologies and their accompanying techniques of listening emerge within a wider cultural milieu that makes them not only possible but also desirable. Considering the development of stethoscopic listening in Western medicine, he suggests that the practice emerged as part of an "Ensoniment"—which, he argues, took place contemporaneously and in conjunction with a wider Enlightenment—in which "people harnessed, modified, and shaped their powers of auditory perception in the service of rationality" (2003: 2). Auscultation was part of a wider drive in the late eighteenth century to improve medical understanding of anatomy and the signs, symptoms, and progression of disease. At a time when autopsy and dissection were considered central to the advancement of medical knowledge, the stethoscope allowed doctors, through careful listening, to detect physiological changes inside the bodies of living patients. Auscultation, then, emerged as an anatomically informed and scientifically rigorous practice within the medical profession. Grasping this cultural-historical context was essential in making sense of auscultation's presence and ongoing significance within the medical culture I encountered during my fieldwork.

The stethoscope is a technology for the amplification of quiet sounds, enhancing the audibility of—and so allowing access to—previously muffled or silent corporeal processes. The instrument extends the doctor's sensory reach and creates a private auditory space in which the doctor is able to listen intently, undisturbed by the wider sound environment. However, the stethoscope has acquired a significance that far exceeds its practical purpose. The medical students I observed took great pride in wearing and displaying their stethoscopes, often performing auscultation in an ostentatious manner, as a self-conscious performance of the medical habitus. Carrying and using a stethoscope was for them an important symbol of their medical identity. Proficiency in auscultation was also a marker of status and position in the professional hierarchy of doctors within the hospital. Indeed, from a sociological perspective, auscultation created multiple opportunities for the articulation of medical knowledge and professionalism whether among students, within the doctor-patient interaction, or in interactions between doctors.

I found in my own experience of auscultation that the stethoscope created a private auditory space, sealing me in an acoustic bubble, rather as Bull (2000) suggests is the case with personal stereo listening. But lessons also emphasized the importance of looking and touching, not only in placing the stethoscope but also in checking for diagnostic signs that might create the expectation of hearing particular sounds in the patient's body. The act of auscultation, then, involved a close interplay between the senses, which followed from its historical emergence alongside practices of medical gazing related to autopsy and dissection. The fact that auscultation required close tactile and visual contact between doctor and patient (listener and listened-to) also meant that it created what some doctors saw as a valuable point of human contact between themselves and their patients. There was some consensus that auscultation produced an intimate, personal, and humane type of medical interaction. Looking to the future, some doctors with whom I spoke were concerned that new technologies, in particular the introduction of handheld ultrasound devices for use at the bedside, might lead to a phasing out of auscultation and a subsequent consolidation of what they saw as an already growing distance between doctor and patient, produced by a increasing dependence on more sophisticated technology in diagnostic work. In this context, listening was harnessed as an index of sympathetic and empathetic medical practice. For some doctors, auscultation became a symbol of the kind of doctors they felt themselves to be and of the way they felt medicine should be practiced. Their adherence to auscultation became a means of articulating both their own ethical standpoints as doctors and the moral obligations of their profession.

It is well recognized that auditory engagement is a key component of ethnographic fieldwork (Forsey 2010). Cohen and Rapport, for instance, point out that "Geertz's famous answer to the question 'What does the anthropologist do? He writes,' is a curiously thin description of what actually happens. . . . Above all, they listen" (1995: 12). For them, the auditory attention of ethnographers should be directed, first and foremost, toward understanding the words spoken by those under study. My own hospital research certainly involved a good deal of verbally orientated listening in interviews conducted with doctors, patients, medical students and others, but my listening was also directed toward nonverbal (and, for that matter, nonmusical) sounds that occurred within the hospital. I found a carefully situated and emplaced listening—an immersion in the sound environment of the ward—to be essential to developing an empathetic understanding of patient experiences of hospital sounds. At the same time, taking an "ears on" approach in my apprenticeship in stethoscopic listening required me to apply both monitory listening, which Pinch and Bijsterveld describe as listening "used to determine *whether* something is wrong," and diagnostic listening, which "reveals *what* is wrong" (Lachmund 1999: 440; Pinch and Bijsterveld 2012: 14). I found that thinking in terms of listening modes was useful as a strategy for imposing conceptual order on the flux of sounds and approaches to sounds I encountered during fieldwork. It was useful too in linking listening to practical tasks and tangible outcomes in both medicine and ethnography.

The working environment at St Thomas'—a busy inner-city hospital—was fast-paced. For many of the doctors, there was a constant need to move forward, to keep up, to hurry. I began to realize that my research methods would have to fit into the doctors' working patterns. It wouldn't be possible to have frequent periods of sustained interaction. Instead, my research would unfold in brief yet focused moments of contact. I was struck by the analogy of stethoscopic listening here. The use of the stethoscope almost invariably involves short spells of intense concentration and careful, considered listening; my research would require the same. Stethoscopic listening, it seemed, also created an interesting tension between proximity and distance. The technique requires doctor and patient to get close to one another, but also ensures a degree of physical separation and diagnostic detachment. Again there is a parallel here with ethnographic fieldwork, where ethnographer and subject come into close contact while the ethnographer tries to keep some reflexive distance. In addition, the balance of subjectivity (in the experience of sounds) and objectivity (in constituting those sounds as perceptual objects about which rational judgments may be made) that occurs in stethoscopic listening resonates with the balance of subjectivity and objectivity that defines the conduct of successful ethnography. In reflecting on medical listening both as an object of research and a method of conducting ethnographic work, then, seemingly discrete modes of listening were brought close together and began to overlap; at points they even seemed to become integrated or to dissolve into each other. I was reminded that a preoccupation with identifying and separating specific modes of listening, as is such a strong trend in sound studies, may not always be productive. Certainly, thinking in terms of distinct listening modes may not accurately reflect—and indeed may at times distort—the perception of listening as it occurs within the holistic context of lived experience. The embodied, emplaced, and multisensory activity of ethnographic fieldwork brought home the fluid and sometimes unpredictable manner in which listening practices overlap with other aspects of attention, experience, and subjectivity.

References

Adorno, Theodor W. 1976 [1962]. *Introduction to the Sociology of Music*. Trans. E. Ashton. New York: Continuum International.

Adorno, Theodor W. 1991 [1972]. *The Culture Industry: Selected Essays on Mass Culture*. London: Routledge.

Back, Les. 2007. *The Art of Listening*. Oxford: Berg.

Berendt, Joachim-Ernst. 1983. *The World Is Sound: Nada Brahma*. Rochester, VT: Destiny Books.

Bergh, Arild, and Tia DeNora. 2009. "From Wind-up to iPod: Techno-Cultures of Listening." In *The Cambridge Companion to Recorded Music*, ed. Nicholas Cook, Eric Clarke, Daniel Leech-Wilkinson, and John Rink, 102–115. Cambridge: Cambridge University Press.

Bijsterveld, Karin, Alexandra Supper, Stefan Krebs, Joeri Bruyninckx, Melissa Van Drie, and Anna Harris. Forthcoming. *Sonic Skills: Sound and Listening in Science, Engineering and Medicine*.

Bourdieu, Pierre. 1977. *Outline of a Theory of Practice*. Trans. R. Nice. Cambridge: Cambridge University Press.

Bull, Michael. 2000. *Sounding Out the City: Personal Stereos and the Management of Everyday Life*. Oxford: Berg.

Bull, Michael. 2007. *Sound Moves: Ipod Culture and Urban Experience*. London: Routledge.

Chessick, Richard D. 1989. *The Technique and Practice of Listening in Intensive Psychotherapy*. Northvale, NJ: Jason Arondson.

Chion, Michel. 1994. *Audiovision: Sound on Screen*. New York: Columbia University Press.

Clarke, Eric. 2005. *Ways of Listening: An Ecological Approach to the Perception of Musical Meaning*. Oxford: Oxford University Press.

Cohen, Anthony P., and Nigel Rapport. 1995. Introduction to *Questions of Consciousness*, ed. Anthony P. Cohen and Nigel Rapport, 1–20. London: Routledge.

Corbin, Alain. 1998. *Village Bells: Sound and Meaning in the Nineteenth-Century French Countryside*. New York: Columbia University Press.

DeNora, Tia. 2000. *Music in Everyday Life*. Cambridge: Cambridge University Press.

DeNora, Tia. 2003. *After Adorno: Rethinking Music Sociology*. Cambridge: Cambridge University Press.

Douglas, Susan J. 1999. *Listening In: Radio and the American Imagination*. Minneapolis: University of Minnesota Press.

Feld, Steven. 1991. "Sound as a Symbolic System: The Kaluli Drum." In *The Varieties of Sensory Experience: A Sourcebook in the Anthropology of the Senses*, ed. D. Howes, 79–99. Toronto: University of Toronto Press.

Feld, Steven. 1996. "Waterfalls of Song: An Acoustemology of Place Resounding in Bosavi, Papua New Guinea." In *Senses of Place*, ed. S. Feld and K. H. Basso, 91–135. Santa Fe: School of American Research Press.

Feld, Steven. 2003. "A Rainforest Acoustemology." In *The Auditory Culture Reader*, ed. M. Bull and L. Back, 223–239. Oxford: Berg.

Feld, Steven. 2012 [1982]. *Sound and Sentiment: Birds, Weeping, Poetics, and Song in Kaluli Expression*. 3rd ed. Durham: Duke University Press.

Forsey, M. G. 2010. "Ethnography as Participant Listening." *Ethnography* 11(4): 558–572.

Freud, Sigmund. 1958 [1912]. "Recommendations to Physicians Practicing Psycho-Analysis." In The Standard Edition of the Complete Psychological Works of Sigmund Freud. Ed. and trans. J. Strachey, Vol. 12, 109–120. London: Hogarth Press.

Gitelman, Lisa. 1999. *Scripts, Grooves and Writing Machines: Representing Technology in the Edison Era*. Stanford: Stanford University Press.

Gitelman, Lisa. 2006. *Always Already New: Media, History and the Data of Culture*. Cambridge, MA: MIT Press.

Goodman, David. 2010. "Distracted Listening: On Not Making Sound Choices in the 1930s." In *Sound in the Age of Mechanical Reproduction*, ed. David Suisman and Susan Strasser, 15–46. Philadelphia: University of Pennsylvania Press.

Henriques, Julian. 2003. "Sonic Dominance and the Reggae Sound System Session." In *The Auditory Culture Reader*, ed. Michael Bull and Les Back, 451–480. New York: Berg.

Herbert, Ruth. 2012. "Modes of Music Listening and Modes of Subjectivity in Everyday Life." *Journal of Sonic Studies* 2(1), available at http://journal.sonicstudies.org/vol02/nr01/a05, accessed September 17, 2014.

Hirschkind, Charles. 2004. "Hearing Modernity: Egypt, Islam, and the Pious Ear." In *Hearing Cultures: Essays on Sound, Listening and Modernity*, ed. Veit Erlmann, 131–151. Oxford: Berg.

Horning, Susan S. 2004. "Engineering the Performance: Recording Engineers, Tacit Knowledge, and the Art of Controlling Sound." *Social Studies of Science* 34(5): 703–731.

Huron, David. 2002, November 1. "Listening Styles and Listening Strategies." Paper presented at Society for Music Theory 2002 Conference, Columbus, Ohio. Available at www.musicog.ohio-state.edu/Huron/Talks/SMT.2002/handout.html, accessed September 17, 2014.

Ihde, Don. 2007. *Listening and Voice: Phenomenologies of Sound*. Albany: State University of New York Press.

Jackson, Stanley W. 1992. "The Listening Healer in the History of Psychological Healing." *American Journal of Psychiatry* 149(12): 1623–1632.

Johnson, James H. 1995. *Listening in Paris: A Cultural History*. Berkeley: University of California Press.

Kassabian, Anahid. 2013. *Ubiquitous Listening: Affect, Attention, and Distributed Subjectivity*. Berkeley: University of California Press.

Katz, Mark. 2010. *Capturing Sound: How Technology Has Changed Music*. Berkeley: University of California Press.

Kochhar-Lingren, Kanta. 2004. "Performing at the Edge of Hearing: The Third Ear." In *Aural Cultures*, ed. J. Drobnik, 229–239. Banff: XYZ.

Krebs, Stefan. 2012. "'Sobbing, Whining, Rumbling': Listening to Automobiles as Social Practice." In *The Oxford Handbook of Sound Studies*, ed. Trevor Pinch and Karin Bijsterveld, 79–101. Oxford: Oxford University Press.

Lachmund, Jens. 1999. "Making Sense of Sound: Auscultation and Lung Sound Codification in Nineteenth-Century French and German Medicine." *Science, Technology, and Human Values* 24(4): 419–450.

Leppert, Richard. 1995. *The Sight of Sound: Music, Representation and the History of the Body*. Berkeley: University of California Press.

Lewis-King, Michelle. 2013. "Touching and Listening: Pulse Project." *Journal of Sonic Studies* 4(1), available at http://journal.sonicstudies.org/vol04/nr01/a12, accessed September 17, 2014.

Mailman, Joshua B. 2012. "Seven Metaphors for Music Listening: DRAMaTIC." *Journal of Sonic Studies* 2(1), available at http://journal.sonicstudies.org/vol02/nr01/a03, accessed September 17, 2014.

Mauss, Marcel. 1979 [1935]. "Body Techniques." In *Sociology and Psychology: essays by Marcel Mauss*, trans. Ben Brewster, 97–123. London: Routledge and Kegan Paul.

McCartney, Andra. 2004. "Soundscape Works, Listening and the Touch of Sound." In *Aural Cultures*, ed. Jim Drobnik, 179–185. Banff: XYZ.

Moore, Brian C. J. 2003. *An Introduction to the Psychology of Hearing*. London: Academic Press.

Novak, David. 2008. "2.5×6 Metres of Space: Japanese Music Coffeehouses and Experimental Practices of Listening." *Popular Music* 27(1): 15–34.

Oliveros, Pauline. 2005. *Deep Listening: A Composer's Sound Practice*. New York: iUniverse.

Picker, John M. 2003. *Victorian Soundscapes*. New York: Oxford University Press.

Pinch, Trevor, and Karin Bijsterveld, eds. 2012. *The Oxford Handbook of Sound Studies*. Oxford: Oxford University Press.

Porcello, Thomas. 2004. "Speaking of Sound: Language and the Professionalization of Sound Recording Engineers." *Social Studies of Science* 34(5): 733–758.

Reik, Theodore. 1951. *Listening with the Third Ear: The Inner Experience of a Psychoanalyst*. Garden City, NY: Garden City Books.

Rice, Tom. 2003. "Soundselves: An Acoustemology of Sound and Self in the Edinburgh Royal Infirmary." *Anthropology Today* 19(4): 4–9.

Rice, Tom. 2008. "'Beautiful Murmurs': Stethoscopic Listening and Acoustic Objectification." *The Senses and Society* 3(3): 293–306.

Rice, Tom. 2010a. " 'The Hallmark of a Doctor': The Stethoscope and the Making of Medical Identity." *Journal of Material Culture* 15(3): 287–301.

Rice, Tom. 2010b. "Learning to Listen: Auscultation and the Transmission of Auditory Knowledge." In Special Issue: Making Knowledge. *Journal of the Royal Anthropological Institute* 16(s1): S41–S61.

Rice, Tom. 2012. "Sounding Bodies: Medical Students and the Acquisition of Stethoscopic Perspectives." In *The Oxford Handbook of Sound Studies*, ed. T. Pinch and K. Bijsterveld, 298–319. New York: Oxford University Press.

Rice, Tom. 2013a. "Broadcasting the Body: The Public Made Private in Hospital Soundscapes." In *Music, Sound and Space: Transformations of Public and Private Experience*, ed. G. Born, 169–185. Cambridge: Cambridge University Press.

Rice, Tom. 2013b. *Hearing and the Hospital: Sound, Listening, Knowledge and Experience*. Canon Pyon: Sean Kingston Press.

Roszak, Theodore. 1993. *The Voice of the Earth*. London: Bantam Press.

Schaeffer, Pierre. 1968. *Traité des Objets Musicaux*. Paris: Editions du Seuil.

Schafer, Murray R. 1977. *The Tuning of the World*. New York: Knopf.

Schwaber, Evelyne A. 1983. "A Particular Perspective on Analytic Listening." In *The Psychoanalytic Study of the Child*, ed. Albert J. Solnit, Ruth S. Eissler, and Peter B. Neubaer, 38: 519–546. New Haven: Yale University Press.

Smith, Bruce R. 1999. *The Acoustic World of Early Modern England*. Chicago: University of Chicago Press.

Smith, Bruce R. 2003. "Tuning into London c. 1600." In *The Auditory Culture Reader*, ed. M. Bull and L. Back, 127–136. Oxford: Berg.

Smith, Bruce R. 2004. "Listening to the Wild Blue Yonder: The Challenges of Acoustic Ecology." In *Hearing Cultures: Essays on Sound, Listening and Modernity*, ed. V. Erlmann, 21–41. Oxford: Berg.

Smith, Mark M. 2001. *Listening to Nineteenth-Century America*. Chapel Hill: University of North Carolina Press.

Smith, Mark M., ed. 2004. *Hearing History: A Reader*. Athens: University of Georgia Press.

Sterne, Jonathan. 2003. *The Audible Past: Cultural Origins of Sound Production*. Durham: Duke University Press.

Sterne, Jonathan, ed. 2012. *The Sound Studies Reader*. London: Routledge.

Stockfelt, Ola. 1997. "Adequate Modes of Listening." In *Keeping Score: Music, Disciplinarity, Culture*, ed. David Schwarz, Anahid Kassabian, and Lawrence Siegel, 129–146. Charlottesville: University Press of Virginia.

Tacchi, Jo. 2003. "Nostalgia and Radio Sound." In *The Auditory Culture Reader*, ed. M. Bull and L. Back, 281–295. Oxford: Berg.

Truax, Barry. 2001. *Acoustic Communication*. Westport: Ablex.

Tuuri, Kai, Manne-Sakari Mustonen, and Antti Pirhonen. 2007. "Same Sound—Different Meanings: A Novel Scheme for Modes of Listening." In *Proceedings of Audio Mostly 2007 2nd Conference on Interaction with Sound*, ed. Henning Köhler, 13–18. Röntgenbau, Ilmenau, Germany: Fraunhofer Institute for Digital Media Technology.

music

Where does music reside within the broader category of sound? Perhaps the most revealing aspect of this question is how rarely it is asked, as the qualities that make certain subsets of sounds "musical" are so often presumed to be self-evident. In a comprehensive survey for the *New Grove Dictionary of Music and Musicians*, Bruno Nettl referenced the entry for "Music, Art of" in two editions of the *Britannica* and observed: "neither article begins with an explicit definition, [instead] assuming that readers know what music is" (2001: 427).

One of the most ubiquitous definitions of music, as "organized sound," came from an experimental composer, Edgard Varèse, and was challenged by another, John Cage, who famously highlighted the arbitrariness of the boundaries between music, noise, and silence in his compositions and writings (Cage 2011 [1961]). Anthropologist John Blacking grounded Varèse's definition in human behavior, describing the relationship of sound structure and social structure as one between "humanly organized sound" and "soundly organized humanity" (1973: 89–116). But with music, there are always more questions and qualifications. When does "organized" sound become "disorganized" and who are the arbiters of organization? Who or what classifies as a "musician" when humans interact with computers and improvising machines? Where does the cry of the muni bird reside in the domain of music?

The realm of sound demarcated as music, which has struck so many as an inviolable and inevitable aspect of human societies, was conceptualized gradually over thousands of years. The association of music with beauty, organization, and intentionality dates at least to antiquity, and studies of music continued to overshadow and envelop studies of sound and hearing until the age of Enlightenment. All throughout the long formalization of Western sciences and aesthetics, it was primarily music (and, to a lesser extent, speech) that provided the grounds for experimentation, analysis, and interpretation in sound. If we accept the premise that there is a field of "music studies," we would have to first recognize that it provided a foundation for the emergence of sound studies, and then ask how these two fields can most productively inform one another.

At this juncture, the core methodologies of music studies—style and repertoire, aesthetic appreciation, and biography—have kept its inquiries relatively isolated from those of sound studies, and nonspecialists are often alienated by the proprietary tools developed to analyze musical texts. Sound studies also came of age after relativism, multiculturalism, and popular culture studies had begun to dismantle the canons and hierarchies that music studies had helped construct. Music studies is a particular and partial discipline, and a disproportionate share of its efforts have been directed at Western culture's most celebrated contribution to global music, variously called "classical," "art," or "serious" music or, in a brutally exclusive shorthand, simply "music." Critiques lodged at this presumption of aesthetic superiority—including the philosophical and sociological studies that situate Western music in the everyday negotiations of bourgeois identity (e.g. Adorno 1978 [1938]; Bourdieu 1987); the ethnomusicological research that weighs the universality and specificity of music making (e.g. Lomax 1968; Feld 1984); the materialist theories of political economy and cultural production (e.g. Adorno and Horkheimer 2002 [1944]; Attali 1985)—scratch the surface of an unruly terrain upon which epistemologies of music and sound have grown as relatively discrete areas.

Music is an idea, not just a form, and like any other idea, music is a problem. Yet the omnipresence and widespread recognizability of music, as a set of performative acts and objects of inscription that invite particular modes of listening, can work to elevate its conceptual status above scrutiny. This entry highlights how music has been naturalized in three principal ways: as science, as art, and as performance. This selective genealogy is aimed at defamiliarizing music rather than deconstructing it: scientific, aesthetic, and social qualities have been attributed to music, and subjecting these ideas to critical analysis is meant to highlight rather than diminish their significance. From a constructivist perspective, the long lineage of music studies has already accomplished much fruitful analysis in advance of sound studies. In turn, sound studies has productively challenged music studies by developing new questions that do not assume a privileged status for music as a formation of sound.

Music as the Science of Sound

In antiquity, music belonged to the quadrivium of *mathematica*—as fundamental to the education of virtuous men as arithmetic, geometry, and astronomy—and Aristotle and Plato's works are often cited to demonstrate the generative role of music in the earliest philosophies of Western aesthetics. Music was also integral to the systematization of science: sonically, pitches were identified, standardized, and differentiated, while textually they were named, assigned visual symbols, and inscribed in a graphical system of notation. Performers and theorists developed laws governing how pitches were classified into modes and ordered consecutively as melody, simultaneously as harmony, durationally as rhythm, and periodically within a given structural form.

As a subject of inquiry and a catalyst for innovation, music instrumentalized science. The Pythagorean quest for universal scientific rationality relied on experiments with a monochord, leading to the discovery of mathematical ratios that were later interpreted as proof that, "the very being of the whole universe [is] bound together by music" as Athenaeus of Naucratis wrote around 192 AD (quoted in Levin 2009: 5). The Platonic concept of *harmonia* and Pythagorean theories of arithmetic and astronomy conjoined in the scientific study of music, which developed, as Adriana Cavarero writes, into "a realm that lends itself to be regulated by forms and norms" (2005: 156). Vibrating strings could unlock the mysteries of the universe only when their sounds were determinable as intervals and classifiable into sets; in other words, when sound was imbued with the properties of music.

Hellenic experimentation set in motion a process of detaching music from sound, amplifying its value, in part, by electing it most suitable for the scientific study of sound. According to Jonathan Sterne, "speech or music had been the general [overarching] categories through which sound was understood," but much later, during the scientific revolution, there was "an inversion of the general and specific in philosophies of sound," with speech and music now downgraded to "special cases" (2003: 23). Music was no longer a science that could explain human and celestial bodies but was itself partially explainable by research in the "superior" sciences. By the eighteenth century, music theorist Jean-Philippe Rameau tested his laws governing harmony with theories developed in the emerging fields of audiology and acoustics, including mathematician Joseph Sauveur's studies of vibrational frequency as a measurement of musical pitch, an indicator of music's diminished status as subsidiary to sound.

The science of systematizing music as sound material reached critical mass with Hermann Helmholtz's work *On the Sensations of Tone as a Physiological Basis for the Theory of Music* in 1863. The book's achievement is its interdisciplinarity, integrating the study of "physical and physiological acoustics on the one hand and of musical science and esthetics on the other" (1885: 1). The yin and yang of science and aesthetics allowed for taxonomies of music, noise, and silence to be distinguished within the larger category of sound. Music was set off as a thing apart—systematized aesthetically, extrapolated scientifically, and philosophically endowed with inherent powers—by scientists from Pythagoras to Helmholtz.

Music as the Aesthetics of Sound

Although the art and science of music are historically entangled (Palisca 1961; Jackson 2006; Hui 2012), Western philosophies of aesthetics have privileged expressive practices of performance, composition, listening, and embodied movement. If the sciences were capable of identifying and standardizing the properties of music that distinguished it from other sounds, it was in the humanities that music was isolated as a distinctive aesthetic object of beauty and organization, and as a human behavioral activity. Whether evaluated as art, as popular culture, as ritual folklore, as individual or collective expression, or as other forms of sociality, music has been considered meaningful because its aesthetic properties convey human emotion.

Throughout the legacy of music studies there has been a ceaseless fascination with the communicative nature of music, which shares the sonorous and expressive qualities of speech but not the supposedly stable referentiality of language (see LANGUAGE). Oral poets, including Homer, were condemned by Plato because their sung vocalizations were a seductive distraction for "those who love sounds," and wind instruments such as Marsyas's *aulos* were morally suspect because they impeded speech (Cavarero 2005: 84). For much of the history of the Catholic Church, a similar tension characterized the relationship of liturgy and music: "when it befalls me to be more moved with the voice than the words sung," wrote Augustine in his *Confessions*, "I confess to have sinned penally, and then had rather not hear music." In the sixteenth-century Counter-Reformation, the Church deliberated over musical reforms that prioritized the intelligibility of the word of God over the aesthetic beauty of musical sound (Lockwood 1984; Monson 2006).

Attempts to translate sound into visual icons can be found in many cultures, such as ancient Sumerian scripts for notating melodies played by the lyre or *guqin* tablature from the time of Confucius. The system of Western staff notation, an arrangement of vertical lines and dots spread across five horizontal lines, developed as the most elaborately organized, slavishly adhered to, widely disseminated, and zealously contested technique for entextualizing sound (Ellingson 1992). An intellectual tradition of analyzing musical texts as an autonomous language—eventually named "music theory" and for centuries directed almost exclusively at Western art music—relies on separating notes from "extramusical" contexts (performance, discourse, biography, etc.), to the extent that the sensory domain of sound is wholly abandoned in favor of the textual domain of musical notation. Since the Romantic period, music theory has congealed into an elaborate and proprietary semiotic system, analogous to grammatical, syntactic, and other abstractions of language (cf. Meyer 1957). Formalism reaches its apex in analyses of entirely instrumental, or "absolute" music, which, Susan McClary writes, is "purported to operate on the basis of pure configurations, untainted by words, stories, or even affect" (1993: 326).

The presumed lack of referentiality feared by Plato was celebrated by metaphysicists such as E. T. A. Hoffmann for "tak[ing] us out of the everyday into the realm of the infinite" (1989 [1814]: 237). When the University of Vienna hired music critic Eduard Hanslick in 1861 and named him the first professor of music history and aesthetics, they established a precedent for locating music studies squarely within the humanities. Hanslick's successor Guido Adler subdivided music research into what would develop into the standard disciplines of music theory, musicology, and ethnomusicology (Mugglestone 1981). The impact and solidity of this legacy—measurable, perhaps, in the sheer number of publications and academic conferences dedicated to any one of "The Three B's" (Bach, Beethoven, and Brahms)—can have the effect of alienating those joining the new ranks of popular music studies, sound studies, and science and technology studies. Progressive research remains to be done on the magnitude to which music studies was able to construct highly formalized systems for entextualizing sound and subjecting it to analysis, and for generating descriptive language and technical conceptualizations of sound that have been integral to Western cultural imperialism.

Within the geopolitics of capitalist empire, music studies provided the basis for Eurocentric claims of cultural superiority, while music of others from elsewhere was evaluated in negative relation, as a foil for the Enlightenment project and as fodder for rationalizing colonization. Matthew Arnold's Romanticist valorization of "pure music," created by exceptional individuals, as "the best which has been thought and said in the world" (1869: viii) was based on comparisons to religious, ethnic, racial, and nationalist others whose cultural practices were vilified and then deployed as justification for racism, enslavement, eugenics, and other forms of structural violence. The sounds of Italian organ grinders in London or of indigenous chanters in the New World could be heard as so much noise, just as the invention of "African rhythm" (as metronomic, syncopated, polyrhythmic, and participatory) could only be conceived against the reciprocal and unmarked construction of European rhythm, whatever that might be.[1]

More sympathetic listeners, especially those affiliated with the social sciences, applied the disciplining strategies of Western music studies to recuperate "savage" sounds as music. In the United States, early studies of American Indian music by Alice Fletcher and Francis La Flesche (1893) and slave spirituals by William Francis Allen, Charles Pickard Ware, and Lucy McKim Garrison (1867) relied on the entextualization of orally transmitted music into Western notation, which then provided the basis for countering claims of deculturation. W. E. B. Du Bois began each chapter of *The Souls of Black Folk* with a quote from a "sorrow song" paired with its melody in musical notation, and he devoted the last chapter to "these weird old songs in which the soul of the black slave spoke to men" (1903: 250; see also Weheliye 2005).

Aesthetic distinctions of music and sound were entangled with Western scientific standards that worked in tandem to either affirm or deny the humanity of others. When Alexander Ellis translated Helmholtz's book into English in 1885, he added an appendix that included analysis of non-Western scales using a new metric of measuring intervals in units called cents (Hui 2012). The quantization of pitch also fueled contentious debates about tuning, leading to agreement on a fixed reference pitch, A at 440 Hz (Jackson 2006). Music, as rationalized and standardized sound, circulated to far-flung lands via emergent technologies such as musical instruments (the piano and the wind instruments of marching bands were especially pervasive) as well as scientific instruments (tuning forks, metronomes, etc.). Western standards set sail into a sea of other cultural standards, asserting the universality of music while attempting to impose order on its many varieties (many of which, at the end of the twentieth century, would be celebrated as "world music").

Systematized analysis was used selectively to support aesthetic presumptions of elite music as more harmonically complex and emotionally subjective than so-called folk and popular musics (Becker 1986). Starting in the mid-twentieth century, ethnomusicologists began wagering an extended campaign against the presumption that musical complexity can be measured objectively, and when sociologists such as Bourdieu (1987) began "studying up," contextualizing notions of "taste" within negotiations of class and social status, classical music could be reimagined as the folk music of Euro-American elites.

Music as the Social Life of Sound

Like all sound, music is in the air, out in the world, and thus always socially mediated. Music takes on particular social significances because it habitually draws attention to its own mediation, especially its forms of performance, inscription, and reception. That music is not only subject to these forms of mediation but is constructed by them is a principal contention of social scientists and others invested in the comparative study of music in culture or, more pointedly, music as culture (Merriam 1977).

The study of non-Western musics, and folk or popular musics of the West, began as an offshoot of both aestheticism and the physical sciences, but it was primarily in anthropology, comparative musicology and ethnomusicology that music was recontextualized in spaces of production and reception. Ethnographers dispatched to "the field" reported back with abundant evidence of music's ubiquity: tuneful prayers and lullabies could be heard the world over, and music was present at weddings and funerals regardless of religious, ethnic, racial, or geographic identification. From travelers' accounts to commercial sound recordings, comparative studies naturalized the idea that music is a universal form of human behavior while simultaneously highlighting its diverse and culturally specific evaluations. This dialectic between universalism and relativism, with "salvage ethnography" providing materials for assessing similarity and difference, became a guiding principle of music studies in the long twentieth century. Music was again codified and used as a tool to accomplish certain ends, now for the comparative study of culture's relation to human evolution and social organization.

Whether through writing, reading, or other forms of inscription, musical research was one component of a larger anthropological imperative to preserve cultural practices deemed to be under threat of disappearance from encroaching modernity (Darnell 2001). Musical traditions were constructed as valuable residues of proud cultures as they fell victim to the inevitable march of progress; efforts to protect and institutionalize these endangered musics inadvertently reaffirmed the power of the "center" (and its signature music) through a paternalistic gesture to the "periphery." That music was a critical node of mediation in this mutual construction of the West and the Rest is evidenced in ethnomusicologist Ali Jihad Racy's (1993) reconstruction of an extraordinary meeting of Western and Middle Eastern music scholars at the Congress of Arab Music in Cairo in 1932.

The Congress was called by King Fu'ād of Egypt as part of a series of reforms that, in the words of the Academy of Oriental Music director Mustafá Ridā, "will bring the country to a zenith of cultural refinement and lead it to compete in the arena of civilized nations" (Racy 1993: 70). Seven technical committees were formed to address such problems as determining a fixed musical scale, adopting notational symbols, building a canon of Arabic compositions, assessing the appropriateness of specific musical instruments, and recording indigenous songs. The Recording Committee (which included Béla Bartók and two esteemed members of the Berlin school of comparative musicology, Erich von Hornbostel and Robert Lachmann) instructed local performers to avoid "music that does not adhere to Eastern melodies" and "which emulates objectionable European music in its worst form" (72), while the Melodic and Rhythmic Modes Committee condensed what member Ahmad Amīn al-Dīk called a "confusing multiplicity" of Arabic modes, ultimately winnowing down the official number of Egyptian maqāmāt to fifty-two (74).

There was unrest on the Musical Instruments Committee, where Western and Arab members disagreed over the suitability of the piano. Curt Sachs, who along with Hornbostel had developed a global instrument classification scheme (Hornbostel and Sachs 1961 [1914]), was among the Europeans who objected that the Western instrument would "disfigure the beauty of Arab music," while the Egyptians argued that instruments such as the *oud* and *qānūn* were inadequate in conveying a range of emotions (Racy 1993: 76). Muhammad Fathī appealed to the Westerners by referring back to a time when Europeans modeled their instruments on those of the Middle East: "if your instruments had developed from ours, today we would like to develop our instruments from yours, so do not be stingy toward us" (79). Music, here, served as a laboratory for experiments in modernity, a site where culture's mediating role in power relations and identity formations was pressed into service for postcolonial projects of state formation.

By the 1950s and 1960s, there was enough comparative data on the music of specific cultures for Alan Lomax to undertake his ambitious cantometrics project, which took the relativist argument that musical structures are manifestations of social structures to its logical extreme (Lomax 1968; see also Feld 1984). In ensuing decades, ethnomusicology and cultural anthropology became increasingly responsive to postcolonial critiques of orientalism and essentialism, questioning the fixity of musical forms and social identities and situating people and their music in relations of power (cf. Askew 2002; Ebron 2002; Weidman 2006). From within the Western classical tradition, some of the most effective challenges to the sanctimony of music have come from musicians creating avant-garde compositions, "noise," and "free" improvisation (Kahn 1999; see NOISE). But music's identity as one among many forms of sound remains underexamined; to recast Bruno Nettl's observation, we largely proceed from the assumption that we know what music is.

Music as Sound

This historical genealogy, with all its emphasis on the disciplining of music in service of various epistemological orderings, is intended to map out some locations where music has taken up residence within the larger domain of sound. The question of music's status as a scientific, aesthetic, and social object and practice has been productively raised by those contextualizing music simply as sound. As a concluding gesture, I turn to three areas of sound studies that have made a critical intervention into music studies: multilayered soundscapes, recorded sounds in circulation, and sites where music appears to shed many of the associations outlined above.

In some of the earliest sound studies research, beginning in the 1960s, R. Murray Schafer (1977) developed his theory of the soundscape that situated music within an ecological expanse populated with multiple sound sources. Building partly on Schafer, Steven Feld (2012 [1982], 1996) studied the Kaluli in a remote rainforest in Bosavi, Papua New Guinea, observing how they evaluated voices (weeping, poetics, and song), environmental sounds (waterfalls and bird calls), and instruments (percussion) within an integrated sensorium. Though Schafer and Feld have created soundscape compositions that can be heard in performance venues and on music devices, music is but one resident within the broad territories of sound they invoke. While the soundscape concept has since been subject to extended critique (see SPACE), on arrival it served as a rejoinder to a much longer history of disarticulating music from the general category of sound.

Music's exceptionalism has been questioned in media studies that position music among many forms of sound, which change through practices of inscription and circulation. Lisa Gitelman (2006) has shown that Edison imagined his phonograph as an extension of inscription machines from print media into the domain of sound, invented primarily for the purpose of dictation in the workplace and then redefined by users as a reproducer of music for domestic entertainment. Jonathan Sterne (2003) shows how machines for musical reproduction were invented in a broader context of sound technologies—the stethoscope, the telegraph, the telephone—and it is with the phonograph that he moves from speech and heartbeats to music as a form of mass culture that crystallized, if not wholly redefined, sound as a commodified object. David Suisman (2010) suggests that even before the talking machine was introduced, the extraction, inscription, and commodification of sound already rested on a musical foundation evidenced by the sheet music publishing industry, which signaled music's reproducibility to a rising consumer class, and by the player piano as an early leader in musical inscription and reproduction. Music is the domain of sound that has been most consistently and thoroughly monetized—whether as live performance, textual inscription, phonography, and so on—and in each of these formulations, music retains a distinct identity but is also refigured as an object of consumer desire entangled in webs of media and technology.

Rapidly developing technologies of mediation have opened up other possibilities for music to shed its role as a privileged domain of sound. At the massive Mall of America in suburban Minneapolis, a highly orchestrated flow of programmed music creates a background of "muzak" that is heard by shoppers in ways that dissociate from perceived norms of musical listening.

Over public loudspeaker systems, recorded music "certainly isn't meant for contemplative listening," observes Sterne; "it also isn't always 'heard' in an entirely passive fashion—rather, it tends to pass in and out of the foreground of a listener's consciousness" (1997: 30), to the point where "music exerts effects primarily or solely as sound" (24). In a far more insidious example, in U.S. military detention camps, continuous and deafening audio playback is meant to shatter the subjectivities of detainees and provide access to actionable intelligence. "It is not at all clear that the music aimed at prisoners in detention camps has functioned *as music*," writes Suzanne Cusick, "Rather, it has more often functioned as *sheer sound* with which to assault a prisoner's sense of hearing" (2008). As former prisoner Ruhal Ahmend said of his experience with what interrogators call "futility music," "*It doesn't sound like music at all*" (quoted in Cusick 2008), and is most productively situated within a larger spectrum of "acoustic violence" (Daughtry 2014).

These examples, as much as Feld's soundscape of human and bird song and Edison's phonograph, underscore music's sounded-ness without assuming an implicit musical order. Music is a shifting subset of sounds that assume particular properties depending on one's orientation to them. In recognizing this, sound studies can engage with the ways that music has been naturalized as distinct, while drawing attention to the arbitrariness of the conceptual separation between music and sound.

Note

1. On Italian organ grinders in Victorian London, see Picker (1999–2000). On the "invention of African rhythm" see Agawu (1995).

References

Adorno, Theodor W. 1978 [1938]. "On the Fetish-Character in Music and the Regression of Listening." In *The Essential Frankfurt School Reader*, ed. Andrew Arato and Eike Gebhardt, 270–299. New York: Urizen Books.

Agawu, Kofi. 1995. "The Invention of African Rhythm." *Journal of the American Musicological Society* 48(3): 380–395.

Allen, William Francis, Charles Pickard Ware, and Lucy McKim Garrison. 1867. *Slave Songs of the United States*. New York: A. Simpson and Co.

Arnold, Matthew. 1869. *Culture and Anarchy: An Essay in Political and Social Criticism*. London: Smith, Elder and Co.

Askew, Kelly. 2002. *Performing the Nation: Swahili Music and Cultural Politics in Tanzania.* Chicago: University of Chicago Press.

Attali, Jacques. 1985. *Noise: The Political Economy of Music.* Trans. Brian Massumi. Minneapolis: University of Minnesota Press.

Becker, Judith. 1986. "Is Western Art Music Superior?" *The Musical Quarterly* 72(3): 341–359.

Blacking, John. 1973. *How Musical Is Man?* Seattle: University of Washington Press.

Bourdieu, Pierre. 1987. *Distinction: A Social Critique of the Judgement of Taste.* Cambridge, MA: Harvard University Press.

Cage, John. 2011 [1961]. "Experimental Music." In *Silence: Lectures and Writings.* Fiftieth anniversary ed. Middletown: Wesleyan University Press.

Cavarero, Adriana. 2005. *For More Than One Voice: Toward a Philosophy of Vocal Expression.* Stanford: Stanford University Press.

Cusick, Suzanne. 2008. "Musicology, Torture, Repair." *Radical Musicology* 3, available at http://www.radical-musicology.org.uk, accessed September 30, 2014, 24 pars.

Darnell, Regna. 2001. *Invisible Genealogies: A History of Americanist Anthropology.* Lincoln: University of Nebraska Press.

Daughtry, Martin. 2014. "Thanatosonics: Ontologies of Acoustic Violence." *Social Text* 32(2): 25–51.

Du Bois, W. E. B. 1903. *The Souls of Black Folk.* Chicago: A. C. McClurg.

Ebron, Paulla A. 2002. *Performing Africa.* Princeton: Princeton University Press.

Ellingson, Ter. 1992. "Notation." In *Ethnomusicology: An Introduction,* ed. Helen Myers, 153–64. New York: W.W. Norton.

Feld, Steven. 1984. "Sound Structure as Social Structure." *Ethnomusicology* 28(3): 383–409.

Feld, Steven. 1996. "Waterfalls of Song: An Acoustemology of Place Resounding in Bosavi, Papua New Guinea." In *Senses of Place,* ed. Steven Feld and Keith Basso, 91–136. Santa Fe: School of American Research Press.

Feld, Steven. 2012 [1982]. *Sound and Sentiment: Birds, Weeping, Poetics, and Song in Kaluli Expression.* 3rd ed. Durham: Duke University Press.

Fletcher, Alice, and Francis La Flesche. 1893. "A Study of Omaha Indian Music." *Archaeological and Ethnological Papers of the Peabody Museum* 1(5): 237–287.

Gitelman, Lisa. 2006. *Always Already New: Media, History, and the Data of Culture.* Cambridge, MA: MIT Press.

Helmholtz, Hermann von. 1885. *On the Sensations of Tone as a Physiological Basis for the Theory of Music.* 2nd English ed. Trans. Alexander J. Ellis. New York: Longmans, Green.

Hoffmann, E. T. A. 1989 [1814]. "Beethoven's Instrumental Music." In *E. T. A. Hoffman's Musical Writings,* ed. David Charlton, 96–103. Cambridge: Cambridge University Press.

Horkheimer, Max, and Theodor W. Adorno. 2002 [1944]. "The Culture Industry: Enlightenment as Mass Deception." In *Dialectic of Enlightenment: Philosophical Fragments,* 94–136. Trans. Edmund Jephcott. Stanford, CA: Stanford University Press.

Hornbostel, Erich M. von and Curt Sachs. 1961 [1914]. "Classification of Musical Instruments." *The Galpin Society Journal* 14: 3–29. Trans. Anthony Baines and Klaus P. Wachsmann.

Hui, Alexandra. *The Psychophysical Ear: Musical Experiments, Experimental Sounds, 1840–1910.* Cambridge, MA: MIT Press, 2012.

Jackson, Myles W. 2006. *Harmonious Triads: Physicists, Musicians, and Instrument Makers in Nineteenth-Century Germany*. Cambridge, MA: MIT Press.

Kahn, Douglas. 1999. *Noise Water Meat: A History of Sound in the Arts*. Cambridge, MA: MIT Press.

Levin, Flora R. 2009. *Greek Reflections on the Nature of Music*. Cambridge: Cambridge University Press.

Lockwood, Lewis. 1984. *Music in Renaissance Ferrara, 1400–1505*. Oxford: Oxford University Press.

Lomax, Alan. 1968. *Folk Song Style and Culture*. New Brunswick: Transaction.

McClary, Susan. 1993. "Narrative Agendas in 'Absolute' Music: Identity and Difference in Brahms's Third Symphony." In *Musicology and Difference: Gender and Sexuality in Music Scholarship*, ed. Ruth A. Solie, 326–344. Berkeley: University of California Press.

Merriam, Alan. 1977. "Definitions of 'Comparative Musicology' and 'Ethnomusicology': An Historical-Theoretical Perspective." *Ethnomusicology* 21: 189–204.

Meyer, Leonard. 1957. *Emotion and Meaning in Music*. Chicago: University of Chicago Press.

Monson, Craig. 2006. "Renewal, Reaction, and Reform in Catholic Sacred Music." In *European Music 1520–1640*, ed. James Haar, 401–421. London: Boydell and Brewer.

Mugglestone, Erica. 1981. "Guido Adler's 'The Scope, Method, and Aim of Musicology' (1885): An English Translation with an Historico-Analytical Commentary." *Yearbook for Traditional Music* 13: 1–21.

Nettl, Bruno. 2001. "Music." In *The New Grove Dictionary of Music and Musicians*, ed. Stanley Sadie, 2nd ed., vol. 17: 425–37. London: Macmillan.

Palisca, Claude V. 1961. "Scientific Empiricism in Musical Thought." In *Seventeenth Century Science and the Arts*, ed. Hedley Howell Rhys, 91–137. Princeton: Princeton University Press.

Picker, John M. 1999–2000. "The Soundproof Study: Victorian Professionals, Work Space, and Urban Noise." *Victorian Studies* 42(3): 427–453.

Racy, Ali Jihad. 1993. "Historical Worldviews of Early Ethnomusicologists: An East–West Encounter in Cairo, 1932." In *Ethnomusicology and Modern Music History*, ed. Steven Blum, Philip V. Bohnlam, and Daniel M. Neuman, 68–91. Urbana: University of Illinois Press.

Schafer, R. Murray. 1977. *The Tuning of the World*. New York: Knopf.

Sterne, Jonathan. 1997. "Sounds Like the Mall of America: Programmed Music and the Architectonics of Commercial Space." *Ethnomusicology* 41(1): 22–50.

Sterne, Jonathan. 2003. *The Audible Past: Cultural Origins of Sound Reproduction*. Durham: Duke University Press.

Suisman, David. 2010. "Sound, Knowledge, and the 'Immanence of Human Failure': Rethinking Musical Mechanization through the Phonograph, the Player-Piano, and the Piano." *Social Text* 28: 13–34.

Weidman, Amanda. 2006. *Singing the Classical, Voicing the Modern: The Postcolonial Politics of Music in South India*. Durham: Duke University Press.

Weheliye, Alexander G. 2005. "The Grooves of Temporality." *Public Culture* 17(2): 319–338.

noise

Sound studies have found in noise a subject of deep fascination that cuts across disciplinary boundaries of history, anthropology, music, literature, media studies, philosophy, urban studies, and studies of science and technology. Noise is a crucial element of communicational and cultural networks, a hyperproductive quality of musical aesthetics, an excessive term of affective perception, and a key metaphor for the incommensurable paradoxes of modernity. "Wherever we are," John Cage famously claimed, "what we hear is mostly noise. When we ignore it, it disturbs us. When we listen to it, we find it fascinating" (1961: 3). We hear noise everywhere. But what do we listen to when we listen to noise? What kinds of noises does "noise" make?

The Latin root of the word is *nausea*, from the Greek root *naus* for ship. The reference to seasickness captures the basic disorientation of the term: noise is a context of sensory experience, but also a moving subject of circulation, of sound and listening, that emerges in the process of navigating the world and its differences. Evaluations of noisiness vary widely between cultures and historical contexts: for example, many languages do not distinguish noise as a general category of sound.[1] Words like the Indonesian *ramé* instead describe the clamorous noisiness of social life in festivals and marketplaces and imply a healthy and lively atmosphere. Noise is associated with public sociality and carnivalesque performances (e.g., *charivari*) that playfully disturb the norms of everyday life. But as a keynote sound of industrial development and mechanization, noise is also recognized for its anti-social and physiologically damaging effects. It is inherent in technological mediations of sound, but it is also considered accidental and meaningless.

Noise is a material aspect of sound. It is discussed as a generalized property of sound (as "noisiness"); as a distinct sonic object within music, speech, or environmental sounds (as "a noise"); or as a totalizing qualifier for emergent styles (e.g., "that hip-hop stuff is all noise"). But its specific qualities are hard to define. The closest thing to a quantifiable form of noise is the abstraction of "white noise," in which all sound frequencies are present at the same time, at the same volume, across the vibrational spectrum (Kosko 2006). But in practice, noise is always "colored," filtered, limited, and changed by contexts of production and reception. Simple loudness is another factor: at the right decibel level, anything, regardless of its original source, can become noise. Noise, then, is not really a kind of sound but a metadiscourse of sound and its social interpretation. The presence of noise indexes a larger field of differences, even as its own particularities remain undefined. "Noises," as Douglas Kahn puts it, "are too significant to be noises. We know they are noises in the first place because they exist where they shouldn't or they don't make sense where they should" (Kahn 1999: 21).

Noise is an essentially relational concept. It can only take on meaning by signifying something else, but it must remain incommensurably different from that thing that we do know and understand. Even in the fundamentally relativistic context of musical aesthetics, noise is defined by its mutual exclusion from the category of music. Yet noise is inherent in all musical sounds and their mediated reproductions; it has been used as musical material and can even be considered a musical genre in itself. Noise is a productive term of many other dialectical binaries of aurality, each of which outlines a different field of social knowledge. But as a discrete subject in itself, noise resists interpretation. It is the static on the radio; the mass of unbeautiful sounds that surrounds the island of musical aesthetics; the clatter of the modern world that indexes the lost sounds of nature; the chaos that resists social order; the unintegrated entities that exist beyond culture.

I will outline three discursive contexts of noise—aesthetic, technological, and circulatory—each of which has been productive for recent scholarship. Although they overlap in important ways, each follows a divergent trajectory of noise as a term of cultural production and leads to different conclusions about its status as a category of sound.

Aesthetics of Noise

Noise is typically separated from music on the grounds of aesthetic value. Music is constituted by beautiful, desirable sounds, and noise is composed of sounds that are unintentional and unwanted. But if noise is nonmusical, music is noisy, and noise-sounds have always been part of music. In Western scientific thought, a formal categorical division between noises and musical sounds was established in the late nineteenth-century field of acoustics, through the classificatory schema of pioneering scholar Hermann Helmholtz (1885), which separated sound vibrations into "periodic" and "nonperiodic" waveforms. Many of Helmholtz's examples were environmental noises, such as wind and water, which could be distinguished from musical sounds by context. But nonperiodic noise is inherent in most instrumental sounds, such as the puff of air that precedes a flute tone, or the bowing sound on a violin. African *mbiras* use buzzers to add a layer of noise, and electric guitars are often modified with distortion pedals to create a noisier timbre (Berliner 1978; Waksman 2004). Helmholtz's analysis of noise reflected the epistemological sensibilities of Western music theory, which privileged tonal consonance and harmonic development over timbre, rhythm, and texture. Noisemaking percussion instruments such as cymbals and drums typically have a low status in this context, and their sounds are considered less meaningful in musical structures. The aesthetics of noise, then, correspond to different cultural valuations of sound, and reflect historical shifts in discourses of musical innovation.

Noise was explicitly developed as a sound aesthetic in modern music, even as its radical incommensurability with existing musical structures was reiterated throughout the twentieth century (Ross 2007). Italian futurist Luigi Russolo (1883–1947) is often credited as the first to bring noise into music, creating a set of noise instruments (*intonarumori*) to orchestrate the speed and power of industry, warfare, and the city, which he famously rhapsodized in his 1913 manifesto The Art of Noises. But Russolo's exemplary influence did not "emancipate" noise into musical history. Instead, the category of noise has continued to symbolize excessive, emergent, and unexplored materialities of sound, even as noise-sounds have become increasingly crucial in musical composition. Noise has been invoked as a modern aesthetic threshold from Henry Cowell to Edgard Varèse to Cage to *musique concrete* and "sound art" (Kahn 1999; Cox and Warner 2004; LaBelle 2006; Van Nort 2006; Licht 2007; Demers 2010; Rodgers 2010; Voeglin 2010). Noise-sounds have become definitive for the timbres of contemporary popular music through the widespread use of effects, synthesizers, samplers, and studio recording techniques (Gracyk 1996; Zak 2001; Moorefield 2005). But the aesthetics of noise also test the centers of musical coherence against the margins of circulation. Musical styles are scaled according to their noisiness, from the least noisy (i.e., smooth jazz, new age) to the noisiest (and therefore least acceptable) form (i.e., heavy metal, techno).

A specific genre called has "Noise" developed since the 1980s among a transnational group of practitioners and fans who used the term to describe an extreme strain of electronic music (Hegarty 2007; Bailey 2009; Cain 2009; Atton 2011; Goddard et al. 2013) whose circulation between Japan and North America gave rise to the subcategory "Japanoise" (Novak 2013).[2] Since Noise intentionally lacks most features of musical sound and structure (tone, rhythm, structural development, etc.), the noisiness of Noise was difficult to qualify. But recordings are nonetheless evaluated as "good" or "bad" examples of Noise, described as deliberate products of distant music scenes, and aestheticized through particular aspects of their sound. Listeners identify their own affective responses—that a noise, for example, felt "harsh"—as aesthetic terms that help construct Noise as a global network of underground producers and fans. Through their attention to the special differences of noise-sounds, Noise was named and circulated as a capitalized musical genre (albeit a contested and endlessly emergent one), which was further endorsed by subgenres based on sound aesthetics (e.g., "Harsh Noise") and assignations of cultural origin (e.g., "Japanoise").

Technological Environments of Noise

In technological media, noise is a subject of excess and disruption. Information theory established a semiotic difference between meaningful signal and accidental noise (Shannon and Weaver 1949). Noise was the byproduct of technological reproduction that interfered with reception of a message (i.e., static in a radio transmission, distortion over a loudspeaker, or hiss on magnetic tape). The "signal-to-noise" ratio identified the balance of interpretable to uninterpretable sound, in which noise should be reduced as much as possible to maximize the efficiency of communication. But even in its pure distinction from signal, the presence of noise in sound communication is far from meaningless. Attention to noise helped listeners to perceive authentic relationships with technologically mediated sound and resituate music and speech in new "discourse networks" (Altman 1992; Kittler 1992; Sterne 2003; Clarke 2010; Mills 2011).

Noise also provides a kind of metadata that informs listeners about the context of reproduction. The level and quality of noise reveals whether the source of a phone call or radio transmission is local or long-distance, or how and when a recording was made: a sonic "glitch" can expose the contingencies of inscription and playback, even in the purportedly "lossless" transparency of digital media (Evens 2005; Chun 2006; Kelley 2009; Krapp 2011).[3] Noise also describes extraneous distortions and fluctuations in the electronic transmission, inscription, or storage of images, films, television, and video (e.g., "snow"); as in sound, visual noise has been harnessed for aesthetic productions. As such, noise becomes a signifying property of informal or underground media distribution, from Nigerian bootleg video markets to DIY networks of U.S. "independent" music (Larkin 2008; Novak 2011).

Noise is strongly associated with the built environments of industrial cities. While the term can refer to sounds of nature (e.g., thunder and lightning, animal sounds; Rath 2003), noise is usually understood as a technologically produced field of sound, which is superimposed on a natural or social environment. In ecological terms, noise is "pollution" that degrades the sonic balance of nature. But before its harmful subliminal effects can be corrected, noise must first be located and brought back into human consciousness from its ubiquitous but subliminal position in the modern soundscape. Although R. Murray Schafer used decibel meters to measure and map noise in urban soundscapes through pure volume, he further distinguished the effects of noise in the artificial mechanical continuities of background "lo-fi" noises (such as the "flatline" noise of highway traffic or the hum of a refrigerator) that blocked the discrete and transient "hi-fi" signals of nature and community.[4] For Schafer, it is not attention that brings noise into being but an entrained "deafness" to its debilitating presence: "noises are the sounds we have learned to ignore" (1994 [1977]).[5]

As noise was brought further into social consciousness, its recognition contributed to the inexorable fragmentation and privatization of urban space, through zoning, sonic surveillance, and acoustic shielding from public noise (Smilor 1977; Thompson 2002). But although projects of noise abatement helped to establish scientific measurements of noise and legal standards of loudness, regulations typically failed or were found unenforceable. Instead, noise was increasingly characterized as an inevitable byproduct of technological progress. The clamor of modern life cultivated individuated desires for silence and quietude, which reaffirmed the unintelligibility of public life (Foy 2010; Keiser 2010; Prochnik 2010; Sim 2007).

But even as noise has been named as the cause of social and physiological ills from hearing loss to schizophrenia, experiences of technological noise have become integral to contemporary sonic knowledge. Machine operators, for example, must carefully listen to and interpret the noises of machines to assure proper function (Bijsterveld 2008).[6] Far from being regulated itself, mechanical noise is used to regulate and control daily life. Bells, buzzers, and alarms force public senses to attention, while weapons technologies such as the Long Range Acoustic Device (LRAD) can generate a directional field of sound that disorients and disables its victims. In these contexts, noise shifts from being the accidental byproduct of a technological environment to become a deliberate form of coercive violence (Cusick 2008; Goodman 2009).

Social Circulations of Noise

Noise stands for subjectivities of difference that break from normative social contexts. It interpellates marginal subjects into circulation, giving name to their unintelligible discourses even as it holds apart unfamiliar ways of being. In the violence of transatlantic slavery, noise textualized the disorientation of African culture (Cruz 1999; Smith 2001; Radano 2003). Describing the music and speech of slaves as noise allowed European colonists to domesticate an expressive production that was "theoretically understandable [even] as it remained practically inaccessible" (Radano 2003: 93). Once rendered as noise, black music could circulate as authentic cultural material, while continuing to signify its fundamental incommensurability with European civilization. Noise also symbolized class relations throughout early modernity. In Victorian England, noise complaints targeted Italian migrant workers, who were caricatured as street organ grinders; noise echoed the unrest of the brawling, milling crowd, with its rude dialects and unconstrained bodily sounds of work, sex, digestion, and disease (Smith 1999; Picker 2003; Schwartz 2011).

But even as noise retained its status as a marker of difference in postcolonial, multicultural, and cosmopolitan societies, it also became a powerful term of cultural agency. In contemporary projects of resistance, noise is the "voice" of subaltern identity on the margins, where "bringing the noise" is not accidental but an expressive practice and a deliberate act of subversion (Ridenour et al. 1987; Rose 1994, Reynolds 2007; McCaugan and Balance 2009).

The creative force of noise is not only essential to the politics of cultural identity but also in developing alternatives to capitalism. Jacques Attali influentially described noise as a "prophetic" form of difference, which precedes the disciplining "sacrifice" of musical "channelization." As a revolutionary project of disorder, noise reveals the coercive repetitions of musical commodification: "change is inscribed in noise faster than it transforms society," and because of this, "power has always listened to it with fascination" (Attali 1985: 5, 6). Noise also circulates as a critique of globalization. As a symbol of irreducible cultural difference that persists within a universalist socioeconomic agenda, noise inscribes the incommensurabilities of multicultural liberalism (Povinelli 2001). For example, the noise of different languages makes audible the skeptical, disconnected logics of a radical cosmopolitan subjectivity in Zambian cities, where "signifying actors might have social reasons not to establish a bond of communication, but to rupture it" (Ferguson 1999: 210). Because it emphasizes mutual unintelligibility and crosstalk, noise represents the failure to translate cultural meaning from one context to another in both national and transnational circulations (Clifford 1997; Sakai 1997).

All of these different conceptualizations of noise overlap in contemporary global societies. To illustrate, I will conclude with an example from my own recent research on the politics of sound in Japan, which shows how perceptions of noise help determine which sounds, places, activities, and people exist within the boundaries of everyday life, and how noise is folded into political dialogue in contemporary protest movements.

Layers of Noise in Kamagasaki

Kamagasaki is the colloquial name for a neighborhood of homeless and migrant workers in the Nishinari ward of southern Osaka. In the late 1960s, a *yoseba* (day labor market) was assembled to develop the site of the 1970 World Exposition (Banpaku), whose theme was "Progress and Harmony for Mankind." Young single men arrived from around the country, living in flophouses (*doya*), later converted to cheap hotels (Gill 2001; Mizûchi 2003). When construction work slowed, and eventually dried up, the aging workers of Kamagasaki found themselves unemployable, and by the 1990s thousands were living as "rough sleepers" (nojukusha) in homeless tent cities (Fowler 1997; Hasegawa 2006). In nearby Tennoji Park, unemployed workers gathered every weekend to drink and sing in makeshift karaoke stalls that lined the public walkways, separated by a thick plexiglass wall from pay-to-enter gardens and the city's art museum and zoo. As one walked along the edges of the park, distorted voices overlapped with one another in an off-key cacophony of song, mixed with laughter, arguments, the shouted greetings of the touts at each stall, and the grinding, whirring sounds of their portable gas generators. I often encountered this karaoke party in the early 2000s, but when I returned to Osaka in 2007 to document the scene for a collective soundscape recording project, forced evictions had swept away the stalls and singers in police actions that destroyed tent homes and "quieted" the neighborhood (shizuka ni saseru).[7]

In Japan, strong antinoise ordinances have been legislated, but are rarely enforced. If noisiness is typically frowned on as socially unacceptable, noise is also tolerated as a basic feature of Japan's "sound-saturated society" (oto zuke shakai; Nakajima 1996; Plourde 2009). Amplified music is piped into the streets, distorted voices are broadcast from "sound trucks" during electoral campaigns, and trains constantly rumble overhead. But Japanese rarely enter litigation over noise complaints and often hesitate to complain directly about noise (Namba 1987; Dolan 2008). However, public noise complaints were high on the list of reasons cited by the Osaka city government to justify the karaoke stall eviction in Tennoji Park. Though few actual noise complaints were provided, Osaka's 2003 investigative commission determined that the music of the karaoke tents interfered with the experiences of zoo visitors, who were described as "customers" (kyaku) and "citizens" (shimin), in contrast to the disturbing presence of "homeless people" (futeijūsha; Sakai and Haraguchi 2004).

The karaoke party, of course, was only one element of the noisy Kamagasaki soundscape, and only one reason why this area has been repeatedly targeted by governmental policy and police enforcements. Over the past decades, as residents have been harassed, tent homes destroyed, occupancy permits canceled, and unemployment insurance revoked, riots have repeatedly brought thousands into the streets to confront police with stones, shouts, and fire. The yoseba in Kamagasaki has become a symbol of general precarity in neoliberal Japan, as its founding generation of workers slowly dies off, and the neighborhood grows quieter each day.

But the noise of Kamagasaki has not been entirely eliminated. Public concerts have been organized in the streets, nonprofit arts groups cultivate public spaces for socialization and performance, and the local rapper Nishinari Shingo narrated the struggle with his album *Welcome to Ghetto* (2006). Further layers were added in 2008, when a younger generation of activists joined a riot by day laborers during the G8 Summit in Japan, using the tactics of "sound demos," in which protesters beat drums, play instruments, and dance to loud amplified music blasted out of PA systems on small trucks (Hayashi and McKnight 2005). In 2012, sound demos became a key tactic for antinuclear protesters who occupied sonic space by drumming on empty nuclear waste disposal cans, blaring horns, and chanting slogans in Hibiya Park, near then-Prime Minister Noda Yoshihiko's residence, every Friday. Noda initially dismissed the demonstrations as just "a loud noise": but by the end of July 2012, after crowds built to over one hundred thousand people, he began describing the sounds of the protests as "unheard voices" to which he would "carefully listen" (Noda 2012).[8]

By disturbing the appreciation of nature, the sounds of people became noise; through technological amplification, voices became noise; by being perceived as unaesthetic sound, music became noise. This noise echoed through the city, and then the country; it was heard as a symptom and a public disturbance; and then, as a metaphor for democratic participation, it became a voice and the sound of the people.[9]

The Hub of a Wheel

The concept of noise is like the hub of a wheel: its differences radiate in every direction, and each appears to extend to a separate end point. For its divergent angles to spin together, the central term of "noise" must bear the weight of their separate trajectories. But without attention to its specific manifestations, noise can only reinforce the structuralism of cultural binaries. It becomes the discursive borderline that separates one kind of person, or sound, or place absolutely from another and ultimately reduces all of the "noncultural" elements that cannot be folded into normative systems of meaning. Noise is a powerful antisubject of culture, raising essential questions about the staging of human expression, socialization, individual subjectivity, and political control. But noise does not merely oppose or interfere with the norms of musical and cultural interpretation. Noise is culture; noise is communication; noise is music.

Notes

1. In Greek, Arabic, and Latin, for example, there is no abstract general term for noise, only words that contextualize particular kinds of noisy sound, such as murmurs, cracks, the hubbub of a crowd, animal cries, etc. (Burnett 1991).

2. Although there have been extensive debates as whether or not "Noise" is music, the genre is also referred to as "Noise music" and "Noise-rock" (Novak 2013).

3. Foucault critiqued the cybernetic signal-to-noise analogy in medical surveillance as a diagnostic listening that filters and suppresses the general noises of the body, in order to objectively classify the informational message of a specific physical condition (Foucault 1994).

4. Truax (1984) further describes the stressful effects of noise on human perception within an auditory field. Because the interpretation of a sonic environment simultaneously requires recognition of noise (to notice that it is there) and denial (to subconsciously separate or block its presence in order to receive information), noise constantly demands to be interpreted, even as it interferes with the listener's ability to hear differences of signal.

5. Sound maps and decibel measurements of cities were basic tools in developing proposals for urban planning and noise abatement policy in Schafer's World Soundscape Project (WSP). But Schafer and his students also took a creative approach to the remediation of noise with electroacoustic soundscape compositions and a curriculum for "ear cleaning" that included environmental "soundwalks" and exercises to retrain hearing (Schafer 1994 [1977]; Truax 1984).

6. Recognizing specific qualities of noise is especially crucial in technological soundscapes of warfare, where soldiers and noncombatants learn to distinguish shots and explosions by weapon type and distance (Pieslak 2009; Daughtry 2012).

7. In the case of the Tennoji Park karaoke stalls, the excuse was street cleaning for the World Rose Convention. Operators were given no chance to appeal the decision and were evicted despite relocating to the street entrance to the park, out of earshot of the zoo (Novak 2010; Haraguchi 2011).

8. For "unheard voices" Noda used the term "koe naki koe," literally meaning "voices with no voices." Ironically, this phrase is politically resonant with Japan's 1960s protest culture and for antiwar and antiestablishment demonstrators, among whom it has been used to suggest something like "the silent majority." Noda met with protesters to work toward a nuclear phaseout policy but lost the election to pronuclear candidate Abe Shinzō in December 2012. Organizers are increasingly split on tactics of public interference. Some hope to "speak out" in dialogue with the Japanese government and nuclear energy companies, who, they argue, must eventually "listen"; others argue that protest should make as much noise as possible to disturb daily life, "occupy" public consciousness, and directly interfere in undemocratic governmental actions.

9. Although sound demos were developed around Japanese policies that allow amplified PAs on moving sound trucks typically associated with right-wing neo-nationalist groups (Smith 2014), there are strong connections to global resistance movements, including Occupy Wall Street's "human microphone" technique, which was developed to bypass restrictions on amplified sound in New York City parks (King 2012).

References

Attali, Jacques. 1985. *Noise: The Political Economy of Music*. Trans. Brian Massumi. Minneapolis: University of Minnesota Press.

Atton, Chris. 2011. "Fan Discourse and the Construction of Noise Music as a Genre." *Journal of Popular Music Studies* 23(3): 324–342.

Bailey, Thomas Bey William. 2009. *Micro-Bionic: Radical Electronic Music and Sound Art in the 21st Century*. London: Creation Books.

Berliner, Paul. 1978. *The Soul of Mbira*. Berkeley: University of California Press.

Bijsterveld, Karin. 2008. *Mechanical Sound: Technology, Culture, and Public Problems of Noise in the Twentieth Century*. Cambridge, MA: MIT Press.

Burnett, Charles. 1991. "Sound and Its Perception in the Middle Ages." In *The Second Sense: Studies in Hearing and Musical Judgement from Antiquity to the Seventeenth Century*, ed. Charles Burnett, Michael Fend, and Penelope Gouk, 43–69. London: Warburg Institute.

Cage, John. 1961. *Silence: Lectures and Writings by John Cage*. Middletown: Wesleyan University Press.

Cain, Nick. 2009. "Noise." In *The Wire Primers*, ed. R. Young, 29–36. London: Verso.

Chun, Wendy. 2006. *Control and Freedom: Power and Paranoia in the Age of Fiber Optics*. Cambridge, MA: MIT Press.

Clarke, Bruce. 2010. "Information." In *Critical Terms for Media Studies*, ed. W. J. T. Mitchell and M. B. N. Hansen, 157–171. Chicago: University of Chicago Press.

Clifford, James. 1997. *Routes: Travel and Translation in the Late Twentieth Century*. Cambridge, MA: Harvard University Press.

Cox, Christopher, and Daniel Warner, eds. 2004. *Audio Culture: Readings in Modern Music*. New York: Continuum.

Cruz, Jon. 1999. *Culture on the Margins: The Black Spiritual and the Rise of American Cultural Interpretation*. Princeton: Princeton University Press.

Cusick, Suzanne. 2008. " 'You Are in a Place That Is Out of the World . . .': Music in the Detention Camps of the Global War on Terror." *Journal of the Society for American Music* 2: 1–26.

Daughtry, Martin. 2012. "Belliphonic Sounds and Indoctrinated Ears: The Dynamics of Military Listening in Wartime Iraq." In *Pop and the World Falls Apart: Music in the Shadow of Doubt*, ed. E. Weisbard, 111–145. Durham: Duke University Press.

Demers, Joanna. 2010. *Listening through the Noise: The Aesthetics of Experimental Electronic Music*. New York: Oxford University Press.

Dolan, Daniel. 2008. "Cultural Noise: Amplified Sound, Freedom of Expression and Privacy Rights in Japan." *International Journal of Communication* 2: 662–690.

Evens, Aden. 2005. *Sound Ideas: Music, Machines, and Experience*. Minneapolis: University of Minnesota Press.

Ferguson, James. 1999. *Expectations of Modernity: Myths and Meanings of Urban Life on the Zambian Copperbelt*. Berkeley: University of California Press.

Foucault, Michel. 1994. "Message ou Bruit." In *Dits et Écrits*, 557–560. Paris: Gallimard.

Fowler, Edward. 1997. *San'ya Blues: Laboring Life in Contemporary Tokyo*. Ithaca: Cornell University Press.

Foy, George M. 2010. *Zero Decibels: The Quest for Absolute Silence*. New York: Scribner.

Gill, Tom. 2001. *Men of Uncertainty: The Social Organization of Day Laborers in Contemporary Japan*. Albany: State University of New York Press.

Goddard, Michael, Benjamin Halligan, and Nicola Spelman, eds. 2013. *Resonances: Noise and Contemporary Music*. New York: Bloomsbury.

Goodman, Steve. 2009. *Sonic Warfare: Sound, Affect, and the Ecology of Fear*. Cambridge, MA: MIT Press.

Gracyk, Theodore. 1996. *Rhythm and Noise: An Aesthetics of Rock*. Durham: Duke University Press.

Haraguchi, Takeshi. 2011. *Kamagasaki no susume* [Advancing Kamagasaki]. Kyoto: Rakuhoku Shuppan.

Hasegawa, Miki. 2006. *"We Are Not Garbage!" The Homeless Movement in Tokyo, 1994–2002*. New York: Routledge.

Hayashi, Sharon, and Anne McKnight. 2005. "Goodbye Kitty, Hello War: The Tactics of Spectacle and New Youth Movements in Urban Japan." *Positions* 13(1): 87–113.

Hegarty, Paul. 2007. *Noise/Music: A History*. New York: Continuum.

Helmholtz, Hermann von. 1885. *On the Sensations of Tone as a Physiological Basis for the Theory of Music*. 2nd English ed. Trans. Alexander J. Ellis. New York: Longmans, Green.

Kahn, Douglas. 1999. *Noise Water Meat: A History of Sound in the Arts*. Cambridge, MA: MIT Press.

Keizer, Garret. 2010. *The Unwanted Sound of Everything We Want: A Book about Noise*. New York: Perseus.

Kelley, Caleb. 2009. *Cracked Media: The Sound of Malfunction*. Cambridge, MA: MIT Press.

King, Homay. 2012. "Antiphon: Notes on the People's Microphone." *Journal of Popular Music Studies* 24(2): 238–246.

Kittler, Friedrich A. 1996. *Gramophone, Film, Typewriter*. Trans. Geoffrey Winthrop-Young and Michael Wutz. Stanford: Stanford University Press.

Kittler, Friedrich. 1990. *Discourse Networks 1800/1900*. Stanford: Stanford University Press.

Kosko, Bart. 2006. *Noise*. New York: Viking Penguin.

Krapp, Peter. 2011. *Noise Channels: Glitch and Error in Digital Culture*. Minneapolis: University of Minnesota Press.

LaBelle, Brandon. 2006. *Background Noise: Perspectives on Sound Art*. New York: Continuum.

Larkin, Brian. 2008. *Signal and Noise: Media, Infrastructure, and Urban Culture in Nigeria*. Durham: Duke University Press.

Licht, Alan. 2007. *Sound Art: Beyond Music, between Categories*. New York: Rizzoli.

McCaugan, Mac, and Laura Balance. 2009. *Our Noise: The Story of Merge Records, the Indie Label That Got Big and Stayed Small*. Chapel Hill: Algonquin Books.

Meintjes, Louise. 2003. *Sound of Africa!: Making Music Zulu in a South African Recording Studio*. Durham: Duke University Press.

Mills, Mara. 2011. "Deafening: Noise and the Engineering of Communication in the Telephone System." *Grey Room* 43: 118–143.

Mizûchi, Toshio. 2003. "The Historical Transformation of Poverty, Discrimination, and Urban Policy in Japanese Cities: The Case of Osaka." In *Representing Local Places and Raising Voices from Below*, ed. T. Mizûchi, 12–30. Osaka: Osaka City University.

Moorefield, Virgil. 2005. *The Producer as Composer: Shaping the Sounds of Popular Music*. London: MIT Press.

Nakajima, Yoshimichi.1996. *Urusai nihon no watashi* [Myself, of noisy Japan]. Tokyo: Shinchôbunko.

Namba, Seiichiro. 1987. "On the Psychological Measurement of Loudness, Noisiness and Annoyance: A Review." *Journal of the Acoustical Society of Japan* 8(6): 211–222.

Nishinari, Shingo. 2006. *Welcome to Ghetto*. CD. Libra Records.

Noda, Yoshihiko. 2012, July 11. "Listening carefully to a range of views." Available at Noda's website, http://nodasblog.kantei.go.jp/2012/07/120711.html, accessed July 24, 2012.

Novak, David. 2013. *Japanoise: Music at the Edge of Circulation*. Durham. Duke University Press.

Novak, David. 2011. "The Sublime Frequencies of New Old Media." *Public Culture* 23(3): 603–634.

Novak, David. 2010. "Listening to Kamagasaki." *Anthropology News* 51(9): 5.

Picker, John. 2003. *Victorian Soundscapes*. New York: Oxford University Press.

Pieslak, Jonathan. 2009. *Sound Targets: American Soldiers and Music in the Iraq War*. Bloomington: Indiana University Press.

Plourde, Lorraine. 2009. "Difficult Music: An Ethnography of Listening for the Avant-Garde in Tokyo." Ph.D. diss., Columbia University.

Povinelli, Elizabeth. 2001. "Radical Worlds: The Anthropology of Incommensurability and Inconceivability." *Annual Review of Anthropology* 30: 319–334.

Prochnik, George. 2010. *In Pursuit of Silence: Listening for Meaning in a World of Noise*. New York: Doubleday.

Rath, Richard. 2003. *How Early America Sounded*. Ithaca: Cornell University Press.

Radano, Ronald. 2003. *Lying Up a Nation: Race and Black Music*. Chicago: University of Chicago Press.

Reynolds, Simon. 2007. *Bring the Noise*. London: Faber and Faber.

Ridenhour, C., C. Benante, F. Bello, H. Shocklee, S. Rosenfeld, J. Bellardini, D. Spitz, and E. Sadler. 1987. "Bring the Noise." Def Jam Recordings.

Rodgers, Tara. 2010. *Pink Noises: Women on Electronic Music and Sound*. Durham: Duke University Press.

Rose, Tricia. 1994. *Black Noise*. Hanover: Wesleyan University Press and University Press of New England.

Ross, Alex. 2007. *The Rest Is Noise*. New York: Farrar, Straus and Giroux.

Russolo, Luigi. 1986 (1913). *The Art of Noises*. London: Pendragon Press.

Sakai, Naoki. 1997. *Translation and Subjectivity: On Japan and Cultural Nationalism*. Minneapolis: University of Minneapolis Press.

Sakai, Takashi, and Takeshi Haraguchi. 2004. "Forced Removal of Karaoke from Tennoji Park." *Sekai* 726:192–200.

Schafer, R. Murray. 1994 (1977). *The Soundscape: Our Sonic Environment and the Tuning of the World* [original title *The Tuning of the World*]. Rochester, VT: Destiny Books.

Schwartz, Hillel. 2011. *Making Noise: From Babel to the Big Bang and Beyond*. New York: Zone.

Shannon, Claude Elwood, and Warren Weaver. 1949. *The Mathematical Theory of Communication*. Chicago: University of Illinois Press.

Sim, Stuart. 2007. *Manifesto for Silence: Confronting the Politics and Culture of Noise*. Edinburgh: Edinburgh University Press.

Smilor, Raymond W. 1977. "Cacophony at Thirty-Fourth and Sixth: The Noise Problem in America 1900–1930." *American Studies* 18: 23–28.

Smith, B. R. 1999. *The Acoustic World of Early Modern England*. Chicago: University of Chicago Press.

Smith, Michael Mark. 2001. *Listening to Nineteenth-Century America*. Chapel Hill: University of North Carolina Press.

Smith, Nathaniel M. 2014. "Facing the Nation: Sound, Fury, and Public Oratory among Japanese Right-Wing Groups." In *Sound, Space, and Sociality in Modern Japan*, ed. Joseph D. Hankins and Carolyn Stevens, 37–56. New York: Routledge.

Sterne, Jonathan. 2003. *The Audible Past: Cultural Origins of Sound Reproduction*. Durham: Duke University Press.

Thompson, Emily. 2002. *The Soundscape of Modernity: Architectural Acoustics and the Culture of Listening in America, 1900–1933*. Cambridge, MA: MIT Press.

Truax, Barry. 1984. *Acoustic Communication*. Norwood: Ablex.

Van Nort, Doug. 2006. "Noise/Music and Representation Systems." *Organised Sound* 11(2): 173–178.

Voegelin, Salome. 2010. *Listening to Noise and Silence: Towards a Philosophy of Sound Art*. New York: Continuum.

Waksman, Steve. 2004. "California Noise: Tinkering with Hardcore and Heavy Metal in Southern California." *Social Studies of Science* 34(5): 675–702.

Zak, Albin. 2001. *The Poetics of Rock: Cutting Tracks, Making Records*. Berkeley: University of California Press.

phonography

Phonography belongs to a family of interrelated terms—including *phonograph*, *phonographic*, and *phonogram*—that combine the Greek *phonē* (sound, voice) with *graphē* (writing) or the related *gramma* (something written) and are usually glossed in terms of "sound-writing" or "voice-writing." This terminology is generally understood as referring not simply to writing about sound as subject matter but to the writing *of* sound—that is, to the project of embodying the transient motion or perception of sound itself in writings as enduring objects. "Writing sound" is arguably an oxymoron, like "deafening silence," and ideas have varied widely over time as to just what it might entail. However, phonography has almost always been defined contrastively, relative to some other practice of inscription that is perceived as less aurally expressive and that the phonographic approach is often intended to improve on or "remediate" (in the sense advanced by Bolter and Grusin 2000). Consider the following account of a public speaking event, published in 1848: "The Hon. Kettle M. Potts then came forward—upon which the uproar was most terrific, and may be expressed Phonographically in this way, ooooooooaurrrr, oooooooooooauurrrr, ooooooooaurrrrrrr, ooooooooooaurrrrrrrr, oooooooaooaooaroooaurrrrrr, (thumping) mmp, mmp, mmp, mmp, mmp, mmp, (clapping) kwak, kwak, kwak, kwak, kwak, kwak" ("Speech" 1848). What made this text "phonographic" was the author's effort to inscribe the noises of the crowd mimetically, through conspicuously detailed sequences of sounds. During the mid-nineteenth century, writings in this spirit were sometimes characterized as visual "reproductions" of sound, reflecting their creators' aspiration to depict sound on paper as directly and holistically as they knew how. Since then, the concept of what it means to "record" and "reproduce" sound has co-evolved with new audio technologies—most notably Thomas Edison's phonograph—that introduced novel possibilities of aural mediation. Phonography itself is now identified with the practice of inscribing sound in terms of a waveform that can then be automatically "reproduced" as sound and is intended for listening rather than for visual reading. Phonography has come to be associated less with writing sounds down than with fixing them repeatably *as* sounds.

Ideas about phonography as sound-writing cannot easily be disentangled from ideas about writing in general. Within the Western tradition, "true" writing has usually been defined as a representation of spoken language that substitutes materially fixed signs for ephemeral aural ones (e.g., Coulmas 1989: 560; Logan 2004; Daniels 2009: 36). This would arguably make *all* writing sound-writing to some extent. But a few theorists have disputed the traditional view, bearing in mind apparent counterexamples, such as mathematical writing, and have distinguished "forms of writing related specifically to spoken language" from other forms (Harris 1995: 13; see also Harris 2001; Powell 2009). Moreover, strategies for writing spoken languages have themselves relied on sound per se to varying degrees. Since the early nineteenth century, linguists have applied "phonographic" terminology to the writing of words based on their aural patterns, as contrasted with pictographic or ideographic writing that represents them on the basis of their referential meanings.[1] Beginning with the rebus principle in ancient Sumer—in which, for example, an image of a reed (*gi*) was used to represent "return" (also *gi*)—different writing systems have implemented the phonographic strategy with different degrees of granularity, completeness, and consistency. This has been the basis for their classification into syllabaries, alphabets, abjads, and so forth.

Some commentators have gone beyond classification to judge writing systems according to how phonographic they are. "Writing is the painting of the voice," claimed Voltaire; "the more close the resemblance the better it is" (1824: 5, 170). Theorists who share Voltaire's opinion often equate steps toward a one-to-one relationship between oral and written signs with evolutionary progress and steps away from this ideal with retrogression. However, they differ as to whether this linguistic evolution has run its course or is still under way. One school of thought treats the phonographic ideal as a fait accompli, a past milestone in the history of Western civilization, as when Robert Logan writes that "the Greek alphabet, complete with vowels, represents a unique achievement in man's capacity for rendering his spoken language in totally accurate written form; it went beyond anything that preceded it and has not been equaled since" (2004: 106). Eric Havelock and other scholars in this tradition have associated alphabetic writing—as the apotheosis of phonographic writing—with a variety of historical "effects," including the democratization of literacy and the capacity for abstract logic (for a critical overview of the arguments, see Halverson 1992).

But others have instead taken the phonographic ideal as a mandate for reforming or improving on existing writing systems, often by replacing "arbitrary" orthographic conventions (*eight*, *ate*) with one-to-one mappings of sound to sign (*āt*) and introducing written characters whose forms somehow reflect their pronunciations. One example is the "phonography" introduced by Isaac Pitman in the late 1830s and valued by stenographers as a means of writing rapidly enough to capture a speaker's words verbatim—that is, "to *reproduce* the words of the orator as they fall upon the ear" ("Rapid Writing" 1869–71: 101, emphasis added). Pitman's strategy centered on establishing rational relationships between the forms of written characters and speech sounds; for example, he translated the audible distinction between voiced and unvoiced consonants (e.g., *b* versus *p*) into a visible distinction between thick and thin strokes. Although the practical demands of stenographic work led to routine compromises of "phonographic" principle (Gitelman 1999), proponents of Pitman's system likened its transparency to that of photography, claiming that "the very simplest elementary forms are employed to carry directly to the eye, the sounds themselves and consequently the words written; and on the other hand to transfer the ear sounds heard without intervention or interpretation. What is called spelling is altogether annihilated, the spoken syllable being the sounds themselves, and the written one the same daguerreotyped upon paper" ("Phonography" 1849: 391). Despite the photographic analogy, Pitman's system continued to depend on manual inscription, so its ability to capture aural reality was limited to what human beings could observe and write down. This was also true of other similarly motivated writing systems, including Victor de Stains's "phonographic" system of musical notation (1842: 157–208) and Melville Bell's "Visible Speech," which aimed to depict pronunciation in terms of the precise mechanical configurations of the vocal organs.

But there were also attempts to make sound or music record itself through indexical self-writing processes more closely analogous to photography. Some mid-nineteenth-century "phonographs" that fall into this category were designed to record the keystrokes of extemporaneous piano or organ performances automatically on moving paper sheets.[2]

However, acousticians came to define "phonography" more specifically as capturing the vibratory motions that constitute sound itself as a physical phenomenon: for instance, by causing a stylus attached to a plucked string to inscribe its movements as a row of dots or wavy line.[3] The most versatile "phonograph" of this sort was invented in the 1850s by French typographer Édouard-Léon Scott de Martinville, who attached his stylus not to a string but to an "artificial ear"—a working replica of the physiological mechanism of hearing—to exploit the *tympanic principle*, or the understanding that the eardrum faithfully transduces aerial sound vibrations as part of the signal chain of audition.[4] In the best known form of Scott's invention, sound was directed into a funnel while a stylus attached to an eardrum-like membrane at the opposite end traced its movements on a paper wrapped around a rotating cylinder. The result was a graph of time versus amplitude, or the degree of the membrane's displacement from a rest position; this is what we still mean today by an audio *waveform*. Scott distanced his work from manual forms of phonography by naming his process *phonautography* ("sound-*self*-writing"), his instrument a *phonautograph*, and his inscriptions *phonautograms*—specimens, as he wrote, of a new "natural writing or stenography" (Feaster 2009: 44).[5] But others applied phonographic terminology to Scott's work (e.g., "Chronique" 1857; Bourget and Bernard 1860: 460), and outside of linguistics, stenography, and language pedagogy, "phonography" is now identified primarily with the inscription of sound through data that could be expressed as a waveform—arguably the ultimate nonarbitrary form for writing sound. Like Pitman's shorthand, however, the phonautograph's waveforms were intended as writings for the eye to read. This branch of "phonography" was aptly characterized at the time as the art of capturing sound-pictures, just as photography was the art of capturing light-pictures (Logeman 1860).

Thomas Edison's phonograph of 1877 deflected the trajectories I've been examining into some radically new paths. It recorded sound using the same stylus-and-membrane mechanism as Scott's phonautograph, except that its stylus indented a sheet of tinfoil vertically into a groove rather than tracing a laterally modulated line on paper. But unlike phonautograms, these inscriptions weren't for static, visual apprehension. Instead, a stylus retraced them while conveying its motions to a membrane that imparted a corresponding sound wave to the surrounding air. Edison's phonograph was thus the first instrument to "reproduce" recorded sounds in the sense of rephenomenalizing them or playing them back.

Under the influence of Edison's phonograph and subsequent technologies such as the gramophone, the phonographic "reproduction" of sound came to mean playback exclusively. It may now be difficult for us even to imagine "sound reproduction" meaning anything but the kind of tympanic transduction associated with telephones and gramophones, and Jonathan Sterne's influential work on the "cultural origins of sound reproduction" (2003) assumes it means exactly that.

But I want to suggest that the equation of "sound reproduction" with this process is itself culturally contingent, in part because we find the same label applied to other things in the past. I've often told audiences that Scott's phonautograph "could record sound but not reproduce it," and I'm sure this hasn't caused any confusion. But I've also seen the phonautograph itself described in print during its heyday as "a new means of *reproducing* the human voice and other sounds in such a manner as to be visible to the eye"—one that "produces in its own peculiar characters a faithful *reproduction* of the sound" (*Literary Gazette* 3 [1859]: 359, emphasis added). It turns out that the words *write*, *record*, and *reproduce* were used interchangeably in this context, all referring to the intersemiotic translation of sounds into visible inscriptions. Phonography since Pitman has been linked consistently to the "reproduction" of sound; it is what it means to "reproduce" a sound that has changed over time.

The very status of phonography as writing has been recalibrated in light of its reorientation from "reproduction" on paper to "reproduction" as sound. For theorist Roy Harris, the records of gramophones don't count as writings, not because they aren't for visual apprehension—neither is Braille—but because human beings aren't biomechanically capable of reading them (1995: 116).[6] Conversely, Theodore Adorno sees the gramophone record not only as writing, but as writing that positively "relinquishes its being as mere signs," "utterly illegible" but also entirely nonarbitrary. Through its mediation, he writes, music becomes "inseparably committed to the sound that inhabits this and no other acoustic groove" (1990: 56, 59). The tangible relationship between sound and groove is also important for Eric Rothenbuhler and John Durham Peters, who define phonography itself as analog sound recording with its physically indexical embodiment of waveforms, as opposed to digital sound recording with its arbitrary symbolism of ones and zeroes (Rothenbuhler and Peters 1997). Analog recordings are themselves "embedded in a network of conventions," as Thomas Hankins and Robert Silverman observe of mechanically recorded graphs in general (1995: 140); but even in the era of playback, some theorists still understand nonarbitrary, indexical, natural *inscription* as an essential feature of phonography.

Writing was one early metaphor for what Edison's phonograph did, but another was human simulation or imitation (Lastra 2000: 16–60), in that it appeared to *imitate* human activities, whether as a writing machine, a hearing machine, a reading machine, or a talking machine. But phonography was simultaneously differentiated from imitation in another sense. Before Edison's phonograph, any representation of sound by means of sound—such as "descriptive" music, the theatrical thundersheet, or performances by the mimic who could "*reproduce* the sound of any musical instruments and of many animals*" ("Sam Loyd" 1911; emphasis added)—had required a conscious exercise of mimetic ingenuity. Early phonography exploited such traditions of aural mimesis for subject matter, much as early photographic portraiture used painted backgrounds; in explicit contrast, Edison's publicists argued that "the Phonograph does not imitate—it *Reproduces* sound" (*Phonogram* 3 [June 1901]: 29).

At issue here is the understanding that phonographic "reproduction" constitutes the capture of real sounds, and is not mere imitation (as with earlier aural mimesis) or inscription (as with the phonautograph). It is this understanding that has prompted people to speak of the phonograph as "bottling" or "canning" actual sound, or even as bringing dead voices "back to life."[7] But even authentic copies of real sounds are still *copies*, so the same paradigm also invites judgments about which characteristics of originals can be satisfactorily preserved in "reproductions" and which cannot. Scholars have usefully examined the construction of phonographic "fidelity" as a measure of audible likeness between original and copy (Thompson 1995; Siefert 1995). But even perfect audio fidelity wouldn't address the intrinsic and total loss of aura posited by Walter Benjamin's theory of mechanical reproduction (1969). I've put forward the additional concept of *performative* fidelity to recognize the degree to which the social force associated with a sound is accepted as carrying over into its reproduction: for example, the question of whether phonographic music can substitute functionally for "live" music (Feaster 2012b). The belief that it can is a precondition for several of the productive "effects" of the phonograph on music identified by Mark Katz: tangibility, portability, (in)visibility, repeatability, and manipulability (2004: 8–47).

But the idea that phonography is essentially a matter of making copies of sounds has been contested, starting with the question of whether it *can* in fact duplicate sonic phenomena. Aerial sound waves have a complex three-dimensional structure, but phonographic technology can only record and rephenomenalize them in two dimensions, from a perspective analogous to that of the ear (or, in the case of stereo, a pair of ears). Accordingly, some theorists assert that phonography never "reproduces" sounds but instead represents them, as a photograph represents a person's face (Williams 1980; Altman 1992). Their arguments give us another reason to treat "sound reproduction" as a culturally contingent label.

The simple equation of phonography with the recording and reproduction of sound also omits the creative elements of phonographic practice and culture. These include the art of the recordist—a role equivalent to that of the photographer—as well as phonomanipulative techniques analogous to photomanipulation, such as speed-shifting, reversing, mixing, and sampling, which have been employed sporadically since the nineteenth century (Feaster 2011) and are now common in DJ production (see, e.g., Katz 2012). Another relevant set of practices involves what I call *phonogenicity*. Phonogenic subjects are to phonography what photogenic subjects are to photography: but unlike those who understand phonogenicity as an inherent property of certain voices (e.g., Chion 1994: 101), I locate it primarily in voicings of communicative behavior for sonic mediation across time and space, analogous to posing or acting for the camera. A prime example is the answering machine message "I am not here right now," which could never be uttered truthfully as live speech (Sidelle 1991).

The study of recordings in terms of phonogenic strategy can provide insights into their changing aesthetics and intended social uses. For instance, early studio recordings of dance music with calls were drastically abridged to fit single cylinders; these recordings simulated the shouts of dancers and announcements of imaginary events. This enabled listeners to eavesdrop on fictional scenes in what I call the *descriptive mode*, comparable to watching a play. By 1900, these dances were instead being presented at full length on multiple discs or cylinders, and fictional announcements and shouts of dancers were omitted, marking a shift to what I call the *substitutive mode*, where a phonogram is designed to substitute functionally for its subject—in this case, by coordinating an actual dance (Feaster 2007: 461–486). Neither approach entailed simply "reproducing" dances; instead, people adopted phonogenic strategies to represent events in different ways.

Evan Eisenberg foregrounds such creative practices by defining phonography itself as "the art of recorded music," which he views "not as a reproduction of the concert but as an independent art, as distinct from live music as film is distinct from theater" (1987: 105). Lee B. Brown builds on Eisenberg's definition by identifying "works of phonography" as "sound-constructs created by the use of recording machinery for an intrinsic aesthetic purpose, rather than for an extrinsic documentary one" (2000). But others equate phonography with field recording endeavors that privilege the discovery and capture of sound over its creative production, as with the recording of "soundscapes" and "soundwalks" by groups that sometimes adopt "phonographic" names, such as Chicago Phonography and the Seattle Phonographers Union; R. Murray Schafer's World Soundscape Project is the most famous endeavor of this kind. For these groups, the essence of phonography lies in its documentation of the world's sounds as they are. Even so, they see transparency of "recording and reproduction" as a philosophical and aesthetic choice, not as something inherent in technology. For soundscape recordists, as for Eisenberg and Brown, phonography is a distinctive set of cultural practices—although what is considered phonography by the former is precisely what it is not for the latter.

The mutual incompatibility of these definitions concerns me less than their partiality, which they share with Rothenbuhler and Peters's stress on analog recording. Each singles out some part of a broader domain as "phonographic"—the analog part, the artfully constructed part, the documentary part—without defining what the broader domain is. If the common denominator for these different versions of phonography was ever the recording of sound for subsequent playback, that interpretation no longer obtains. Even international copyright law now recognizes the existence of "phonograms that are not fixations of sounds" and that consist instead of "data which can be used to generate sounds even though no 'real' sounds have yet been produced" (World Intellectual Property Organization 1996). The intent is presumably to include works of electroacoustic synthesis, which seems reasonable enough. But if we accept this judgment, then phonography can generate sounds that have no connection to any "original" sounds, and thus can't be said to "reproduce" them. There is still a transduction of sound in such cases, but with a difference: there's no use of a membrane to pick up aerial sounds, but only an output that transduces the signal as sound through a loudspeaker. I call this process eduction, meaning the elicitation of sound "from a condition of latent, rudimentary, or merely potential existence" (Simpson and Weiner 1989: 5, 75). I've argued that "sound reproduction" is a culturally contingent label and that its meaning has changed over time—for instance, from "reproduction" on paper to "reproduction" as sound. It now appears to be changing yet again, by coming to refer not just to the sonic "reproduction" of original sounds but to *any* tympanic eduction of sound—*any* output from a loudspeaker, for instance, regardless of its origin.

Phonography, then, is still coevolving with different meanings of "sound reproduction" as they arise, rather than being tethered to any one of them. As the definition of "phonography" has continued to change and expand, so has the scope of its history. In my book/CD *Pictures of Sound* (2012a), I identify various historical images that represent sound in "phonographic" formats, and that we can educe "phonographically," even though this wasn't what their creators intended. The inspiration for this project came from my participation in the First Sounds initiative, which made news in 2008 by playing back a rendition of "Au Clair de la Lune" as sung into a phonautograph in 1860 and captured as a waveform on paper.[8] I've since found that even some medieval musical notations can be interpreted as graphs of time versus frequency, transformed mathematically into waveforms, and educed "phonographically" to yield semblances of the encoded music (Feaster 2012a). We can thus access inscriptions made a thousand years ago just as we access modern "sound recordings," using an epistemology of eduction and mediated listening that didn't exist when they were created, but that is still more or less compatible with their technical form.

One continued benefit of the etymological association of phonography with writing is that it points to the importance of critical reading. Phonograms may not give us transparent echoes of the past, but neither are they fully opaque; analyzing them in an informed way will sometimes be intellectually demanding. This is equally true whether we are speaking of alphabetic writing, phonetic stenography, phonautograms, wax cylinders, or vinyl LPs. The future productivity of phonography as a concept within sound studies will depend largely on our willingness to seek critical distance from the cultural tendency to equate it only with the sonic "copying" of original sounds, and instead attend seriously to those practices—such as phonogenic behavior, phonomanipulation, and electroacoustic composition—that run against the grain of that paradigm, to define phonography through its nuanced strategies of sonic representation.

Notes

1. The earliest instance I've seen of this usage appears in *Le Journal des sçavans* (1823): 381. However, the word "phonography" had itself been put forward less successfully at the end of the seventeenth century as a name for the study of phonological change over time, the resulting divergence of pronunciation from spelling, and the implications for reading and writing; see Ekwall 1907.

2. The example usually cited is the "electro-magnetic phonograph" of Joseph Beverley Fenby, patented in England in 1863; but a similar "phonograph" attachment for organs and pianos had also been patented in France by Jean-Henri Duprat de Tressoz in 1840.

3. In 1863, for instance, Austrian physicist Franz Josef Pisko formally defined a "phonograph" as "any contrivance that makes it possible . . . for a sounding body itself to write down its vibrations" (1863: 2; my translation). The first published results of such an experiment appear in Duhamel (1840), but the idea itself dates back at least to Young (1807: 1190–1191).

4. The importance of the tympanic principle for modern audio technology is well articulated in Sterne (2003: 31–85); however, I will argue in a forthcoming article that the tympanic "reproducibility" of sound was not as obvious a corollary of mid-nineteenth-century acoustic theory as his account suggests and was perceived by leading experts as a naïve and discredited idea before its empirical demonstration by the Bell telephone in 1876.

5. The connection of Scott's work to shorthand has sometimes been overstated due to the fact that he has been credited with writing a history of shorthand that was actually the work of his father (Scott de Martinville 1849); however, he was still probably familiar with that book, which cited several prior uses of "phonography" in the stenographic sense.

6. The same consideration shaped early debates over the relevance to phonograms of copyright laws designed expressly to protect "writings"; see Gitelman (1999: 97–147).

7. These tropes were widespread in the late nineteenth century, but for some specific examples see Sterne (2003: 287–333).

8. Contra Sterne and Akiyama (2012), our playback of this phonautogram did not entail much subjective "reconstruction"; it had an objective time reference (inscribed by a 250 Hz tuning fork) and did not have the words written in alongside the trace for guidance.

References

Adorno, Theodore W. 1990. "The Form of the Phonograph Record." Trans. Thomas Y. Levin. *October* 55: 56–61.

Altman, Rick. 1992. "The Material Heterogeneity of Recorded Sound." In *Sound Theory Sound Practice*, 15–31. New York: Routledge.

Benjamin, Walter. 1969. "The Work of Art in the Age of Mechanical Reproduction." In *Illuminations*, ed. Hannah Arendt, trans. Harry Zohn, 217–251. New York: Schocken Books.

Bolter, Jay David, and Richard Grusin. 2000. *Remediation: Understanding New Media*. Cambridge, MA: MIT Press.

Bourget, J., and Félix Bernard. 1860. "Sur les vibrations des membranes carrées." *Annales de chimie et de physique* 60: 449–479.

Brown, Lee B. 2000. "Phonography, Rock Records, and the Ontology of Recorded Music." *Journal of Aesthetics and Art Criticism* 58: 361–372.

Chion, Michel. 1994. *Audio-Vision: Sound on Screen*. Trans. and ed. Claudia Gorbman. New York: Columbia University Press.

"Chronique." 1857. *L'Ami des Sciences* 3: 770.

Coulmas, Florian. 1989. *The Blackwell Encyclopedia of Writing Systems*. Oxford: Blackwell.

Daniels, Peter D. 2009. "Grammatology." In *The Cambridge Handbook of Literacy*, ed. David R. Olson and Nancy Torrance. New York: Cambridge University Press, 25–45.

Duhamel, M. 1840. "Vibrations d'une corde flexible, chargée d'un curseur." *Comptes rendus hebdomadaires des séances de l'Académie des sciences* 11: 15–19.

Eisenberg, Evan. 1987. *The Recording Angel: Explorations in Phonography*. New York: McGraw Hill.

Ekwall, Eilert, ed. 1907. *Dr. John Jones's Practical Phonography*. Neudrücke frühneuenglischer Grammatiken, vol. 2. Halle: Max Niemeyer.

Feaster, Patrick. 2007. " 'The Following Record': Making Sense of Phonographic Performance, 1877–1908." Ph.D. diss., Indiana University.

Feaster, Patrick, ed. and trans. 2009. *The Phonautographic Manuscripts of Édouard-Léon Scott de Martinville*. Bloomington: FirstSounds.org. Available at https://archive .org/details/ThePhonautographicManuscriptsOfEdouard-leonScottDeMartinville, accessed September 23, 2014.

Feaster, Patrick. 2011. " 'A Compass of Extraordinary Range': The Forgotten Origins of Phonomanipulation." *ARSC Journal* 42(2):163–203.

Feaster, Patrick. 2012a. *Pictures of Sound: One Thousand Years of Educed Audio: 980–1980*. Atlanta: Dust-to-Digital.

Feaster, Patrick. 2012b. " 'Rise and Obey the Command': Performative Fidelity and the Exercise of Phonographic Power." *Journal of Popular Music Studies* 24(3): 357–395.

Gitelman, Lisa. 1999. *Scripts, Grooves, and Writing Machines: Representing Technology in the Edison Era*. Stanford: Stanford University Press.

Halverson, John. 1992. "Havelock on Greek Orality and Literacy." *Journal of the History of Ideas* 53(1): 148–163.

Hankins, Thomas L., and Robert J. Silverman. 1995. *Instruments and the Imagination*. Princeton: Princeton University Press.

Harris, Roy. 1995. *Signs of Writing*. London: Routledge.

Harris, Roy. 2001. *Rethinking Writing*. London: Continuum.

Katz, Mark. 2004. *Capturing Sound: How Technology Has Changed Music*. Berkeley: University of California Press.

Katz, Mark. 2012. *Groove Music: The Art and Culture of the Hip-Hop DJ*. New York: Oxford University Press.

Lastra, James. 2000. *Sound Technology and the American Cinema: Perception, Representation, Modernity*. New York: Columbia University Press.

Logan, Robert K. 2004. *The Alphabet Effect: A Media Ecology Understanding of the Making of Western Civilization*. Cresskill, NJ: Hampton Press.

Logeman, W. M. 1860. "Phonographie." *Album der Natuur*, 247–251.

"Phonography." 1849. *Friends' Weekly Intelligencer* 5: 390–391.

Pisko, Fr. Josef. 1863. "Über einige neuere akustische Gegenstände." *Jahresbericht über die wiener Kommunal-Oberrealschule auf der Wieden* 8: 1–36.

Powell, Barry B. 2009. *Writing: Theory and History of the Technology of Civilization*. Malden, MA: Wiley-Blackwell.

"Rapid Writing." 1869–71. *Rapid Writer* 1: 101–102.

Rothenbuhler, Eric W., and John Durham Peters. 1997. "Defining Phonography: An Experiment in Theory." *Musical Quarterly* 81: 242–264.

"Sam Loyd, the Puzzle Marvel." 1911. *Register* (Adelaide, South Africa). June 20.

Scott de Martinville, [Auguste-Toussaint]. 1849. *Histoire de la sténographie depuis les temps anciens jusqu'a nos jours*. Paris: Charles Tondeur.

Sidelle, Alan. 1991. "The Answering Machine Paradox." *Canadian Journal of Philosophy* 21: 525–539.

Siefert, Marsha. 1995. "Aesthetics, Technology, and the Capitalization of Culture: How the Talking Machine Became a Musical Instrument." *Science in Context* 8: 417–449.

Simpson, J. A., and E. S. C. Weiner, eds. 1989. *The Oxford English Dictionary*. 2nd ed. 20 vols. Oxford: Oxford University Press.

"Speech of the Hon. Kettle M. Potts." 1848. *John-Donkey* 1: 276.

Stains, V. D. de. 1842. *Phonography; or The Writing of Sounds*. London: Effingham Wilson.

Sterne, Jonathan. 2003. *The Audible Past: Cultural Origins of Sound Reproduction*. Durham: Duke University Press.

Sterne, Jonathan, and Mitchell Akiyama. 2012. "The Recording That Never Wanted to Be Heard and Other Stories of Sonification." In *Oxford Handbook of Sound Studies*, ed. Trevor Pinch and Karin Bijsterveld, 544–560. New York: Oxford University Press.

Thompson, Emily. 1995. "Machines, Music, and the Quest for Fidelity: Marketing the Edison Phonograph in America, 1877–1925." *Musical Quarterly* 79: 131–171.

Voltaire, M. de. 1824. *A Philosophical Dictionary*. 6 vols. London: John and Henry L. Hunt, 1824.

Williams, Alan. 1980. "Is Sound Recording Like a Language?" *Yale French Studies* 60: 51–66.

World Intellectual Property Organization. 1996. "Basic Proposal for the Substantive Provisions of the Treaty for the Protection of the Rights of Performers and Producers of Phonograms to Be Considered by the Diplomatic Conference." Available at www.wipo.int/meetings/en/html.jsp?file=/redocs/mdocs/diplconf/en/crnr_dc/crnr _dc_5-chapter1.html, accessed on September 17, 2014.

Young, Thomas. 1807. *A Course of Lectures on Natural Philosophy and the Mechanical Arts*. 2 vols. London: William Savage.

radio

Radio as Wireless Sound

Radio encompasses a broad range of audio and musical media, from commercial, community, and pirate broadcasting to the compositional and conceptual horizons opened up by the invention of wireless sound. Emerging from point-to-point wireless telegraphy in the late nineteenth century, by the 1920s wireless sound was understood as both a military necessity and a commercial opportunity, sparking corporate empires and public anxiety alike as radio came to animate and transform broad domains of social life across North America and Europe, and then much of the world. Yet if radio is easily figured as a modern sound or broadcast technology, its global significance depends on its articulation with a range of historical, cultural, geographic, and resolutely local considerations. What coheres as "radio," that is, differs between 1950s North Africa and 1950s North America, or between 1990s Indonesia, Japan, or Australia, as does the shape radio takes as technology, as institution, and as meaningful sound. And while radio often disappears into the background, moving to the limits of awareness as a supplement to that which it mediates, it also frequently reasserts itself as a force in social life that provokes reflection on mediation itself. Given this technosocial variability and unsettled history, in what terms might we define "radio" as "wireless sound"?

In technical terms, all forms of wireless telegraphy, wireless telephony, and radio—and even cellular telephony and Internet networking— depend on electromagnetism. Today, just as a century ago, radio transmitters transform sound (and increasingly, images and data as well) into modulated frequencies of electromagnetic energy, which are amplified and transmitted as radio waves. This same process is exploited by all broadcasters, from national networks that depend on satellite or digital audio codec redistribution to address a mass audience to sound artists utilizing 50-milliwatt microtransmitters within a gallery space (Kogawa

1994). Radio receivers demodulate and transduce the electromagnetic signal into audible sound (see TRANSDUCTION). Radio receivers are thus often figured as technologies for listening to sound, but what they hear are inaudible frequencies: wireless transmissions of electromagnetic radiation, which they make acoustically perceivable for human ears.

In the twenty-first century, the term *wireless* typically refers to the digital networks of wireless internet, mobile telephony, and data transmission, but these newer technologies continue to depend on the same forms of electromagnetic energy as radio. Cell phones act as both radio receivers and transmitters. Baby monitors, wireless modems, and remote controlled garage door openers all depend on the modulation, transmission, reception, and demodulation of electromagnetic energy; so too do military applications from radar to missile guidance (see Kittler 1994). In general terms, wireless refers as much to a newly expanded capacity for mobile communications as to the capacity of sound to be transfigured and transmitted as electromagnetic energy. In thinking about "the wireless" and radio as technologies of sound, then, it pays to recall their deep sedimentation within the material culture of the present.

To do ethnographic work on radio is to encounter the diverse ways its technologies remain a vital feature of local cultural imaginaries—a foundation for broader mediascapes as well as for a range of everyday "acoustemologies," what Steven Feld figures as "the agency of knowing the world through sound" (1996, 2012 [1982]; see also ACOUSTEMOLOGY). Indeed, radio is almost everywhere today. Wireless sound accompanies revolution and war in North Africa, weddings in Zambia (Spitulnik 2002), housework and homework in England (Tacchi 2012), and prayer and healing in North and South America (Blanton 2012). For much of the past one hundred years, radio has also offered a key to the future—its technologies catalyzing and mobilizing new forms of collective subjectivity. In North America, radio could thus generate both the warmth of Franklin D. Roosevelt's "fireside chats" and the panic attributed to Orson Welles's 1938 *War of the Worlds* broadcasts (Sconce 2000).

Yet radio is often described as anachronistic and secondary to online and televisual media. Certainly, this belies its centrality to contemporary Western material and media culture, but it also engenders a teleology of media in which radio can be imagined as a backwards phenomena, at both a spatial and temporal remove from the present (Fisher 2004; see also Hilmes 1997). To think through radio sound then is also to consider how its particular technological capacities inform a range of media ideologies (Gershon 2010; Kunreuther 2012) and are understood in relation to other televisual and digital media (Tacchi 2012).

In all these ways, radio as wireless sound involves particular modes of listening and transmission; a range of institutions and social powers; those publics and other forms of collective subject that radio's sounds have entailed, and a constellation of technologies and expertise needed to master its powers (Bessire and Fisher 2012; see also Born 2005). Here I canvass the complex exchanges between wireless sound and social life to suggest that imaginings of how radio might or should work are central to how radio does work; they are not just inconsequential glosses on its powers but fundamental to its diverse social constitution.

Radio's Social Historicity

Radio itself is a spatial metaphor. It indexes the cultural imagination of a radial, "broadcast" signal that gathers its audience through concentric waves of sound. R. Murray Schafer can thus equate radio transmitters with church bells, each extending sound over a given, resolutely social territory (1993 [1977]: 92; see also Corbin 1998). As such, for much of the twentieth century radio's penumbra indexed the publics, communities, or collective selves within range of its spatial address. "Radio Alice" in 1970s Bologna, "the Voice of Fighting Algeria," and "Aunty Beeb" (BBC) each relate a social institution to a collective subject—the molecular political formations of anarchist politics, Algerian anticolonial nationalists, and the British "nanny" state, respectively (Fanon 1959; Guattari 1978; Born 2004). Radio sound may resonate with the power and aura of the state (Tsing 2003; Kunreuther 2010, 2012), with a nation's movement into the future (Bolton 1999; Mrázek 2002), or with the transfiguration of national publics as saleable media markets (Berland 1990, 1993; Kittler 1994). The wireless can thus signify a way of sounding and also the audiences those sounds gather or otherwise entail (Berland 1994).

Yet from Marconi's 1901 transatlantic communication until the post–World War II consolidation of commercial radio, radio's powers seemed unsettled. The "wireless" was not merely the transmission of sound through the "ether" but offered a capacity to hear previously unheard sounds—to listen in on the ether itself. The magic of wireless mediation thus animated a broad concern with domains beyond human perception (Sconce 2000;

Sterne 2003; compare Houdini 1922). In later years, as wireless sound became radio and came to signify mass culture, national publics, and the commercialization of audiences as market share, radio took on a more anxious tenor as its voices spoke to a new mass subject. For some listeners, radio evoked the claustrophobic copresence of unimaginable numbers of people, of being always and everywhere "in reach." As an ironic corollary to this claustrophobia, radio sound also evoked loneliness and separation: for North Americans, its static and hiss could index distance and isolation to make a mass audience feel alone together (Sconce 2000; see also Hilmes 1997; Douglas 2004).

The perceptual vertigo of radio's mass address also called forth the first studies of mediatized sound as such. Adorno famously critiqued radio's sonic miniaturization of musical culture, but he also joined Benjamin and Brecht in seeing its capacity for rendering a mass public as an intelligent interlocutor, and radio as an experimental horizon of radical shifts in human being (Brecht 1932; Mehlman 1993). Rudolf Arnheim's treatise on radio as a sound art (1936) developed a gestalt framework for radio analysis (Cardinal 2007; Spitulnik 2012), and for futurists Velimir Khlebnikov, Vladimir Mayakovsky, and F. T. Marinetti, radio promised to transform humanity in its fusion with new mechanical apparatuses—cars, trains, and radio machines (M. Fisher 2009).

More recently, Friedrich Kittler suggests that radio itself quickly receded to the limits of awareness. He draws on Heidegger, for whom radio accomplishes a spatial magic, causing huge distances to be abolished by minuscule movements—"flicks of the wrist" (1994: 81). Heidegger's thinking does momentarily pivot, in *Being and Time*, on radio's miniaturization of distance. With wireless sound, remote things become "ready-to-hand," and for Heidegger this lends intentionality a spatial complexity and expansiveness (1962: 140). "With the 'radio,' for example," he writes, "Dasein has so expanded its everyday environment that it has accomplished a 'deserverance' of the 'world'" (140). The world is at once closer yet also set at a remove as an object toward which one may act.[1] Radio here figures as sensory prosthesis, akin to eyeglasses (141). Though perched on one's nose, they disappear in making the distant wall more present. Just so for radio, insofar as it makes far-removed sounds seem themselves closer to hand than the very receiver that brings them near. The mediation of sound thus disappears with the distances conquered by radio, and wireless sound itself gains a kind of naturalized, unproblematic character.[2]

After the "event" of radio, in Kittler's reading of Heidegger's mediatized ontology, all histories must be histories of technology, to the extent that "being" itself has become enmeshed with its technologies.[3]

Alongside these philosophical provocations and interests in the de- and re-naturalization of technology, one can also suggest that wireless sound is also always wired sound. Indeed, from the first mass marketed Regency transistor radio receivers to the digital plasticity of sound production in contemporary radio studios, the wireless depends on a large material infrastructure (Larkin 2008; LaBelle 2010). Attention to this materiality can allow one to better grasp efforts to denaturalize radio technologies. For instance, national radio studios provided Pierre Schaeffer, composer, engineer, and administrator at Radiodiffusion Télévision Française, with the tools and space to craft a new "concrete" music (Schaeffer 2012). In the latter half of the twentieth century artists such as John Cage, La Monte Young, and many others famously drew on radio as a compositional tool, a technology for producing sound as sound and introducing Cageian "chance operations" into performance (Cage 1961; Strauss and Mandl 1993; Augaitis and Lander 1994; Kahn and Whitehead 1994; Weiss 1995; Kahn 1999). For some, such as Nicolas Collins and Alvin Lucier, the construction of bespoke radio instruments assisted the aural investigation of the world's "hidden magnetic music" (Collins 2009). While "radio" generally works by acquiring intentionally transmitted electromagnetic signals, Collins and Lucier sought out unintentionally generated electromagnetic frequencies (Collins lists their origins as "lightning, sunspots, Aurora borealis, meteorites, subway trains, and a gaggle of household appliances" [2009: 11]).

To review such well-known philosophical and art world work is to foreground the de- and re-naturalization of wireless sound across the twentieth and early twenty-first centuries. For instance, Kittler (1994) suggests that radio came to be understood as always already there, like "water from a tap," a naturalized convenience and absent to consciousness. But radio has also been a site of constant activist and artistic denaturalization (Augaitis and Lander 1994), "theft" (Friz 2009), and reinvention (Kogawa 1994; Collins 2009). And for all that radio might seem vanish to consciousness, like the spectacles on one's face, it functions less transparently than either Heidegger or Kittler imagined when seen ethnographically across the last half of the twentieth century. As such, its sonic character appears susceptible to, and even constituted by, a range of media ideologies that have redefined radio less as a transparent medium and more as a site for reflection, agitation, and provocation (see Morris 2000; Fisher 2009; Gershon 2010; Kunreuther 2010).

In colonial and postcolonial contexts, radio sound provided a link to a metropolitan homeland and its presumed civilizational center. Figured as a modern, even "cozy" item of furniture (Mrázek 2002), radio was a domestic bulwark against the wilds of the colony. In Nigeria radio served a modernizing project as part of a broader colonial and postcolonial infrastructure (Larkin 2008). And radio could also animate different nationalist aspirations in the postcolony. Thus, if for the Dutch colonist radio sound served as an auditory icon of everything that the colony was not as yet, for the Indonesian nationalist radio's technologies served as a promise of what a new nation might become. To be a "radio mechanic," here, mastering both the expertise and material equipment of national development, was to participate in the technological magic of modernity (Mrázek 2002; see also Barker 2005; Larkin 2008, 2009).

Radio may also elicit public participation and enable consequential forms of collective self-abstraction, and this has informed development projects across the twentieth century. This capacity underwrote UNESCO efforts to empower and enable marginalized peoples around the globe through community radio (see Schramm 1964; UNESCO 1997; Tufte and Mefalopulos 2009). As instruments of "modernization" and nation building, radio technologies are indeed key platforms for counter-hegemonic "voices" and forms of participatory democracy. As a source of community copresence and self-representation (Huesca 1995) radio has proved a powerful technology for creating "fissures" in state-derived or commercial mediascapes (Rodriguez 2001).

However, radio rarely vanishes to the voices and agencies its mediation supplements (cf. Derrida 1974). Indeed, its powers of mediation may derive as much from its apprehension as from its actual technological capacities (Tsing 2003). Laura Kunreuther writes compellingly of Nepali radio, describing how its local meaning derives in part from the conjoined significance of FM technologies and the direct language of FM DJs (2010, 2012). The value of direct language to FM radio's immediacy emerges from local senses that directness is a prerequisite of democratization and economic liberalization. FM radio thus embodies practices necessary for democracy, and this informs a Nepali ideology of communication (Durham Peters 1999; Morris 2000; Tsing 2003; Axel 2006; Kunreuther 2012).[4]

In a short but important chapter of his book *A Dying Colonialism*, Frantz Fanon recounts the transformation of radio in Algeria from a beacon of colonial civilization into a "voice" of Algerian agency. For Fanon, radio meant more than the fact of a self-present population. Rather, the particular grain of technologized sound—here in the static of a radio signal jammed by the French colonial forces—resonated with revolutionary sensibilities. "For an hour the room would be filled with the piercing, excruciating din of the jamming. Behind each modulation, each active crackling, the Algerian would imagine not only words, but concrete battles. The war of the sound waves, in the gourbi, re-enacts for the benefit of the citizen the armed clash of his people and colonialism" (Fanon 1959: 87–88). Yet in Fanon's account, no actual voice makes itself clear: instead, the din of amplified electromagnetic noise informed the coherence of institution, audition, and desire as mass-mediated counter-publicity.

Fanon's work analyzes radio sound with less anxiety than either Adorno or Arnheim, yet he shares with this early criticism a "form-sensitive" interest in radio sound (see Warner 2005). Algeria's revolution was perhaps the iconic postcolonial moment—a cataclysmic upheaval that echoed across the latter half of the twentieth century. And in static and noise, radio sounds made the violence of French colonization audible and gave shape to a postcolonial Algerian collective subject. Fanon's account suggests that the "voice of fighting Algeria" should thus be understood as both an aural screen for mediatized self-abstraction and an index of collective agency.

Mediated sound, though, is also the object of studio labor (Meintjes 2003; Sterne 2003; Greene and Porcello 2005). As such, radio is amenable to ethnographic study as a site of cultural production and the forms of social reification and reflexivity such production can entail (Fisher 2012). I conclude with a brief account of Aboriginal radio production in order to illustrate the value of bringing together form-sensitive and ethnographic research on radio as a domain of cultural production. As Fanon's writings suggest, formal accounts can inform but not supplant historical and ethnographic interests in the shape of radio sound.

Indigenous Radio and the Remediation of Kinship

The origins of Aboriginal radio are diverse. Early Indigenous encounters with radio occurred as part of the spread of settler colonial infrastructure and resource extraction to Australia's North. This serendipitous exposure was compounded in 1984 by a satellite footprint that reached across the central desert and into some of the most "traditional" Aboriginal communities in Australia. Anxieties about the encroaching cultural imperialism that this might entail spurred governmental and activist efforts to enable Aboriginal participation in media production. But Aboriginal radio was also shaped by the goal of Aboriginal self-determination within a fairer, more inclusive Australia. The overwhelming majority of contemporary Indigenous media projects emerged from the initiatives of Aboriginal activists and advocates during the 1970s and 1980s, who created Indigenous stations to transform the place of Indigenous people in settler-Australia. Their successes have led to a present in which Aboriginal people live within a cosmopolitan media world of their own making (Batty 2003; Fisher 2012).

Yet this Indigenous media world entails a range of technical skills and social imperatives that are not necessarily evident in the sounds of radio itself. At the time of my most sustained fieldwork in 2004, Microsoft Windows–based software programs such as Cool Edit Pro and Sound Forge were combined with analog broadcast desks to constitute the heart of both broadcast and production studios in many Indigenous stations and Indigenous media training programs.[5] This technical complexity of Aboriginal radio production was joined with a social one: making radio required Aboriginal producers to embrace a representational task of representing a broader Aboriginal public to itself and to a broader settler-Australia. And this meant frequent reflection on how radio might be made to "sound Aboriginal."

Working with trainers on vocal styles for live to air radio or editing a digital timeline in Sound Forge or Cool Edit led to many conversations on how Aboriginal radio ought properly to sound. In part, this meant negotiating local cultural dynamics of respect and propriety. To speak for others demands reserve and respect, and this was accomplished in the cultivation of a professional radio voice, a "broadcast standard" (Bell 1983). As one trainer frequently intoned: "avoid hard language; watch out for the pops and whistles where the microphone meets the body; hold your mouth slightly away from the mic; careful with your 'ahs' and 'ums.' " Though heard by some non-Indigenous observers as a "mainstream" sound, to sound professional on Aboriginal radio is also to respectfully represent one's community and one's elders.

But this standard is joined with a rougher "poetics of imperfection" (Salazar and Cordova 2008) that foregrounds radio's material apparatus, and at once indexes and surmounts its technical mediation of Aboriginal voices. In request shows, programers include the distortion of a telephone receiver, the idiosyncrasies of colloquial speech, and the vocal tics, "ums," and "ahs" that are elsewhere purposefully avoided. These programs grew from efforts to "link up" incarcerated Aboriginal men and women with their families and extended kin outside prisons and retain this aim as a central preoccupation. Transcribed, a request may read as follows, the broadcast distorted by telephonic noise: "I'd like to make a special request for all the boys in Ipswich, all me mates and that. And we're having a good time at the moment, and I'd like to request any song from Charley Pride. Thank you." The DJ pairs this request for "the boys in Ipswich" (an allusion to the prison located there) with a second request for the same singer but reads this into the studio mic: "Another request for Charley Pride from Travis Henry to his grandmother, Betty Henry and his mother and Aunty and Uncles. 'Chrystal Chandeliers.'" These requests and their curation by the producer create a register of familial connection that is both intimate and representative of a broader Aboriginal counter-public (D. Fisher 2009). The intimate character of Aboriginal self-abstraction becomes even more clear in Christmas greetings, prerecorded in prisons for later airplay.

> Hello my name is Les and I'd like to say a big hello and a merry Christmas call to all the fellas at Bourke and Gunya and especially my mother and father there at Bre. And I wish that I was home there, with youse there now, and I miss youse all and, uh, I wish I was home there with youse now. So, yeah, so I'd like to say merry Christmas to youse-all, at Bre and Gunya and Bourke there.[6] And I'd like to put over a big hello to Judy over there. And you want ta' keep strong, and be happy, and you'll be out soon. So for all the best of Christmas and New Year's my baby, from your sweetheart always, Les.

In contrast with the effort to cultivate a broadcast standard, request programs "link up" listeners with representations of intimate connection. The value of this practice rests in a broader privileging of kinship as a diacritic of Aboriginal distinction. The broader effort to make Aboriginal radio "sound Aboriginal"—and to matter to Indigenous listeners—means pairing the respect locally encoded in a broadcast standard with frequent allusions to kinship as a foundation for Aboriginal difference in the twenty-first century, as something Aboriginal people "have" that whitefellas do not (D. Fisher 2009). DJs curate forms of kinship address and toponymic allusion to make broadcasts speak of kin and country—to sound at once intimate and distinctly Aboriginal. As I heard numerous times in the studio, "it's who we are."

As a form of cultural work with wireless sound, Aboriginal radio requires some complicated representational and pragmatic negotiation. In this process, radio studios become sites of metapragmatic discourse and the frequent denaturalization of both radio sound and Indigenous speech. In Northern Australia, then, radio should be understood as a site of cultural reproduction where the technology, its sounds, and the subjects to which it speaks, are all de- and re-naturalized in the daily labor of producing wireless sound.

Notes

1. "'De-severing' amounts to making the farness vanish—that is, making the remoteness of something disappear, bringing it close" (Heidegger 1962: 139).

2. Similarly, radio equates in this passage of *Being and Time* with the sidewalk, both figuring as existential grounds of being-in-the-world, and both most available to reflection when least "ready-to-hand."

3. In Kittler's summation: "any talk of the subject (even in its conceptual liquidation as an 'existence') would again present a falsified image of man, whom technology subjugates as much as it needs him, as the master of technology" (1994: 82).

4. The capacity to speak directly, in a fashion untroubled by syntactical artifice and indirection, is held to be a cornerstone of a democratic and economically vibrant Nepal. And this style of speaking is also held to be an inherent aspect of FM radio's new voices. For Kunreuther, this value of directness also emerges against the ground of an enduring Nepali poetics of indirectness, now figured as abetting forms of antidemocratic political subterfuge. This indirectness becomes associated with state-controlled AM radio broadcasters.

5. Both software programs have since been purchased by international media corporations Adobe and Sony. Adobe has changed the name of Cool Edit to Adobe Audition, and Sound Forge is now marketed as Sony Sound Forge.

6. "Bre and Gunya and Bourke" refers here to the New South Wales country towns Brewarrina, Enngonia, and Bourke.

References

Adorno, Theodor. 1941. "The Radio Symphony: An Experiment in Theory." In *Radio Research 1941*, ed. Paul F. Lazarsfeld and Frank N. Stanton, 110–140. New York: Arno.

Adorno, Theodor. 2009. *Current of Music: Elements of a Radio Theory*. Ed. Robert Hullot-Kentor. Cambridge: Polity Press.

Arnheim, Rudolf. 1972 [1936]. *Radio, an Art of Sound*. New York: Da Capo.

Augaitis, Daina, and Dan Lander, eds. 1994. *Radio Rethink: Art, Sound and Transmission*. Banff: Walter Philips Gallery, Banff Centre for the Arts.

Axel, Brian Keith. 2006. "Anthropology and the Technologies of Communication." *Cultural Anthropology* 21 (3): 354–384.

Bachelard, Gaston. 1971. "Reverie and Radio." In *From Right to Dream*. New York: Grossman.

Barker, Joshua. 2005. "Engineers and Political Dreams: Indonesia in the Satellite Age." *Current Anthropology* 46(5): 703–727.

Batty, Philip. 2003. "Governing Cultural Difference." Ph.D. diss., University of South Australia.

Bell, Allan. 1983. "Broadcast News as a Language Standard." *International Journal of the Sociology of Language* 40: 29–42.

Benjamin, Walter. 1999. "Reflections on Radio." In *Walter Benjamin Selected Writings*, vol. 2, 1927–1932, ed. Michael Jennings, Howard Eilad, and Gary Smith, 543–544. Cambridge, MA: Harvard University Press.

Berland, Jody. 1990. "Radio Space and Industrial Time: Music Formats, Local Narratives and Technological Mediation." *Popular Music* 9(2): 179–192.

Berland, Jody. 1993. "Contradicting Media: Towards a Political Phenomenology of Listening." In *Radiotext(e)*, ed. Neil Strauss and David Mandl, 209–217. New York: Semiotext(e).

Berland, Jody. 1994. "Toward a Creative Anachronism: Radio, the State and Sound Government." In *Radio Rethink: Art, Sound and Transmission*, ed. D. Augaitis and D. Lander, 33–45. Banff: Walter Phillips Gallery, the Banff Centre for the Arts.

Bessire, Lucas, and Daniel Fisher, eds. 2012. *Radio Fields: Anthropology and Wireless Sound in the 21st Century*. New York: New York University Press.

Blanton, Andrew. 2012. "Appalachian Radio Prayers: The Prosthesis of the Holy Ghost and the Drive to Tactility." In *Radio Fields: Anthropology and Wireless Sound in the 21st Century*, ed. L. Bessire and D. Fisher, 215–232. New York: New York University Press.

Bolton, Lissant. 1999. "Radio and the Redefinition of Kastom in Vanuatu." *Contemporary Pacific* 11(2): 335–360.

Born, Georgina. 2005. "On Musical Mediation: Ontology, Technology, Creativity." *Twentieth Century Music* 2(1): 7–36.

Born, Georgina. 2004. *Uncertain Vision: Birt, Dyke, and the Reinvention of the BBC*. London: Random House.

Brecht, Bertholt. 1993 [1932]. "Radio as a Means of Communication." In *Radiotext(e)*, ed. Neil Strauss and Davi Mandl, 15–16. New York: Semiotext(e).

Cage, John. 1961. *Silence*. Middletown, CT: Wesleyan University Press.

Cardinal, Serge. 2007. "Radiophonic Performance and Abstract Machines: Recasting Arnheim's Art of Sound." *Liminalities: A Journal of Performance Studies* 3 (3), available at http://liminalities.net/3–3/cardinal.pdf, accessed September 25, 2014.

Collins, Nicolas. 2009. *Handmade Electronic Music: The Art of Hardware Hacking*, 2nd ed. New York: Routledge.

Corbin, Alain. 1998. *Village Bells: Sound and Meaning in the Nineteenth-Century French Countryside*. New York: Columbia University Press.

Critical Art Ensemble. 2001. *Digital Resistance: Explorations in Tactical Media*. New York: Autonomedia.

Derrida, Jacques. 1974. *Of Grammatology*. Trans. Gayatri Spivak. Baltimore: Johns Hopkins University Press.

Durham Peters, John. 1999. *Speaking into the Air: A History of the Idea of Communication*. Chicago: University of Chicago Press.

Douglas, Susan J. 2004. *Listening In: Radio and the American Imagination*. Minneapolis: University of Minnesota Press.

Fanon, Frantz. 1959. *A Dying Colonialism*. Trans. Haakon Chavalier. New York: Grove Press.

Feld, Steven. 1996. "Waterfalls of Song: An Acoustemology of Place Resounding in Bosavi, Papua New Guinea." In *Senses of Place*, ed. K. Basso and S. Feld, 91–125. Santa Fe: SAR Press.

Feld, Steven. 2012 [1982]. *Sound and Sentiment: Birds, Weeping, Poetics, and Song in Kaluli Expression*, 3rd ed. Durham: Duke University Press.

Fisher, Daniel. 2004. "Local Sounds, Popular Technologies: History and Historicity in Andean Radio." In *Aural Cultures*, ed. Jim Drobnick, 207–218. Banff: YYZ Books.

Fisher, Daniel. 2009. "Mediating Kinship: Country, Family, and Radio in Northern Australia." *Cultural Anthropology* 24(2): 280–312.

Fisher, Daniel. 2012. "From the Studio to the Street: Producing the Voice in Indigenous Australia." In *Radio Fields: Anthropology and Wireless Sound in the 21st Century*, ed. L. Bessire and D. Fisher, 69–88. New York: New York University Press.

Fisher, Margaret. 2009. "Futurism and Radio." In *Futurism and the Technological Imagination*, ed. Gunter Berghaus, 229–262. Amsterdam and New York: Rodopi.

Friz, Anna. 2009. "Radio as Instrument." *Wi: Journal of Mobile Media* (summer 2009), available at http://wi.hexagram.ca/?p=39, accessed September 25, 2014.

Gershon, Ilana. 2010. "Media Ideologies: An Introduction." *Journal of Linguistic Anthropology* 20(2): 283–293.

Greene, Paul, and Thomas Porcello. 2005. *Wired for Sound: Engineering and Technologies in Sonic Cultures*. New Middletown, CT: Wesleyan University Press.

Guattari, Félix. 1978. "Popular Free Radio." *La Nouvelle Critique* 115 (296): 77–79.

Heidegger, Martin. 1962. *Being and Time*. New York: HarperCollins.

Hilmes, Michele. 1997. *Radio Voices: American Broadcasting, 1922–1952*. Minneapolis: University of Minnesota Press.

Houdini, Harry. 1922. "Ghosts That Talk, by Radio." *Popular Radio*, October 1922, 100–107.

Huesca, Robert. 1995. "A Procedural View of Participatory Communication: Lessons from Bolivian Tin Miners' Radio." *Media, Culture and Society* 17(1): 101–119.

Kahn, Douglas. 1999. *Noise Water Meat: A History of Sound in the Arts*. Cambridge, MA: MIT Press.

Kahn, Douglas, and Gregory Whitehead, eds. 1994. *Wireless Imagination: Sound, Radio, and the Avant-Garde*. Cambridge, MA: MIT Press.

Kittler, Friedrich. 1994. "Observations on Public Reception." In *Radio Rethink: Art, Sound and Transmission*, ed. Diana Augaitis and Dan Lander, 75–85. Banff: Walter Phillips Gallery.

Kogawa, Tetsuo. 1994. "Toward a Polymorphous Radio." In *Radio Rethink: Art, Sound and Transmission*, ed. Daina Augaitis and Dan Lander, 286–299. Banff: Walter Philips Gallery.

Kunreuther, Laura. 2010. "Transparent Media: Radio, Voice, and Ideologies of Directness in Postdemocratic Nepal." *Journal of Linguistic Anthropology* 20(2): 334–351.

Kunreuther, Laura. 2012. "Aurality under Democracy: Cultural History of FM Radio and Ideologies of Voice in Nepal." In *Radio Fields: Anthropology and Wireless Sound in the 21st Century*, ed. L. Bessire and D. Fisher, 48–68. New York: New York University Press.

LaBelle, Brandon. 2010. *Acoustic Territories: Sound Culture and Everyday Life*. New York: Continuum.

Larkin, Brian. 2008. *Signal and Noise: Media, Infrastructure, and Urban Culture in Nigeria*. Durham: Duke University Press.

Larkin, Brian. 2009. "Islamic Renewal, Radio, and the Surface of Things." In *Aesthetic Formations: Media, Religion, and the Senses*, ed. Birgit Meyer, 117–136. New York: Palgrave MacMillan.

Luykx, Aurolyn. 2001. "Across the Andean Airwaves: Satellite Radio Broadcasting in Quechua." In *Endangered Languages and the Media: Proceedings of the Fifth Foundation for Endangered Languages Conference, 20–23 September 2001*, ed. C. Moseley, N. Ostler, and H. Ouzzate, 115–119. Bath: Fel.

Mehlman, Jeffrey. 1993. *Walter Benjamin for Children: An Essay on His Radio Years*. Chicago: University of Chicago Press.

Meintjes, Louise. 2003. *Sound of Africa! Making Music Zulu in a South African Recording Studio*. Durham: Duke University Press.

Morris, Rosalind. 2000. "Modernity's Media and the End of Mediumship? On the Aesthetic Economy of Transparency in Thailand." *Public Culture* 12(2): 457–475.

Mrázek, Rudolf. 2002. *Engineers of Happy Land: Technology and Nationalism in a Colony*. Princeton: Princeton University Press.

Murillo, Mario. 2008. "Weaving a Communication Quilt in Columbia: Civil Conflict, Indigenous Resistance, and Community Radio in Northern Cauca." In *Global Indigenous Media: Cultures, Poetics, and Politics*, ed. Pamela Wilson and Michelle Stewart, 145–159. Durham: Duke University Press.

O'Connor, Alan. 2006. *The Voice of the Mountains: Radio and Anthropology*. Lanham, MD: University Press of America.

Rodriguez, Clemencia. 2001. *Fissures in the Mediascape: An International Study of Citizen's Media*. Cresskill, NJ: Hampton.

Salazar, Juan, and Amalia Cordova. 2008. "Imperfect Media: The Politics of Indigenous Video in Latin America." In *Global Indigenous Media: Cultures, Poetics, and Politics*, ed. Pamela Wilson and Michelle Stewart, 39–57. Durham: Duke University Press.

Schaeffer, Pierre. 2012. *In Search of a Concrete Music*. Berkeley: University of California Press.

Schafer, R. Murray. 1993 [1977]. *The Soundscape: The Tuning of the World*. Rochester, VT: Destiny Books.

Schramm, Wilbur. 1964. *Mass Media and National Development*. Stanford: Stanford University Press.

Sconce, Jeffrey. 2000. *Haunted Media: Electronic Presence from Telegraphy to Television*. Durham: Duke University Press.

Spitulnik Vidali, Debra. 1998. "Ideologies in Zambian Broadcasting." In *Language Ideologies: Practice and Theory*, ed. B. B. Schieffelin, K. Woolard, and P. Kroskrity, 163–188. Oxford: Oxford University Press.

Spitulnik Vidali, Debra. 2002. "Mobile Machines and Fluid Audiences: Rethinking Reception through Zambian Radio Culture." In *Media Worlds: Anthropology on New Terrain*, ed. Faye Ginsburg, Lila Abu-Lughod, and Brian Larkin, 337–354. Berkeley: University of California Press.

Spitulnik Vidali, Debra. 2012. " 'A House of Wires upon Wires': Sensuous and Linguistic Entanglements of Evidence and Epistemologies in the Study of Radio Culture." In *Radio Fields: Anthropology and Wireless Sound in the 21st Century*, ed. L. Bessire and D. Fisher, 250–267. New York: New York University Press.

Sterne, Jonathan. 2003. *The Audible Past: Cultural Origins of Sound Reproduction*. Durham: Duke University Press.

Sterne, Jonathan. 2012. *MP3: The Meaning of a Format*. Durham: Duke University Press.

Strauss, N., and D. Mandl, eds. 1993. *Radiotext(E)*. New York: Semiotext(E).

Tacchi, Jo. 2012. "Radio in the (i)Home: Changing Experiences of Domestic Audio Technologies in Britain." In *Radio Fields: Anthropology and Wireless Sound in the 21st Century*, ed. L. Bessire and D. Fisher, 233–249. New York: New York University Press.

Tsing, Anna. 2003. "The News in the Provinces." In *Cultural Citizenship in Island Southeast Asia*, ed. Renato Rosaldo, 192–222. Berkeley: University of California Press.

Tufte, Thomas, and Paolo Mefalopulos. 2009. *Participatory Communication: A Practical Guide*. World Bank Working Paper 170. Washington, DC: World Bank.

UNESCO. 1997. *World Communication Report: The Media and the Challenge of the New Technologies*. Paris: UNESCO.

Warner, Michael. 2005. *Publics and Counterpublics*. New York: Zone Books.

Weiss, Allen. 1995. *Phantasmic Radio*. Durham: Duke University Press.

religion

The modern concept of religion is founded upon a certain moral skepticism in regard to sonority. Emerging during the seventeenth and eighteenth centuries, as one in the constellation of categories that together gave shape to what we now recognize as a modern moral and political order, religion is understood first and foremost to be a matter of belief, of the silent affirmation of religious truths within the private, inner space of individual subjectivity (Asad 1993; Masuzawa 2005). While sounds and gestures may accompany religious observances and modes of worship, they are to be viewed as inessential to, when not outright destructive of, those expressions of religious adherence. Inasmuch as "true religion" finds its essence in the motions of conscience within the silent interior of the subject, the prominence of sounds within religious life marks the fall from genuine faith into the seductions of religious enthusiasm or the machinations of religious power. Within the context of European colonialism, this same criterion undergirds the distinction between the religious lives of Europeans (quiet) and the forms of so-called primitive religion (noisy) said to be characteristic of non-Europeans, which became a topic of scholarly inquiry for Victorian anthropologists in the nineteenth century.

I begin with these brief comments on the concept of religion not to suggest that the modern history of religion is silent, which it certainly is not. Rather, my aim is to highlight a sensory epistemology that, since the early modern period, has played a significant role in shaping the way religious practices are evaluated, criticized, defined, and emplaced within secular social and political orders. In light of this "auditory suspicion" (Schmidt 2000) within the institutions that regulate the place and meaning of religion within modern society, recent explorations of the sonic dimensions of religious practice have provided a unique and crucial vantage point for a broader reconsideration of the category of religion, as well as provincializing its own normative sensory commitments. In particular, studies of religion that thematize the acoustic dimensions of religious knowledge have heightened our awareness of the material and embodied dimensions of religious practices and of the roles of both representational and nonrepresentational dimensions of sound within them. The ear, as conceived within this scholarship, is far more than a simple entryway for a divine message. Rather, it is the practical and conceptual site where the task of molding the human senses in accord with the demands of a religious tradition is to be carried out; it is where the sensory architectures of distinct forms of religious life are to be built. Over the following pages, I highlight some of the different ways that scholars attentive to sound have enriched and extended our understanding of both the religious and the secular.

Sound Discourse

While scholars attuned to religious sonorities have expanded our appreciation for the extrarepresentational dimensions of religious knowledge and practice, they have also sharpened our reading of religious discourse. Religious traditions have often exploited the symbolic resources of different perceptual models, drawing on the phenomenological specificities of sight, hearing, touch, taste, and smell in order to articulate cosmological or theological concepts. Debates within Christianity—for example, concerning the opposing dimensions of Christ's nature as both human and divine—have at different historical junctures pivoted on the contrasting deployment of visual and auditory metaphors. Extending a tradition that went back at least as far as the philosophy of the ancient Greeks, early Christian scholars understood vision to be predicated on a relationship of immediacy and continuity between viewing subject and object (Onians 1951). In contrast, the phenomenology of hearing emphasized a distance and discontinuity between perceiving subject and perceived object and, thus, the nonpresence of the one to the other. As David Chidester has noted, this phenomenological distinction provided the symbolic resources for Christian theological arguments as early as the Nicaean controversy, in the fourth century, wherein those scholars emphasizing the humanity of Christ—hence the distance and difference separating God the father from Christ the son—elaborated their viewpoint using metaphors drawn from such a verbal/auditory model (Chidester 1992: 43–50). Thus Arius, the most prominent exponent of this position at Nicaea, drew on a phenomenology of speech in his reading of the biblical notion of the

"Word of God" in order to depict the non-copresence of God (speaker) and Christ (hearer): "He is to Himself what He is, that is, unspeakable. So that nothing which is called comprehensible does the Son know how to speak about" (cited in Chidester 1992: 47). Notably, contemporary philosophical inquiry into the limits of discursive reason often proceeds via this same phenomenological pathway: as most theories of the subject are grounded in metaphors of visual perception (the gaze, mirroring, the subject position, the spectacle), contemporary theorists tend to introduce aural or sonic metaphors precisely at the junctures where speech is seen to encounter its limit (Kahn 1992).[1]

The use of acoustic and auditory perceptual metaphors for the elaboration of distinct concepts of transcendence, divinity, or cosmology within religious traditions can be found throughout history, a striking and early example being the Pythagorean notion of the "music of the spheres." Extending Pythagoras's mathematical analysis of harmonic ratios, his followers envisioned the cosmos to be a fundamentally musical structure with each celestial body contributing its unique tone to the great harmonic unity (Gouk 1988; Barker 2004). Humankind's enmeshment in the illusion of material reality prevented it from hearing the celestial harmonies. Only with the gradual attuning of the soul through a rigorous disciplinary regime could humans once again achieve the refinement of the ear necessary to hear and participate in the universal song of creation. Sonic cosmologies had a determining impact on early modern European inquiries into the properties of the physical universe, including Newtonian mechanics, and remain prominent within a variety of religious traditions (Beck 1993; Barker 2004).

Attunement

Some aspects of the harmonic theories of the ancient Greeks also left an imprint on Jewish, Christian, and Muslim thinkers, which is most evident in the conceptualization of the tasks of worship (and ethical life more broadly) as demanding "attunement" to a divinely constructed world (Carruthers 1990; Gouk 1999; Smith 1999; Nancy 2007; Erlmann 2010). Ethical attunement across these traditions, as well as others, has often entailed the development of capacities of moral discernment grounded in acts of "sensitive" or "spiritual" listening. Islamic ethical writings, for example, often include exercises through which Muslims may hone their ability to hear and respond to the divine word as embodied in the Quran. An important reference here is the twelfth-century theologian Abu Hamid al-Ghazali, who advises: "if [a Muslim] hears [the recitation of] a verse of prostration by another person he will prostrate himself when the reciter prostrates. He will prostrate only when he is physically and ritually clean. . . . Its perfect form is for him to utter *allahu akbar* [God is Great!] and then prostrate himself and, while prostrate, supplicate with that supplication which is appropriate to the verse of prostration recited" (al-Ghazali 1984). Through repeated practice, the ethical listener within this tradition endows the sensitive heart—understood as the organ of ethical-passional audition—with the affective attributes enabling of Muslim worship and social existence (Graham 1987; Chittick 1989; Hirschkind 2006). Throughout the Middle East today, popular Islamic sermons, recorded and circulated on cassette tapes, CDs, or via MP3 files, are often employed within practices of ethical listening. Through such innovations, long-standing Islamic traditions of listening have been accommodated to the spaces and temporalities of a modern social, political, and religious order, and recalibrated to the rhythms and functional modalities of its technological forms.

Ethical attunement may require competence not only in recognizing and responding to the divine or supernatural but also to the sounds of particular natural environments. For the Kaluli of Papua New Guinea, as Steven Feld has beautifully described, the sounds of the forest environment—bird songs, the sounds of other animals, natural sounds such as waterfalls, rivers, and wind—have both practical and mystical dimensions; knowledge of these sounds, as well as of those that are human-made (e.g. singing, whooping, weeping, and drumming), is essential to adult competency (Feld 2012 [1982], 1984). Within both of these traditions, the Islamic and the Kaluli, an art of listening mediates one's relation to a practical and moral world, one with both natural and supernatural dimensions. More than serving as a vehicle for a symbolic content, sound and aurality are part of the material-sensory world that human life must accommodate and respond to in the course of constructing a valued form of life.

Soundmaking

Within different religious traditions, human attunement is not just achieved through the refinements of the auditory sense but also entails the creation and orchestration of sounds, whether musical, verbal, percussive, or otherwise. The recitation of the Quran with all of its required affective-gestural contours endows the reciter with the qualities of heart that allow her to draw closer to God and so bring her actions ever more closely in alignment with God's will (Gade 2004; Hirschkind 2006). In Java, gamelan performances historically provided (and, to a lesser extent, still provide) an occasion wherein listeners could achieve a meditative condition conducive to heightened states of knowledge and perception. Blending elements from Sanskritic aesthetics, Sufi mystical disciplines, and Tantric Buddhism, Javanese meditative practice took the music of the gamelan as a *yantra*, a vehicle for the presencing of the deity, to be achieved through a particular style of relaxed and passive hearing (Becker 1997: 43–48). Ideas about the agency of music, drumming, chanting, and general noisemaking—as practices that attune human perceptual faculties and expressive repertoires in accordance with a society's place in a divinely ordered universe—are found throughout the world, often in conjunction with doctrines of an acoustically ordered cosmology.

Distinct kinds of sound often define and identify distinct locations within religious topographies. Depictions of heaven and hell in eschatological writings of Christianity and Islam, for example, have often been acoustically configured. Demonic laughter, pain-riddled screams, horrifying shrieks and roars, and even farts have announced the descent into underworld for Muslims and Christians across the centuries. Religious acoustemologies frequently have parallels in social life. Referring to a medieval Christian context, Hillel Schwartz notes: "the hornblowing and potbanging of charivari that hounded weddings of codgers to teenagers, as well as the 'rough music' of drums, pans, pot spoons, lids, and caldrons that hounded husbands or wives that abandoned their spouses—these were replayed as sound-effects for performances of medieval miracle, morality, and mystery plays at the same time that artists were painting musical instruments into the hands of angels" (Schwartz 2011: 70). Schwartz's description reminds us that the sonic figuration of eschatological space may find an echo in the moral space of daily life, where ethical deviancies in this life—cross-generational marriage or spousal abandonment—can engender acoustic results similar to those encountered in the afterlife.

The intervention of the divine or the demonic into human life often occurs through the medium of sound. For Christians in the nineteenth-century United States, divine acoustics often took the form of thunderclaps, heavenly bells and trumpets, or the sublime voices of angels.

Sometimes the human voice may become a vehicle for a divine speech beyond human comprehension, as in the phenomenon of glossolalia, or as the shrieks and screams of demons issuing from the mouth of the possessed (de Certeau 1996; Csordas 1997). Or the otherworldly may avail itself of the human faculty of speech, as when practitioners of Vodoun serve as mediums for ancestral spirits who come to both offer guidance and demand money or service (Brown 2001). Religious traditions have distinct repertoires of natural and unnatural sounds that signal the presence or activity of spiritual or otherworldly forces.

The Acoustic Flow of Community

The temporal rhythms and spatial contours that constitute the daily patterns of religious life within many traditions are often acoustically produced and regulated (Schafer 1977; Feld 1996; Smith 1999). In his pioneering study of church bells in nineteenth-century rural France, Alain Corbin describes how bell ringing constituted the acoustic architecture of rural life, punctuating the flow of everyday activities in accord with the temporality of Christian piety, both Catholic and Protestant (Corbin 1998). The ring of village bells demarcated and sacralized communal space: the sense of belonging and affective attachment that bound individuals to a specific community and geography was rooted in the shared sensory experience of the communal bell, with its distinct tonal qualities and specific histories (96–101). The bell also protected and preserved communal space against otherworldly threats, such as demons or witches who fled in horror from its ring, thereby deepening the feelings of security and belonging among community residents (101–110). In Islamic societies, the call to prayer intoned from neighborhood mosques (often with the buzz and distortion of poor-quality amplification) aligns the community with the rhythm of religious duty, reminding the faithful to not abandon themselves to the chronology of worldly pursuits (Lee 2003).

The acoustic scaffolding of religious community, however, does more than simply integrate adherents into a communal way of life. In contexts of religious tension and conflict, sound can become a provocation, a threat, or a weapon. Brian Larkin has described how in Jos, Nigeria— where tensions between Muslims and Christians constantly threaten to burst forth into bloodshed—residents must learn to cultivate an inattention to the competing messages blasting from loudspeakers of Sufi,

Salafi, and Pentecostal groups (Larkin 2014). Within this volatile context, where religiously organized violence has often been triggered by calls for mobilization broadcast over loudspeakers, it is only by screening out the excess of amplified religious noise that one can overcome the sense of threat sufficiently to go about one's daily routine. Religious broadcasts, however, do not always act to exacerbate religious antagonisms but may also serve as a medium through which "acoustic coexistence" may be established, as documented by Steven Feld in his observations and recording of the acoustic interplay of a mosque and church near his home in Ghana (Feld 2012 [1982]). Feld's account of the sonic sparring that unfolded over the course of months between these neighboring institutions of Muslim and Christian worship suggests something far more akin to an argument than a battle, one carried out not in words but through the medium of amplified pious sounds.

The Secular

Scholars concerned with religion have increasingly turned their attention to the entwined category of the secular. Challenging the conventional wisdom that defines the secular simply as the reality revealed once the veils of religious error were lifted, these scholars have approached this category in terms of a unique historical ontology, articulated by a constellation of practices, sensibilities, and concepts (see Asad 2003; Taylor 2007). Talal Asad, for example, has sought to locate the emergence of the secular in relation to a set of shifting attitudes to the body (e.g. to pain, sex, death), to new concepts of the human enshrined in legal discourse, and to the ideas about inspiration and creativity that shaped literary expression among nineteenth-century Romantic writers (Asad 2003). On one hand, Asad draws our attention to historical shifts in the conceptual grammar through which theological notions acquired new, nontranscendental meanings; on the other, he points out the new sensory habits and commitments that accompanied and gave force to these secular concepts within knowledge and practice.

How might an attention to sound contribute to our understanding of the secular? Eric Leigh Schmidt has approached this question through an exploration of what could be called the secularization of the ear in nineteenth-century America (Schmidt 2000). Schmidt links the decline of the once commonplace experience of hearing God's speech among American Christians to a gradual retuning of aural sensibilities by both popular and scientific discourses (including the emerging field of acoustics) and by new forms of popular entertainment that highlighted the illusionist auditory effects achievable by technological artifice. As popular attractions at nineteenth-century fairs and exhibitions, contrivances such as talking statues and speaking trumpets demonstrated how otherworldly voices could be simulated via technical means. These demonstrations, Schmidt argues, "offered both a naturalistic vocabulary and a distancing amusement that helped support a stance of incredulity in the face of the clamoring voices of religious inspiration and the sweeping rise of revivalistic fervor" (150). Through such popular and scientific means, Americans were schooled in what Schmidt calls "auditory suspicion," which impacted the way religious experiences of divine communication were interpreted and valorized. This shift in the field of religious epistemology was one element in a broader transformation that secured the authority of the emergent forms of sociability and knowledge of a modern secular society.

Note

1. As Douglas Kahn has observed, for the analyst interested in audition itself, this way of theoretically framing the aural constitutes a serious obstacle: "How can we then rely on the same theories and philosophies to query the very sounds heard during such moments of inarticulation?" (1992: 4). A phenomenon that swells, bounces, engulfs, dissipates, sound—listening's intimate—does not offer itself willingly to visually grounded language.

References

Asad, Talal. 1993. *Genealogies of Religion: Discipline and Reasons of Power in Christianity and Islam.* Baltimore: Johns Hopkins University Press.

Asad, Talal. 2003. *Formations of the Secular: Christianity, Islam, Modernity.* Stanford, CA: Stanford University Press.

Barker, Andrew, ed. 2004. *Greek Musical Writings II: Harmonic and Acoustic Theory.* Cambridge: Cambridge University Press.

Beck, Guy L. 1993. *Sonic Theology: Hinduism and Sacred Sound.* Columbia: University of South Carolina Press.

Becker, Judith. 1997. "Tantrism, Rasa, and Javanese Gamelan Music." In *Enchanting Powers: Music in the World's Religions*, ed. L. Sullivan, 15–59. Cambridge, MA: Harvard University Press.

Brown, Karen McCarthy. 2001. *Mama Lola: A Vodou Priestess in Brooklyn.* Berkeley: University of California Press.

Carruthers, Mary. 1990. *The Book of Memory: A Study of Memory in Medieval Culture.* Cambridge: Cambridge University Press.

Chidester, David. 1992. *Word and Light: Seeing, Hearing, and Religious Discourse.* Chicago: University of Illinois Press.

Chittick, William. 1989. *The Sufi Path of Knowledge.* Albany: State University of New York Press.

Corbin, Alain. 1998. *Village Bells: Sound and Meaning in the Nineteenth-Century French Countryside.* New York: Columbia University Press.

Csordas, Thomas. 1997. *The Sacred Self: A Cultural Phenomenology of Charismatic Healing.* Berkeley: University of California Press.

de Certeau, Michel. 1996. "Vocal Utopias: Glossolalias." *Representations* 56: 29–47.

Erlmann, Veit. 2010. *Reason and Resonance: A History of Modern Aurality.* Brooklyn: Zone Books.

Feld, Steven. 1984. "Sound Structure as Social Structure." *Ethnomusicology* 28(3): 383–409.

Feld, Steven. 1996. "Waterfalls of Song: An Acoustemology of Place Resounding in Bosavi, Papua, New Guinea." In *Senses of Place,* ed. K. Basso and S. Feld, 91–136. Santa Fe, NM: School of American Research Press.

Feld, Steven. 2012 [1982]. *Sound and Sentiment: Birds, Weeping, Poetics, and Song in Kaluli Expression.* 3rd ed. Durham: Duke University Press.

Feld, Steven. 2012. *Waking in Nima.* VoxLox.

Gade, Anna. 2004. *Perfection Makes Practice: Learning, Emotion, and the Recited Quran in Indonesia.* Honolulu: University of Hawaii Press.

al-Ghazali, Abu Hamid. 1984. *The Recitation and Interpretation of the Quran: Al Ghazali's Theory.* Trans. Muhammad Abul Quasem. London: KPI Press.

Gouk, Penelope. 1988. "The Harmonic Roots of Newtonian Science." In *Let Newton Be!,* ed. J. Fauvel, R. Flood, M. Shortland, and R. Williams, 102–125. Oxford: Oxford University Press.

Gouk, Penelope. 1999. *Music, Science, and Natural Magic in Seventeenth-Century England.* New Haven: Yale University Press.

Graham, William A. 1987. *Beyond the Written Word: Oral Aspects of Scripture in the History of Religion.* Cambridge: Cambridge University Press.

Hirschkind, Charles. 2006. *The Ethical Soundscape: Cassette-Sermons and Islamic Counterpublics.* New York: Columbia University Press.

Kahn, Douglas. 1992. "Introduction: Histories of Sound Once Removed." In *Wireless Imagination,* ed. Douglas Kahn and Gregory Whitehead, 2–29. Cambridge, MA: MIT Press.

Larkin, Brian. 2014. "Techniques of Inattention: The Mediality of Loudspeakers in Nigeria." *Anthropological Quarterly* 87(14): 989–1014.

Lee, Tong Soon. 2003. "Technology and the Production of Islamic Space: The Call to Prayer in Singapore." In *Music and Technoculture,* ed. Rene Lysloff and Leslie Gay, 109–124. Middletown, CT: Wesleyan University Press.

Masuzawa, Tomoko. 2005. *The Invention of World Religions.* Chicago: University of Chicago Press.

Nancy, Jean-Luc. 2002. *A l'ecoute.* Paris: Editions Galilee.

Onians, Richard. 1951. *The Origins of European Thought: About the Body, the Mind, the Soul, the World, Time, and Fate.* Cambridge: Cambridge University Press.

Schafer, R. Murray. 1977. *The Tuning of the World.* New York: Random House.

Schmidt, Leigh Eric. 2000. *Hearing Things: Religion, Illusion, and the American Enlightenment.* Cambridge, MA: Harvard University Press.

Schwartz, Hillel. 2011. *Making Noise: From Babel to the Big Bang and Beyond.* Brooklyn: Zone Books.

Smith, Bruce. 1999. *The Acoustic World of Early Modern England: Attending to the O Factor.* Chicago: Chicago University Press.

Taylor, Charles. 2007. *A Secular Age.* Cambridge, MA: Harvard University Press.

resonance

"Listening does not figure in the encyclopedias of the past, it belongs to no acknowledged discipline," Roland Barthes writes (1985: 260). The sentence appears at the end of the article "Listening," in which Barthes makes a distinction between two forms of listening: a listening concerned with "signification," or the recognition of a given code, and "signifying," a listening that constantly produces new signifiers without fixing their meaning. Barthes's argument might be extended beyond listening to the acoustic realm more broadly. Our everyday speech and linguistic inventories are infused with words that, like "listening," do not belong to any acknowledged discipline, have no fixed meaning, and whose etymological roots are rarely recognized. One of these is "resonance."

Derived from the Latin *resonare*, "resound," resonance is a key term in the natural sciences. Thus physicists, the OED tells us, talk about resonance when "a particle is subjected to an oscillating influence (such as an electromagnetic field) of such a frequency that a transfer of energy occurs or reaches a maximum." In astronomy, resonance occurs when two orbiting bodies exert a regular, periodic gravitational influence on each other. And in chemistry, resonance describes the complex phenomenon of so-called delocalized electrons within certain molecules that, instead of being associated with a single atom, are represented by several "resonance structures."

In the humanities, resonance more recently has become part of a rich metaphorology that seeks to replace the binaries of structuralist thought with a notion of discourse that is diametrically opposed to a distancing and objectifying form of knowledge. In one of his later texts, new historicism theorist Stephen Greenblatt, for instance, evokes resonance to signal a shift from Foucauldian notions of the implication of knowledge with power to the idea of wonder as a figure for the impossibility of incorporating radical strangeness (Greenblatt 1990). Resonance, Greenblatt argues, highlights the inescapably limiting yet indispensably productive intimacy of words with other words and things and their circulation in culture as a source of authority, legitimacy, and value.

Although his primary concern is with reading, seeing, and feeling, Greenblatt briefly acknowledges the etymological roots of resonance in the acoustic domain. And, indeed, from the early modern period to the early twentieth century resonance occupied a prominent position in a sprawling conceptual terrain, encompassing virtually all of European science, art, and philosophy. It was this prolonged and often controversial reflection on acoustic resonance that enabled scientists, scholars, artists, and philosophers to invent, shape, and define their respective fields of practice and their relationships to each other. For generations of thinkers, resonance was deeply meaningful and a key site of contestation over some of the most intractable issues concerning the social order and subjecthood. Hence, to retrace the hidden history of resonance promises to provide fresh insight into the role of sound in Western thought and cultural practice, a role that has been overlooked by predominantly ocularcentric discourses and paradigms.

Resonance enters modern discourse at the exact moment when the theory of music leaves its accustomed place in the quadrivium, the ancient theory of learning composed of music, geometry, arithmetic, and astronomy. At the turn of the seventeenth century, music's status in the order of knowledge shifted from what a ninth-century tract had called the offspring of "mother arithmetic" (*Musica Enchiriadis and Scolica Enchiriadis* 1995: 65) to a more ambiguous position. Musical harmony ceased to be the objective reflection of the divine cosmos (and as such the province of geometry and arithmetic) and instead became the subject of two interconnected yet distinct discourses. As a source of pleasure, music became the object of aesthetic judgment, but at the same time it became the object of scientific inquiry into the natural causes of such pleasure. Resonance was the key factor mediating between these discourses.

Initially, during the early stages of the Scientific Revolution around the turn of the seventeenth century, the pioneers of modern physics focused their interests on the nonacoustic properties of pendulums. It was only several decades after Galileo Galilei's seminal work *Discorsi* (1632)—in which he elaborated on the claim that all pendulums are isochronous—that the acoustic dimension of such pendulums as musical strings (along with the speed and propagation of sound and other issues) came under more intense scrutiny. And it took another half century for the idea of resonance to find its way into the discourse of medicine or, as it was commonly known, the "practice of physick." An all-encompassing sympathetic resonance interlinking vibrating fibers, nerves, and fluids was held to operate throughout the human body. In fact, as the physics of vibrating, resonant matter had become a cornerstone of the new experimental science at the heart of the Scientific Revolution, "natural philosophers" increasingly invoked resonance for a larger, metaphysical agenda.

René Descartes's work is a good example of this agenda and the difficulty of assigning to resonance a stable place within it. Although infamous for having single-handedly invented an entity we now call mind and for having degraded the body to a mere machine separate from the disembodied mind, the philosopher never quite renounced the notion of mind and body being cojoined in some higher unity. From his maiden work, the *Compendium musicae* of 1618 (Descartes 1961), to his last writings on the fetus, resonance is the main operative mechanism for this unity. Thus, although in the opening paragraph of the *Compendium* he acknowledges, with one foot still in the quadrivium, the alleged resonant properties or *sympathia* of drum skins or friendly voices, he dismisses the study of such material aspects as the domain of ordinary *physicii* and hence as irrelevant to the study of music (1). Yet *sympathia* also joined body to mind. In a collection of posthumous fragments on the formation of the fetus, he describes the "rapport" between the movements of the mother's heart and the individual body parts of the unborn child as a form of *sympathia* (Descartes 1985: 7–14).

Resonance was thus called upon to do double duty. On the one hand the concept of resonance, having been derived from core epistemological virtues such as intuition, observation, and experiment, names the natural mechanism governing the interaction of vibrating matter, such as strings, nerves, and air. As such resonance is the "Other" of the self-constituting Cartesian ego as it discovers the truth (of musical harmony, for instance) and reassures itself of its own existence as a thinking entity. On the other hand resonance names the very unity of body and mind that the cogitating ego must unthink before it uncovers the truth (of resonance, for example.)

The Cartesian dilemma shaped scientific and philosophical discourse for centuries, but it was in the physiology of hearing and musical aesthetics that the precarious intimacy of reason with resonance was particularly evident. Thirty-three years after Descartes's death, a young scientist by the name of Joseph-Guichard Duverney published *Traité de l'organe de l'ouïe* (Treatise of the organ of hearing), the first description of the inner ear that offered hitherto unparalleled insights into a host of features such as the structure of the basilar membrane (the membrane dividing the cochlea into two ducts), the mysterious phenomenon of "sounds that do not exist" (i.e., tinnitus), and most important, the physiology of auditory resonance. Because the basilar membrane, Duverney argued, is trapeze-shaped, "we may suppose that since the wider parts may be vibrated without the others participating in that vibration they are capable only of slower undulations which consequently correspond to the low notes; and that on the contrary when its narrow parts are struck their undulations are faster and hence correspond to high notes; so that, finally, according to the different vibrations in the spiral lamina, the spirits of the nerve, which spread through its substance, receive different impressions which in the brain represent the different appearances of pitches" (96–98). Although the perception of lower pitches originates in the "narrow parts" of the membrane, Duverney's theory—now commonly labeled the "place resonance theory" of hearing, because the sensation of pitch is produced in a one-to-one correspondence between the wave frequency of air and that of specific parts of the inner ear (Wever 1965)—became the dominant model for the biomechanics of the human ear for much of the eighteenth and nineteenth centuries. During that time it also proved extremely attractive to a long line of thinkers struggling to come to terms with Descartes's powerful legacy. For instance, the Enlightenment sensualist philosopher Denis Diderot openly flirted with the image of a simultaneously reasoning and physically resonating philosopher. Much like what Descartes had exemplified in his famous thought experiment in the *Meditations*, Diderot pictured this hybrid thinker as someone who "listens to himself in silence and darkness" while his ideas make each other "quiver" in the way the strings of a harpsichord "make other strings quiver" (1951: 879). Meanwhile, a contemporary of Diderot, composer Jean-Philippe Rameau, based an entire theory of music on his idea of an "instinct" for harmony. The "natural" predilection for major triads and, he claimed by way of an intricate argument, even minor chords was rooted in the resonance between the "sounding body," or *corps sonore*, of a string and the fibers of the basilar membrane. Even as late as 1863, Hermann von Helmholtz in his work *On the Sensations of Tone* advanced a highly influential theory of music that rested entirely on the ingenious way he interwove Fourier analysis, Corti's discovery of the hair cells, Ohm's acoustic law, and his mentor Johannes Müller's theorem of specific sense energies into the most advanced scientific theory of auditory resonance (Steege 2012).

In contrast to Descartes, Diderot, and Rameau, however, Helmholtz enlarged the sensualist model of sensory of perception by adding what he called a "psychic" dimension. The senses, he argued, do not provide us with carbon copy–like representations of reality, as the thinkers of the Enlightenment had claimed. The senses merely produce signs that we interpret, on the basis of lifelong practical experience, as corresponding to the outside world. Thus, we consider the sound of a violin to mean "violin" because we unconsciously combine the upper partials that determine the instrument's timbre into the sound we associate with a violin. In and of itself the sound of the violin does not represent any outside reality. But even though Helmholtz's theory of signs, almost in passing, initiated a major paradigm shift in nineteenth-century philosophy (the so called neo-Kantian turn) while simultaneously providing a scientific rationale to emerging liberalism (Erlmann 2010: 217–270; Steege 2012), resonance retained its central position in the metaphysics of the subject.

The place resonance theory of hearing suffered a major setback in 1928 when the Hungarian communications engineer Georg von Békésy introduced a non-resonant place theory. The key mechanism of pitch perception, Békésy argued, is not selective resonance but a traveling, nonresonant wave that affects a much wider area of the basilar membrane and the structures lining it than Duverney and Helmholtz had assumed. Because the wavelike motion of the basilar membrane traveling from the lower end of the membrane to its apex continually varies its amplitude along the way, the point at which this movement reaches a maximum depends on the wave frequency: higher tones with shorter wavelengths reach their maximum in the basal part, low tones toward the apex. What remained unclear in this model was how pitch location could be specific enough if the source of the stimulation was not restricted to the crest of the wave but was dispersed over its entire length. Without going into details, one can say that Békésy solved this conundrum by introducing several additional factors that restricted the spread-out impact of wave motion by exerting steady pressure on a smaller section of the membrane and the hair cells nearby (Erlmann 2010: 313–314).

The demise of resonance as the fundamental mechanism of auditory perception did not immediately find a parallel in early twentieth-century thought. Quite the contrary: the growing importance of phenomenology to European philosophy in the wake of work by Edmund Husserl, Martin Heidegger, and Maurice Merleau-Ponty, as well as the fundamental notion that our knowledge of things is inescapably contingent on our experience of these things, seems to have been based on the idea of resonance. As Jacques Derrida argues, it was none other than Heidegger who embraced resonance as a cornerstone of the way philosophy might relate to its Other. Heidegger, Derrida suggests, was the first philosopher who rejected philosophy's obsession with "absolute properness," or the difference, epitomized by the eardrum, between what is proper to oneself and what is the realm of the Other. Heidegger's "otophilology" reorganized philosophy by admitting into its discourse a "privileged metonymy" of domains previously thought of as dichotomies (Derrida 1997: 164).

The hegemony of resonance as the central category connecting scientific, philosophical, and aesthetic discourses, however, did not go uncontested for the nearly three centuries prior to Derrida. During the so-called Romantic era, between 1790 and 1830, alternative concepts of auditory perception, musical experience, and consciousness emerged that echoed Kant's rebuttal of the "barbaric" notion that aesthetic pleasure—and by extension any activity of the transcendental mind—required the "addition of stimuli" (Kant 1924: 62). In other words, "Romantic" theorists rejected wholesale both the Cartesian rationalism and the crude eighteenth-century physiological determinism according to which, as Diderot's and d'Alembert's Encyclopédie authoritatively phrased it, "moral effects are set in relation to physical agents" through sympathetic vibration between matter and mind (Diderot and d'Alembert 1755: 215).

The negation of resonance may seem to be consonant with conventional constructions of Romanticism and Romantic aesthetics as being obsessed with the Absolute and the dissolution of the boundaries between the material and the immaterial. Yet Romantic thinkers did not in principle shirk from figuring the body-mind relationship in terms of a physical correlation as much as they tended to frame this relationship on the basis of a different set of metaphors privileging circulation and flows of energy, electricity, and water. The declining conceptual and metaphorical power of resonance was accompanied and in part caused by a series of influential developments, most notably the discovery by the Italian anatomist Domenico Cotugno of the endolymph (the fluid filling the inner ear), the first detailed description of the round window (the opening at the lower end of the cochlea) by Cotugno's contemporary Antonio Scarpa, the Weber brothers' seminal work on wave motion and, finally, Müller's theory of sense energies (Müller 1826). The importance of these findings goes beyond the fact that they marked a threshold in the transformation of otology from a crude mechanical to a more complex biomechanical model of hearing involving numerous intermediary steps. Also significant is the fact that, in what is perhaps one of the ironies of conceptual history and a striking illustration of the twists and turns of the genealogy of "resonance," these findings strengthened the place resonance theory of hearing *without* invoking resonance. It was thus that the heady mix of Romantic *Naturphilosophie* and sober empirical work, even where it enhanced understanding of the micromechanism of cochlear pitch perception, ultimately perpetuated the Cartesian mind-body split.

Conflicting interpretations of resonance shed new light on contemporary debates about the precarious interrelations between sound, aurality, cognition, subjectivity, and embodiment, and their broader significance for a cultural critique of modernity. Because resonance names the Other against which thought is defined and privileged as philosophy's possibility and core operation, and because resonance concurrently denotes the materiality of auditory perception, resonance is eminently suited to dissolve the binary of the materiality of things and the immateriality of signs that has been at the center of Western thought for much of the modern era. At the very least, resonance compels us to call into question the notion that the nature of things resides in their essence and that this essence can be exhausted by a sign, a discourse, or a logos (Latour 1993). An account of something such as resonance must therefore situate itself in a kind of echo chamber together with other things, signs, discourses, institutions, and practices.

References

Barthes, Roland. 1985. *The Responsibility of Forms*. Berkeley: University of California Press.
Derrida, Jacques. 1997. "Heidegger's Ear: Philopolemology (Geschlecht IV)." In *The Politics of Friendship*. London: Verso.
Descartes, René. 1961. *Compendium of Music* [Compendium musicae]. Trans. Walter Robert. Rome: American Institute of Musicology.

Descartes, René. 1985. *The Philosophical Writings of Descartes, Volume 3.* Trans. J. Cottingham, R. Stoothoff, A. Kenny, and D. Murdoch. Cambridge: Cambridge University Press.

Diderot, Denis. 1951. "Entretien entre d'Alembert et Diderot." In *Œuvres.* Paris: Gallimard.

Diderot, Denis, and Jean le Rond d'Alembert, eds. 1755. "Ebranler." In *Encyclopédie, ou Dictionnaire raisonné des sciences, des arts et des métiers,* 5:215. Paris.

Duverney, Joseph-Guichard. 1683. *Traité de l'organe de l'ouïe.* Paris: Estienne Michallet.

Erlmann, Veit. 2010. *Reason and Resonance: A History of Modern Aurality.* New York: Zone Books.

Erlmann, Veit. 2011. "Descartes's Resonant Subject." *differences* 22(2–3): 10–30.

Greenblatt, Stephen. 1990. "Resonance and Wonder." *Bulletin of the American Academy of Arts and Sciences* 43(4): 11–34.

Kant, Immanuel. 1924. *Kritik der Urteilskraft.* Hamburg: Felix Meiner.

Latour, Bruno. 1993. *We Have Never Been Modern.* Cambridge, MA: Harvard University Press.

Müller, Johannes. 1826. *Zur vergleichenden Physiologie des Gesichtssinnes des Menschen und der Thiere.* Leipzig: Cnobloch.

Musica Enchiriadis and Scolica Enchiriadis. 1985. Trans. Raymond Erickson. New Haven: Yale University Press.

Steege, Benjamin. 2012. *Helmholtz and the Modern Listener.* Cambridge: Cambridge University Press.

Wever, Ernest G. 1965. *Theory of Hearing.* New York: Wiley.

silence

"Silence does not exist," says a character in Andrés Neuman's 2010 novel *El Viajero del Siglo* (Traveler of the century). He was perhaps echoing, in literary rendition, John Cage's famous words on the impossibility of perceiving silence. Yet silence is lived as one of the most intense experiences across cultures. On the one hand, silence invokes a type of plenitude most commonly associated with contemplative techniques of quietness as a means to bring about a transformation of the self (Merton 1996; Corbin 1997). On the other, silence is often associated with a "sinister resonance" (Toop 2010) that invokes a haunting; the dangers and fear of the unknown; the insecurities produced by the ungraspable and by the profound irreversibility of death. We also find this sinister dimension in the constitution of silence as a means of torture, in practices such as extreme isolation, where the sense of self is lost due to sensory deprivation, or in kidnapping, whose expediency depends on the efficacy of silencing techniques as a tortuous means of emotional manipulation. Between these experiential extremes, silence appears as a term "by which we understand our existence as beings in a world larger than ourselves, a world not entirely of our making, whose limits and constraints provide the very limits and constraints of thought itself" (Grosz 2011: 99).

Silence is also used in political language to imply an active politics of domination and nonparticipation. In such use, it is understood as the opposite of "having a voice," where voice is rendered as a sign of identity and presence of the subject (see VOICE) and is contrasted with types of dialogism that have historically been seen in Western modernity as a key dimension of political participation and of the constitution of the public sphere. Psychoanalysis (Dolar 2008; Lagaay 2008) and linguistics (Bajtin [Medvedev] 1994) have complicated such oppositional understandings of voice and silence by intertwining one into the other in the political and affective constitution of the self. Silence can also be used as a significant political, symbolic, and interpretive strategy to respond to situations of conflict (Lévi-Strauss 1983; Sor Juana 2011) in contrast with imposed forms of silencing through coercion.

The tension between the apparent acoustic impossibility of silence and the intensely contrasting experiences it provokes lies at the heart of the types of presence and affect invoked by the term. At the center of this tension lies the fact that a central element of silence is a deployment of the limit. This can been seen in creative uses of the inaudible in music, in the ways silence has been used as a key aspect of the negative dialectics central to the constitution of modernity, and in the understanding of auditory thresholds according different forms of life. In what follows, I contrast and explore the ways such a creative tension appears in different forms and uses of silence.

Silence and Music

The artistic uses of silence in music, visual arts, cinema, and literature share the idea that silence is a creative tool, a formal resource that has the potential of questioning the binary logic of apparent opposites by dissolving one into the other (presence as absence, emptiness as plenitude, quietness as expressivity, silence as intensity of life). This ambivalence has been a crucial site of intervention in the transformation of notions of silence by twentieth-century avant-garde composers, who use different understandings of silence to provoke different effects. In classical understandings of Western art music, silences are perceived—even until today—as "acoustic gaps" and "particularly important loci of expressivity," which are defined as such in relation to the musical material that surrounds them (Margulis 2007: 485). John Cage challenged this interpretation of silence as "the time lapse between sounds useful to a variety of ends" (Cage 2011: 22) through his famous observation pronounced on entering the anechoic chamber at Harvard University in 1951: "I heard two sounds, one high and one low. When I described them to the engineer in charge, he informed me that the high one was my nervous system in operation, the low one my blood in circulation. . . . Until I die there will be sounds. And they will continue following my death. One need not fear about the future of music" (8). Simultaneously, he reaffirmed silence's central role in twentieth-century musical experimentalism, stating: "when none of these or other goals is present, silence becomes something else—

not silence at all but sounds, the ambient sounds" (Cage 2011: 22). Thus how silence is understood depends in good measure on how the relationship between the listener and his or her surroundings are conceptualized. Cage's new understanding of the relation between silence and ambient sound provoked, in turn, new types of creative interventions in the arts.

David Novak explores how the rise of notions of silence in experimental music in postwar Japan and the United States mutually constituted each other. After Cage, particularly his emblematic composition 4′33″ (1952), "silence became the lynchpin of a new postwar American experimentalism" (Novak 2010: 48). This in turn generated responses from Japanese composers that sought to deprovincialize American and European understandings of Japanese silence by elaborating, conceptually and musically, the Japanese notion of ma, translated as "interval" or "space." Such a concept was different from Cage's notion of silence and could be strategically deployed by Japanese composers who sought to gain recognition for their own experimental uses of silence. Silence, like noise, thus shows the central role of the limits of translation of different domains of sound in the global constitution of the avant-garde (see NOISE; Ramos 2014).

One of the effects of Cage's injunction to listen to ambient sounds is the development of soundscape compositions. Alongside the development of soundscape composition through portable recording technology and a growing social interest in ecology, a notion of silence as acoustic materiality has also emerged. The Sound Museum of Silence, a website where contributors post recordings of silence, is based on the idea that a silence is a sound "with a loudness lower than 20 db, the threshold of hearing for human beings" (Inker 2011). Thus, the silences posted on the website are understood as elements of a "soundscape with loudness below 20 dB." The perception of this soundscape depends on the use of electronic amplification devices, such as earphones, that allow humans to hear silences as sounds, and also on visual renditions of silence through spectrographs, that is, through graphic representations that allow one to see such sounds even if one cannot hear them. These silences become audible "not by the acoustics of places (like concert halls) but by techniques of sound reproduction" (Helmreich 2007: 823) and by the prosthetics of sound amplification and visualization. Here, the limits of human hearing are simultaneously highlighted and transformed through technological prosthetics. This particular form of silence brings together a long twentieth-century history of avant-garde experimentalism and sound engineering in cinema

(Buhler et al. 2009), telephony (Mills 2010, 2011), sound reproduction and amplification (Sterne 2003, 2012), and experimental music (Novak 2010), all of which place us in an acoustic world defined not solely by humans but by the interaction between humans and machines.

The Biopolitics of Silence

The use of silence to intervene in the politics of life is central to the constitution of modernity and appears in different forms in multiple fields. One aspect involves the use of physical and psychoacoustic factors of hearing in the development of sound technologies. The clinical history of deafness, for example, was central to the development of auditory amplification and reproduction technologies (see DEAFNESS, HEARING; Sterne 2003, 2011; Mills 2010, 2011). Another aspect involves the intertwined relation between repression and expression—silence and voice—that is central to the understanding of the conscious and the unconscious in psychoanalysis. Artistic movements such as Surrealism, fields of thought such as structuralism, and clinical understandings of the mind have been deeply shaped by this relation that explores the different modes of presence of that which is left unspoken.

Silence is also used in political language to imply an active politics of domination invoked by the verbal form of the term silencing. Sometimes such silencing is straightforward, as in the prohibition of different forms of expression or in silencing by death or disappearance in histories of oppression (Uribe 1993). But central to the biopolitics of silence is the pervasive dialectic between recognition and negation that is constitutive of the modern (Taussig 1999). Modern subjectivity demanded a specific type of listening constituted by silent attention, understood as a crucial dimension of an ideal, rational subject that is in control of the production of meaning (see LISTENING; Johnson 1995; Schmidt 2000). This required the cultivation of an enlightened notion of the senses, which involved the silencing of irrational or noisy forms of listening. Eric Leigh Schmidt, for example, has explored how the idea of "hearing voices" in certain Christian traditions was deemed irrational. An enlightened cultivation of hearing was supposed to allow for the development of a subject that was not possessed by such auditory incantations. This led to the emergence of a silence associated with proper, privatized forms of religious expression

(Bauman 1983; Schmidt 2000). Such silencing of what was deemed an irrational hearing of "voices from afar" also characterizes the history of colonialism. The ability to hear nonhumans in Afrodescendant or Amerindian ontologies, and the assignation of the capacity of hearing to objects, such as musical instruments or plants, were denied and silenced as valid forms of hearing.

A history of the containment of noisy modes of hearing can also be found in the transformation of both musical aesthetics and nature in the eighteenth and nineteenth centuries. Johnson (1995) has explored how Parisian operagoers were transformed, by mid-nineteenth century, from noisy publics into silent attentive audiences capable of forming rational aesthetic judgments. Similarly, the understanding of nature as a passive, silent background involved the rise, in the nineteenth century, of the notion of a passive environment amenable to scientific dissection and to a Romantic "silent" expansion of the soul (Morton 2007; Ochoa Gautier 2014). The idealized form of "devotional silence" permeated different aspects of eighteenth- and nineteenth-century pedagogies and understandings of listening and extends into late modernity, appearing, for example, in R. Murray Schafer's evolutionary notion of the soundscape (Schmidt 2000: 29) where the sounds and silences of nature are gradually polluted through the noisy rise of industrial civilization.

In late liberalism, the politics of silencing have been transformed through the use of new sound weapons, neurobiological research in sensorial perception, and radical economic disenfranchisement. The acoustic overtones of silencing include experiments with loss of sensorial control in the use of sound waves as a weapon and the denial of expressive practices and needs in institutional forms of clinicalization and criminalization of populations that involve radical isolation (Cusick 2006; Goodman 2009). This is not seen only in practices such as solitary confinement in prison; it is also present in the increasing deployment of "economies of abandonment" (Povinelli 2011) through which whole populations are deemed dispensable (Meintjes 2004; Araujo and Grupo Musicultura 2010; Epele 2010).

This repeated history of silencing through denial, negation, and abuse has often led to a political response by different populations through an affirmative biopolitics of life. Processes of redress or reparation often involve a public politics of "unsilencing" in the form of protest, legal processes such as truth commissions or reclamation of rights and lands, and the public use of music performance or artistic display as a response to situations of excessive violence (Ochoa Gautier 2003; Yudice 2004; Silent Jane 2006). But the effects of such politics of redress are highly dependent on the way unsilencing is conceived and deployed. Assisting a community through occasional interventions, such as an artistic workshop for example, is not the same as seeking a deeper transformation by changing the structures of discrimination as an everyday practice (Araujo and Grupo Musicultura 2010).

The dialectic between the history of silencing and the need to recognize this history complicates the personal, aesthetics, and legal values of sound (Moten 2003; Constable 2005). Problems such as establishing boundaries between the denunciation and the spectacularization of violence (Moten 2003) or the difficulty of distinguishing between a politics of participation and the constructions of salvationist intervention (Araujo and Grupo Musicultura 2010) are crucial here. For example, the recognition of Indigenous peoples and Afrodescendants in Colombia has been seen as a crucial step in redressing a past that excluded them from the nation; as a result, the artistic practices (music, weaving, etc.) of different peoples are more widely recognized as valuable in the nation-state today. However, such recognition is often mediated by highly standardized practices of "valid" performance that, ultimately, do not transform these histories of discrimination or translate performance into economic or legal politics of recognition and accountability (Ochoa Gautier 2003).

The processes of redress involve not only a public dimension but also a relation between public denunciation and personal elaboration: here silence appears as the limit of the speakable. Experiences of abuse test the limits of forms of acoustic remembrance and oblivion (Moten 2003; Silent Jane 2006), creating charged silences that tacitly or explicitly entangle the political history of aesthetics, as well as the history of the sensorial and the acousticity of its juridico-political dimensions. In these contexts, music often permits a process of unsilencing that involves political, acoustic, aesthetic, sensorial, and bodily explorations left untouched by talk therapy or direct denunciation. This highlights and mobilizes rather than resolves the tensions and contradictions between the personal, the juridical, and other political aspects of histories of redress and recognition. Further, we begin to see how the dialectic between the deployment of different forms of silence and expression constitutes a biopolitical history of modernity.

Who Perceives Silence

If silence implies a relation between (non)hearing and perception, then it depends on the types of entities or events that produce and perceive it. The identification of auditory thresholds changes notably from one culture and one living entity to another. In Western culture, audition (or lack thereof) is associated mostly with humans and animals; but in some other cultures, entities such as stones, wind, and other types of nonhuman forms also have the capacity to listen, to lose hearing, or to provoke silence. The question then rests on the changing metaphysics and physics of the definition of forms of life across cultures and history. As noted by Lévi-Strauss, in mythical narration "things that emit sound" often act as "operators" that "possess other sensory connotations" and "express, as a totality, a set of equivalences connecting life and death, vegetable food and cannibalism, putrefaction and imputrescibility, softness and hardness, silence and noise" (1983: 153). The presence or absence of sound then stands as the very mediator of the presence or absence of life, showing us how myths (or cosmologies) can tie events into structures. But the acknowledgment of such a relation—based as it is on admitting the agentive acoustic dimensions of nonhuman entities in the affairs of humans— is largely based on an understanding of the relations between humans and nonhumans that unsettles the historically constructed boundaries between nature and culture, the human and the nonhuman, in Western modernity. In such a world, the idea of "hearing things"—which Western metaphysics either silenced or displaced to a separate philosophical terrain by associating it with either "the occult" (Thacker 2011) or the mentally distressed (Schmidt 2000)—is cosmologically mediated by an understanding between humans and nonhumans that allows for their mutual acoustic interaction. Such a relation between nature and culture and between humans and nonhumans makes us rethink the acoustic definition of silence as determined solely by human auditory thresholds. It also recasts the relation between physical acoustics ("nature") and the auditory interpretation of silence ("culture") as dependent on the way such fields are conceptualized. If the experience of silence across different cultures has historically mediated between the experiential intensity of presence and absence associated to life and death, then the redefinition of forms of life currently taking place in Western metaphysics (Shaviro 2012) also implies an ongoing transformation of silence.

Note

The author wishes to thank David Novak, Matt Sakakeeny, Julio Ramos, and the excellent comments of an anonymous reviewer.

References

Araujo, Samuel, and Grupo Musicultura. 2010. "Sound Praxis: Music, Politics, and Violence in Brazil." In *Music and Conflict*, ed. John Morgan O'Connell and Salwa El-Shawan Castelo-Branco, 217–231. Urbana: University of Illinois Press.

Asad, Talal. 2003. *Formations of the Secular: Christianity, Islam, Modernity*. Stanford: Stanford University Press.

Bajtin, Mijail [Pavel N. Medevedev]. 1994. "El método formal en la historia literaria." In *El método formal en los estudios literarios*, 227–264. Madrid: Alianza.

Bauman, Richard. 1983. *Let Your Words Be Few: Symbolism of Speaking and Silence among Seventeenth-Century Quakers*. Cambridge: Cambridge University Press.

Bauman, Richard, and Charles Briggs. 2003. *Voices of Modernity: Language Ideologies and the Politics of Inequality*. Cambridge: Cambridge University Press.

Buhler, James, David Neumeyer, and Rob Deemer. 2009. *Hearing the Movies: Music and Sound in Film History*. Oxford: Oxford University Press.

Cage, John. 2011 [1939]. "Experimental Music." In *Silence: Lectures and Writings*. Fiftieth anniversary ed. Middletown: Wesleyan University Press.

Connor, Steven. 2009, February 14. "Earslips: Of Mishearings and Mondegreens." Talk given at conference "Listening In, Feeding Back," Columbia University. Available at http://www.bbk.ac.uk/english/skc/seeingtosound.htm.

Constable, Marianne. 2005. *Just Silences: The Limits and Possibilities of Modern Law*. Princeton: Princeton University Press.

Conter, Marcelo B., and Gabriel Saikoski. 2012. "Execuções audiovisuais de 4′33″ de John Cage em vídeos para web." Paper presented at IASPM Latin America conference, Córdoba, Argentina, April 18–22.

Corbin, Alain. 1998. *Village Bells: Sound and Meaning in the Nineteenth-Century French Countryside*. New York: Columbia University Press.

Cusick, Suzanne. 2006. "Music as Torture/Torture as Weapon." *TRANS, Revista Transcultural de Música* 10, article 11.

De la Cruz, Sor Juana Inés. 2011 [1690]. *Carta atenagórica y respuesta a Sor Filotea*. Barcelona: www.linkgua-digital.com.

Deleuze, Gilles, and Félix Guattari. 2002 [1988]. *Mil mesetas, capitalismo y esquizofrenia*. París: Pre-textos.

Derrida, Jacques. 2011. *Voice and Phenomenon: Introduction to the Problem of the Sign in Husserl's Phenomenology*. Evanston: Northwestern University Press.

Dolar, Mladen. 2008. *A Voice and Nothing More*. Cambridge, MA: MIT Press.

Epele, María. 2010. *Sujetar por la herida: Una etnografía sobre drogas, pobreza y salud*. Buenos Aires: Paidós.

Esposito, Roberto. 2012. *El dispositivo de la persona*. Madrid: Amorrortou.

Goodman, Steve. 2009. *Sonic Warfare: Sound, Affect and the Ecology of Fear*. Cambridge, MA: MIT Press.

Grosz, Elizabeth. 2011. *Becoming Undone: Darwinian Reflections on Life, Politics and Art*. Durham: Duke University Press.

Helmreich, Stefan. 2007. "An Anthropologist Underwater: Immersive Soundscapes, Submarine Cyborgs and Transductive Ethnography." In *American Ethnologist* 34(4): 821–841.

Hill, Jonathan D., and Jean-Pierre Chaumeil. 2011. "Overture." In *Burst of Breath: Indigenous Ritual Wind Instruments in Lowland South America*, 1–48. Lincoln: University of Nebraska Press.

Hirschkind, Charles. 2006. *The Ethical Soundscape, Cassette Sermons and Islamic Counterpublics*. New York: Columbia University Press.

Inker, Aaron. 2011. Entry in *Below 20, Sound Museum of Silence* (blog). http://20decibel.blogspot.com, accessed November 10, 2013.

Jackson, Michael D. 2002. *The Politics of Storytelling: Violence, Transgression and Intersubjectivity*. Copenhagen: Museum Tusculanum Press.

Johnson, James H. 1995. *Listening in Paris: A Cultural History*. Berkeley: University of California Press.

Lagaay, Alice. 2008. "Between Sound and Silence: Voice in the History of Psychoanalysis." *e-pisteme* 1(1): 53–62.

Lévi-Strauss, Claude. 1983. *The Raw and the Cooked*. Chicago: University of Chicago Press.

Lutfi, Robert A. 2007. "Human Sound Source Identification." In *Auditory Perception of Sound Sources*, ed. William A. Yost, Arthur N. Popper, and Richard R. Fay, 29: 13–42. New York: Springer.

Margulis, Elizabeth. 2007. "Moved by Nothing: Listening to Musical Silence." In *Journal of Music Theory* 51(2): 245–276.

Meintjes, Louise. 2004. "Shoot the Sergeant, Shatter the Mountain: The Production of Masculinity in Zulu Ngoma Song and Dance in Post-apartheid South Africa." In *Ethnomusicology Forum* 13(2): 173–201.

Merton, Thomas. 1996. *Entering the Silence: Becoming a Monk and Writer: The Journals of Thomas Merton*, ed. Jonathan Montaldo. San Francisco: HarperCollins.

Mills, Mara. 2010. "Deaf Jam, from Inscription to Reproduction to Information." In *Social Text* 102, 28(1): 35–58.

Mills, Mara. 2011. "Deafening: Noise and the Engineering of Communication in the Telephone System." *Grey Room* 43:118–143.

Moten, Fred. 2003. *In the Break, the Aesthetics of the Black Radical Tradition*. Minneapolis: University of Minnesota Press.

Neuman, Andrés. 2010. *El viajero del siglo*. Madrid: Alfaguara.

Novak, David. 2010. "Playing Off Site: The Untranslation of Onkyo." *Asian Music* 41(1): 36–59.

Ochoa Gautier, Ana María. 2003. *Entre los deseos y los derechos: Un ensayo crítico sobre políticas culturales*. Bogota: ICANH.

Ochoa Gautier, Ana María. 2014. *Aurality: Listening and Knowledge in Nineteenth-Century Colombia*. Durham: Duke University Press.

Palmié, Stephan. 2002. *Wizards and Scientists: Explorations in Afro-Cuban Modernity and Tradition*. Durham: Duke University Press.

Povinelli, Elizabeth. 2011. *Economies of Abandonment: Social Belonging and Endurance in Late Liberalism*. Durham: Duke University Press.

Ramos, Julio. 2014. "Disconancia afrocubana: John Cage y las rítmicas V y VI de Amadeo Roldán." In *Revolución y cultura I, Epoca V, Año 56 de la Revolución*: 52–63.

Shaviro, Steven. 2012, June 13. "Forms of Life." Entry in *The Pinocchio Theory* (blog), available at www.shaviro.com/Blog/, accessed February 27, 2014.

Schmidt, Leigh Eric. 2000. *Hearing Things: Religion, Illusion and the American Enlightenment*. Cambridge, MA: Harvard University Press.

Silent Jane. 2006. "Beautiful Fragments of a Traumatic Memory: Synaesthesia, Sesame Street and Hearing the Colors of an Abusive Past." In "Dossier: Música, silencios y silenciamientos: Música, violencia y experiencia cotidiana," ed. Ana María Ochoa, TRANS. *Revista Transcultural de Música* 10.

Sound Museum of Silence. 2011. Compilation/archive, Discogs.com, available at www.discogs.com/Various-Below-20-Db/release/3229578, accessed August 15, 2014.

Sound Museum of Silence. Facebook page. www.facebook.com/pages/Sound-museum-of-silence/165145740176093, accessed November 10, 2013.

Sterne, Jonathan. 2003. *The Audible Past: Cultural Origins of Sound Reproduction*. Durham: Duke University Press.

Sterne, Jonathan. 2012. *MP3: The Meaning of a Format*. Durham: Duke University Press.

Taussig, Michael. 1999. *Defacement: Public Secrecy and the Labor of the Negative*. Stanford: Stanford University Press.

Thacker, Eugene. 2011. *In the Dust of this Planet: Horror of Philosophy*, vol. 1. Winchester: Zero Books.

Toop, David. 2010. *Sinister Resonance: The Mediumship of the Listener*. New York: Continuum.

Uribe, Maria Victoria. 1993. *Enterrar y callar: Las masacres en Colombia 1980–1993*. Bogota: Comité Permanente por la Defensa de los Derechos Humanos y Fundación Terre des Hommes.

space

Sound and space—however one defines these terms—are phenomeno-logically and ontologically intertwined. Sounds, after all, are always in motion; they emanate, radiate, reflect, canalize, get blocked, leak out, and so on. This intimate link between sound and space holds true whether one conceives of sound as inextricably linked to the perceptual faculty of hearing or as a "vibration of a certain frequency in a material medium" (Friedner and Helmreich 2012: 77–78).[1] From a hearing-centered stand-point, sound is inherently spatial because the process of audition attaches a spatial "narrative" to each sound (Altman 1992: 19); from a vibration-centered standpoint, sound does not exist without its propagation in space (Henriques 2010).

One need only imagine sound or space without the other term to re-alize their intimate relationship. Imagine sound without space, vibrat-ing everywhere and nowhere. The idea is otherworldly, belonging to the realms of religion, mysticism, and aesthetics. It is the Voice of God speaking directly to the "heart" or "spiritual ear" (Bauman 1983; Ihde 2007 [1976]; Saeed 2012), the dharmic Om and Sufi Hu that enable worshipers to "[forget] all earthly distinctions and differences, and [reach] that goal of truth in which all the Blessed Ones of God unite" (Beck 1993; Inayat Khan 1996: 72). Religious communities have always sought to capture the experience of nonspatial sound through meditation and trance, and by harnessing the despatializing effect of physical reverberation for spiritual transcendence (Blesser and Salter 2007). The goal of a direct, spaceless connection between a sound and its internal reception has also emerged through the use of the electroacoustic loudspeaker to effect a "sonic dom-inance" (Henriques 2003) that envelops and invades the body, dissolving the subject. Amplified sound at high volume and close proximity is used to just this effect in subcultural and experimental music scenes like Japanese Noise (Novak 2013) and Jamaican dancehall (Henriques 2003, 2011) and in forms of military interrogation and torture that employ sonic dominance as a form of violence (Bayoumi 2005; Cusick 2013). These despatialized sonic experiences reaffirm sound's fundamental spatiality not only in their extramundane character but also in their ironic reliance on particular sonic-spatial phenomena like reverberation. Hence, the despatializing reverberations of a grand cathedral stand as an icon—or "earcon"—of a particular kind of architectural space (Blesser and Salter 2007: 83).

Now imagine space without sound—space imbued with absolute, undifferentiated silence. It is perhaps a less mystical idea than that of nonspatial sound. Silence exists in modes of abstract thought outside of the spiritual, including mathematics, theoretical physics, and architectural planning, and is a feature of the known physical universe (sound cannot exist in a vacuum). Moreover, silent, if not exactly *soundless*, space is an everyday experience for the profoundly deaf.[2] But for hearing people, soundless space—evoked in such common experiences as viewing "calm and lifeless" tableaux "through binoculars or on the television screen with the sound turned off" (Tuan 1977: 16)—is as otherworldly as nonspatial sound and similarly implicated in spiritual practice. At least within the realms of human experience and the social, then, sound is constitutive of space, just as space is constitutive of sound.

The decade following the publication of Raymond Williams's *Keywords* (1983) saw *space* emerge as a new keyword that Williams "would surely have included" (Harvey 2006: 270). Space rose to the fore in poststructuralist concerns with relationality and the situated nature of knowledge, following the realization among Marxist and critical theorists that the emerging post-Fordist, globalized era necessitated a "demystification of spatiality and its veiled instrumentality of power" (Soja 1989: 61). Channeling Williams, David Harvey calls space "one of the most complicated words in our language" (2006: 270). Leaving aside its endless metaphorical uses, the word references a range of concepts that philosophers and physicists have long understood as ontologically incommensurable. Space may either be conceived as a kind of framework in which entities are situated or as an effect of the relations between entities, "the universal power enabling them to be connected" (Merleau-Ponty 1958: 284). The former conception, known as *absolute space*, has also been revised as *relative space* in relation to the non-Euclidean geographies of Einstein and others. For Harvey, all these apparently incompatible ontologies of space have analytical purchase on the social world, each corresponding to a particular human engagement with physical world. Henri Lefebvre (1991) offers another multifarious model of social space, describing it as a product of the relations between physical form (the *perceived*), instrumental knowledge (the *conceived*), and symbolic practice (the *lived*).

The increasing recognition of the intimate links between sound and space may be attributed to a confluence of scientific and technological developments in the latter half of the twentieth century, including the development of traveling-wave models of auditory perception and the rise of multichannel audio recording and playback. But the spatiality of sound and sonorous nature of space were rarely recognized in Western thought before the "spatial turn." Frustration at this particular historical deafness comes through in some of the early touchstone works of sound studies. Philosopher Don Ihde, for example, stresses the need to transcend the description of auditory experience as purely temporal; a tradition so powerful, he suggests, that it delayed the discovery of animal echolocation for centuries (2007 [1976]: 58–59). In a similar vein, musical philosopher Victor Zuckerkandl worked to slough off the conception, proffered by Schopenhauer and other Romantics, of "music as a purely temporal art" (1956: 336).

It is difficult to identify any work of sound studies that does *not* deal in some way with space, if only by implicitly incorporating epistemological and ontological commitments with respect to the spatiality of sound. But it is possible to identify certain modalities of space, or spatialities, that have emerged at the center of the field. I describe five such spatialities here: *phenomenal field, the virtual, ecology, territory,* and *circulation*.[3]

Spatialities of Sound

PHENOMENAL FIELD

Edmund Carpenter and Marshall McLuhan introduced the term "acoustic space" (sometimes "auditory space" in Carpenter's work) in the 1950s to refer to the supposed "boundless, directionless, horizonless" sensory world and related "mentality" of pre- and nonliterate cultures, and perhaps literate Westerners in a media saturated world (McLuhan 1960; see also inter alia McLuhan 2004). The idea, further developed in Walter Ong's *Orality and Literacy* (1982) and the writings of music composer R. Murray Schafer (see below), reproduced a set of reductive binary oppositions between the visual and the auditory, positing the former as analytical and the latter as emotional (later critiqued by Feld 1996; Ingold 2000: 248–249; Sterne 2003, 2011).

In contrast, Don Ihde's *Listening and Voice* (2007 [1976]) approaches the question of how sound mediates human perceptions and understandings of physical space by combining Edmund Husserl's phenomenological perspectives with his own investigations of auditory experience. Ihde painstakingly deconstructs the supposed "weakness" of the spatiality of hearing, describing an auditory field that is "bidimensional," being both spherical and directional. At the same time, he rejects any simple opposition between the modalities of hearing and seeing, even in the service of "antivisualism"—a move that has reverberated in the anthropology of the senses.

THE VIRTUAL

An obvious weakness in Ihde's otherwise essential phenomenological account of sound and space is his lack of attention to how the history of "spatialization" practices in audio production has informed modern epistemologies of sound (Born 2013: 14). The use of spatial cues—sonic gestures that simulate "the position of sound sources in the environment and the volume of the space in which a listener is located" (Clarke 2013: 94)—goes back to the earliest days of recorded music and film soundtracks, predating the development of stereophony. Spatial effects produced through reverberation and microphone placement had become a rich site for aesthetic innovation in popular music as early as the 1920s (Doyle 2005). The propagation of multichannel stereophony in the post–World War II period then added another layer of spatiality to an already richly spatial art of audio production, transforming production aesthetics and home listening technologies in popular music (Zak 2001: 148–149; Dockwray and Moore 2010) and fostering a rich array of approaches to electroacoustic music, marked by "multiple-speaker projection techniques, spatial simulation methods, and custom-built architectural installations" (Ouzounian 2007; Valiquet 2012: 406).

A literature on sociotechnical practices of sound reproduction, much of it explicitly aligned with sound studies, explores the production of virtual sonic worlds and their complex interrelations with physical and social spaces. Various works on audio engineering explore the recording studio as a laboratory-like setting in which sounds and human actors are "isolated" in order to be reconfigured in a sonic spacetime (Hennion 1989; Meintjes 2003; Porcello 2004, 2005; Théberge 2004). In addition to outlining the technological production of recorded musical space, this work speaks to the mutual mediation of aesthetic and social space. Louise Meintjes's ethnography of Zulu popular music production, for example, explores struggles over sound in the "seemingly neutral political ground" of the recording studio as intimately bound up with racial and class politics, thereby offering an ear on the quotidian reality of late capitalist, late apartheid South Africa (Meintjes 2003: 9).

Sound studies scholarship also investigates virtual sonic spaces outside of the recording studio. In his studies of personal stereo and MP3 player use in cities, Michael Bull explores how users "create a privatized sound world, which is in harmony with their mood, orientation and surroundings, enabling them to re-spatialize urban experience through a process of solipsistic aestheticization" (Bull 2010: 57–58; see also 2000, 2008). Meanwhile, sound-oriented studies of "new media" explore how the omnidirectional and haptic characteristics of sound are mobilized to foster experiences of "immersion" (Dyson 2009; Grimshaw 2011).

ECOLOGY

Ecology refers to an environment—often the environment, the "natural world"—as a space of relations. The notion of "acoustic ecology" as an object or mode of inquiry has for half a century been tethered to the term soundscape, first popularized by R. Murray Schafer and his World Soundscape Project during the late 1960s and early 1970s. Schafer conceptualized the soundscape as an increasingly "polluted" global environment of humanly perceived sounds that composers and music teachers should work to understand, and ultimately to transform. Inspired by McLuhan's conception of art as "an instrument of discovery and perception" (McLuhan, quoted in Cavell 2003: 185) and John Cage's definition of music as "sounds around us, whether we're in or out of concert halls" (quoted in Schafer 1969: 57), Schafer founded the World Soundscape Project with the aim of assessing sonic environments through rigorous audio documentation and analysis of recorded "soundscapes."

The idea of taking a composer's ear to the environment spawned a variety of approaches to mapping and analyzing inhabited environments, natural ecosystems, and interactions between humans and their environments (see e.g. Wrightson 2000; Atkinson 2007; Pijanowski et al. 2011). Schaferian soundscape-related concepts have also been operationalized in sociocultural analysis, particularly in ethnomusicology. Schafer's notion of "schizophonia," or the anxiety-generating "split between an original sound and its electroacoustical transmission or reproduction" (1977: 90), has proven useful for opening up questions about the dynamics of authenticity and ownership in recorded music (Feld 1994; Moehn 2005), and concepts like "soundmark" and "acoustic community" (Truax 2001) provide ways of thinking about the relationships between emplacement and social orientation, particularly in contexts of social struggle and transformation (Lee 1999; Sakakeeny 2010).

But Schafer's *soundscape* is deeply problematic as a central figure for sound studies. Not only is it grounded in normative ideas of which sounds "matter" and which do not, it groans under the weight of the irony that it is born of the very modern technologies of sound reproduction that Schafer decries as sources of "lo-fi" "pollution" (Helmreich 2010). Even the term's greatest strength—the fact that it "evokes a whole complex set of ideas, preferences, practices, scientific properties, legal frameworks, social orders, and sounds"—is also a weakness insofar as it diminishes the term's heuristic value (Kelman 2010: 228).

Other scholars have sought to describe the interrelations of sound, space, and the social in different ways, often with limited or no engagement with Schafer's term. Sterne (1997), for example, approaches programed music in commercial space as an "architectonics" with attendant modes of listening. Alain Corbin (1998) uses *auditory landscape*, which emphasizes sensory experience and its discursive framing, in his history of church bells in the French countryside. Emily Thompson similarly redefines *soundscape* as "simultaneously a physical environment and a way of perceiving that environment" (2002: 1). Drawing on Schafer but taking a radical turn toward emplacement, Steven Feld (1996) coins the term *acoustemology* (acoustics + epistemology) to describe a way of knowing place in and through the sonic environment. At once a subject-centered approach to ecology and an ecological approach to the subject, *acoustemology* attends to "local conditions of acoustic sensation, knowledge, and imagination embodied in the culturally particular sense of place" (Feld 1996: 91; see also ACOUSTEMOLOGY).

Place might be described as another modality of space but is in truth its own keyword. It is a human engagement with the world that stands apart from, and indeed *prior to*, space. Abstract conceptions of space, time, and spacetime are, in a sense, purified versions of the contextual, contingent, messy experience of place (Casey 1996, 1998). Sound-oriented approaches to place have become an important domain of recent ethnomusicology, which shows how music and sound are crucial in place-making and the poetics of place (see e.g. Stokes 1994; Solomon 2000; Fox 2004; Sakakeeny 2010; Gray 2011; Eisenberg 2012, 2013).

TERRITORY

Territory, a spatial figure that has received significant attention in sound studies, is about boundary making, enclosure, and the production of interiority and exteriority. Deleuze and Guattari (1987) expound on the intimate link between sound and territory in a discussion of the home as a "milieu": "Sonorous or vocal components are very important: a wall of sound, or at least a wall with some sonic bricks in it" (311). Sonic practices territorialize by virtue of combining physical vibration with bodily sensation and culturally conditioned meanings. This is particularly audible in the sonorous enactments of publicity and privacy in inhabited spaces, as scholars of sound have shown in relation to the city (Picker 2003; LaBelle 2010), the car (Bull 2003), the office (Dibben and Haake 2013), the hospital (Rice 2013), and perhaps most powerfully Islam, which mediates the public/private distinction in relation to the sacred, and the sacred in relation to sound (Hirschkind 2006; Bohlman 2013; Eisenberg 2013).

CIRCULATION

The movement of mediated sounds, especially commercially recorded music, reveals how understandings, if not the very natures, of place and territory have changed in the era of intensified globalization. Connell and Gibson (2003) suggest that mediated music is crosscut by opposing dynamics of "fixity" and "fluidity," which shift and change in relation to technological and legal regimes. Nowhere is this more evident than in the case of commercial "world music," whose aesthetics, power dynamics, and complex interrelations with ethnic and national imaginaries reveal globalization's "increasingly complicated pluralities, uneven experiences, and consolidated powers" (Feld 2000: 146; see also Meintjes 1990, 2003; Guilbault 1993; Taylor 1997; Stokes 2004; Ochoa Gautier 2006).

Paul Gilroy (1993) offers another powerful approach to global musical circulation in his formulation of the "Black Atlantic" as a space of transnational, diasporic connection and consciousness grounded in what Alexander G. Weheliye (2005) aptly terms a "sonic Afro-modernity." Gilroy's provocative description of black music in commercial circulation as a mode of nonrepresentational "metacommunication" across diasporic spacetime has been enormously influential and lays the groundwork for recent discussions of phonographic aurality (Weheliye 2005) and cosmopolitan acoustemology (Feld 2012 [1982]).

David Novak's ethnography of transnational underground Noise music introduces a new approach to sonic circulation with the heuristic of "feedback," which he develops in dialogue with the rich anthropological literature on circulation. Feedback—defined as "circulation as an experimental force, which is compelled to go out of control" (2013: 18)—works as both an aesthetic and a cultural logic in Noise. The sounds of Noise, constituted through the technological effect of positive feedback, emerged and are sustained by practices of sounding and listening constituted in contingent and experimental feedback loops connecting Japan and North America.

Noise's feedback loops comprehend two different sonic spatialities— the global circulation of sounds and individual experiences of immersion in sound: "To close the distances of global circulation," Novak argues, "listeners and performers alike become deeply invested in the personal embodiment of sound" (2013: 22). Here we have a powerful example of how sound can serve as a medium through which spatialities articulate or interfere with each other. I will close with an example from my own research in coastal Kenya (Eisenberg 2009, 2010, 2012, 2013) to consider how sound studies might lend a more attentive ear to the interactions of discrete sonic spatialities.

Sound, Space, and Citizenship on the Kenyan Coast

In my research on "cultural citizenship" (social belonging in relation to the nation-state) among marginalized Muslim communities of the Kenyan coast, I employ methods of "participant-audition" to investigate social identification and boundary making in the public spaces of an iconic Muslim Old Town located within Kenya's heterogeneous port city of Mombasa. This task calls for attention to sonic spatialities not only as multiple but also as overlapping and mutually mediating.

A key focus of my research is Mombasa Old Town's quotidian "Islamic soundscape" of electrically amplified muezzin calls and sermons, which marks the neighborhood as a space apart from the surrounding city. Old Town's Islamic soundscape is clearly a territorializing force, fostering an affectively and symbolically significant divide between old and new—and

Muslim and Christian—Mombasa. It is also the basis of an acoustic ecology and attendant acoustemology of place. Pious Muslims on the Kenyan coast, as elsewhere, receive its constituent elements through cultivated bodily techniques. On hearing the call to prayer, for example, women reflexively replace their headscarves, and everyone halts conversations and other noisy activities; many vocalize prescribed verbal responses quietly to themselves. Such "ethical practices" (Hirschkind 2006) continually enact the "public" spaces of Mombasa Old Town as, effectively, "private," in the Islamic sense of bearing "sanctity—reserve—respect" (El Guindi 1999: 77–96). This sets the terms for an everyday spatial politics whereby Old Town's Muslim residents constantly effect a sonorous "communitarian privacy" that stands in tension with Kenya's broadly liberal-democratic understanding of urban space (Eisenberg 2010, 2013).

Layered atop the sonorous spatial practices and politics surrounding the Islamic soundscape in Mombasa Old Town, another kind of soundscape introduces another kind of sonic spatiality, that of popular media circulation. Through musical practices, sonic artifacts of transnational circulation enter into the same public spaces that vibrate with the Islamic soundscape, supplying raw semiotic materials for a different way of imagining one's place in the world. Take, for example, the soundtrack of Arab pop (Nancy Ajram, Amr Diab) and arabesque American hip-hop (tracks produced by Timbaland and Scott Storch) that emanates daily from a popular juice bar and the vehicles of middle-class youth in Old Town's lively Kibokoni district (Eisenberg 2012: 567–569). Exemplifying David Novak's idea of listening as a form of circulation (Novak 2008, 2013), public engagements with these sounds in the spaces of Mombasa Old Town make audible a "discrepant cosmopolitanism" (Clifford 1994; Feld 2012 [1982]) that speaks back to the Black Atlantic cosmopolitanism that prevails among urban youth in noncoastal Kenya. If this cosmopolitanism becomes a cosmopolitics, it does so partly by virtue of its acoustic-ecological and acoustemological contexts (the latter being one of multiplicity and disjuncture). That is to say, the Islamic soundscape and its attendant struggles over the meanings of public space lend Kibokoni's transnational popular music soundtrack a political timbre it might not have otherwise had. And Kibokoni's transnational popular music soundtrack also inflects the Islamic soundscape and attendant struggles, if in more subtle ways.

Spatial practices and politics need not be studied with an overriding emphasis on sound. But it is worth recognizing how sound, as an ethnographic object, enables one to analytically separate, and then reconnect, the "perceived, conceived, and lived" spatialities that Lefebvre (1991) enjoins us to keep always visible and audible in any analysis of space and social relations. As a phenomenon that exists at once within and beyond perceiving subjects, sound cannot but reveal social space as an artifact of material practices complexly interwoven with semiotic processes and the "imaginations, fears, emotions, psychologies, fantasies and dreams" that human beings bring to everything (Harvey 2006: 279; see also Lefebvre 1991).

Notes

1. In philosophy and sound studies alike, one finds multiple, competing ontologies of sound, which mostly seem to turn on the question of location—that is, of whether sound resides in the listening subject, the sounding object, the air (or other material medium) between them, or somewhere else entirely (Sterne 2012b; Casati and Dokic 2012).

2. The distinction I am making between silence and soundlessness here is based on a definition of silence as a lack of audible sound. According to a vibration-centered ontology of sound, the silent experiential world of the profoundly deaf is not soundless (see DEAFNESS; Friedner and Helmreich 2012).

3. The term *phenomenal field* comes from Merleau-Ponty (1958).

References

Altman, Rick. 1992. "The Material Heterogeneity of Recorded Sound." In *Sound Theory, Sound Practice*, ed. Rick Altman, 15–31. New York: Routledge.

Atkinson, Rowland. 2007. Ecology of Sound: The Sonic Order of Urban Space. *Urban Studies* 44(10): 1905–1917.

Attali, Jacques. 1985. *Noise: The Political Economy of Music*. Trans. Brian Massumi. Minneapolis: University of Minnesota Press.

Bauman, Richard. 1983. *Let Your Words Be Few: Symbolism of Speaking and Silence among Seventeenth-Century Quakers*. Cambridge: Cambridge University Press.

Bayoumi, Moustafa. 2005, December 26. "Disco Inferno." *Nation*, available at www.the nation.com/article/disco-inferno?page=0,0, accessed December 21, 2013.

Beck, Guy L. 1993. *Sonic Theology: Hinduism and Sacred Sound*. Columbia: University of South Carolina Press.

Blesser, Barry, and Linda-Ruth Salter. 2007. *Spaces Speak, Are You Listening?: Experiencing Aural Architecture*. Cambridge, MA: MIT Press.

Bohlman, Philip V. 2013. "Music Inside Out: Sounding Public Religion in a Post-Secular Europe." In *Music, Sound and Space: Transformations of Public and Private Experience*, ed. Georgina Born, 205–223. Cambridge: Cambridge University Press.

Born, Georgina. 2011. "Music and the Materialisation of Identities." *Journal of Material Culture* 16(4): 376–388.

Born, Georgina. 2013. Introduction to *Music, Sound and Space: Transformations of Public and Private Experience*, ed. Georgina Born, 1–70. Cambridge: Cambridge University Press.

Bull, Michael. 2000. *Sounding Out the City: Personal Stereos and the Management of Everyday Life*. Oxford: Berg.

Bull, Michael. 2003. "Soundscapes of the Car." In *The Auditory Culture Reader*, ed. Michael Bull and Les Back, 357–374. Oxford: Berg.

Bull, Michael. 2008. *Sound Moves: Ipod Culture and Urban Experience*. New York: Routledge.

Bull, Michael. 2010. "Ipod: A Personalized Sound World for Its Consumers." *Revista Comunicar* 17(34): 55–63.

Casati, Roberto, and Jerome Dokic. 2012. "Sounds." In *The Stanford Encyclopedia of Philosophy*, ed. Edward N. Zalta, available at http://plato.stanford.edu/archives/win2012/entries/sounds/, accessed September 26, 2014.

Casey, Edward S. 1996. "How to Get from Space to Place in a Fairly Short Stretch of Time: Philosophical Prolegomena." In *Senses of Place*, ed. Steven Feld and Keith H. Basso, 13–52. Santa Fe: School of American Research Press.

Casey, Edward S. 1998. *The Fate of Place: A Philosophical History*. Berkeley: University of California Press.

Cavell, Richard. 2003. *McLuhan in Space: A Cultural Geography*. Toronto: University of Toronto Press.

Chion, Michel. 1994. *Audio-Vision: Sound on Screen*. Trans. and ed. Claudia Gorbman. New York: Columbia University Press.

Clarke, Eric F. 2013. "Music, Space and Subjectivity." In *Music, Sound and Space: Transformations of Public and Private Experience*, ed. Georgina Born, 90–110. Cambridge: Cambridge University Press.

Clifford, James. 1994. "Diasporas." *Cultural Anthropology* 9(3): 302–338.

Connell, John, and Chris Gibson. 2003. *Sound Tracks: Popular Music, Identity and Place*. London: Routledge.

Corbin, Alain. 1998. *Village Bells: Sound and Meaning in the Nineteenth-Century French Countryside*. New York: Columbia University Press.

Cusick, Suzanne G. 2013. "Toward an Acoustemology of Detention in the 'Global War on Terror'." In *Music, Sound and Space: Transformations of Public and Private Experience*, ed. Georgina Born, 275–291. Cambridge: Cambridge University Press.

Deleuze, Gilles, and Félix Guattari. 1987. *A Thousand Plateaus: Capitalism and Schizophrenia*. Trans. Brian Massumi. Minneapolis: University of Minnesota Press.

Dibben, Nicola, and Anneli B. Haake. 2013. "Music and the Construction of Space in Office-Based Work Settings." In *Music, Sound and Space: Transformations of Public and Private Experience*, ed. Georgina Born, 151–168. Cambridge: Cambridge University Press.

Dockwray, Ruth, and Allan F. Moore. 2010. Configuring the Sound-Box 1965–72. *Popular Music* 29(2): 181–197.

Doyle, Peter. 2005. *Echo and Reverb: Fabricating Space in Popular Music, 1900–1960*. Middletown: Wesleyan University Press.

Dyson, Frances. 2009. *Sounding New Media: Immersion and Embodiment in the Arts and Culture*. Berkeley: University of California Press.

Eisenberg, Andrew J. 2009. "The Resonance of Place: Vocalizing Swahili Ethnicity in Mombasa, Kenya." Ph.D. diss., Columbia University.

Eisenberg, Andrew J. 2010. "Toward an Acoustemology of Muslim Citizenship in Kenya." *Anthropology News* 51 (9, December): 6.

Eisenberg, Andrew J. 2012. "Hip-Hop and Cultural Citizenship on Kenya's 'Swahili Coast.'" *Africa* 82 (4): 556–578.

Eisenberg, Andrew J. 2013. "Islam, Sound, and Space: Acoustemology and Muslim Citizenship on the Kenyan Coast." In *Music, Sound, and Space: Transformations of Public and Private Experience*, ed. Georgina Born, 186–202. Cambridge: Cambridge University Press.

Elden, Stuart. 2005. "Missing the Point: Globalization, Deterritorialization and the Space of the World." *Transactions of the Institute of British Geographers* 30(1): 8–19.

Emmerson, Simon. 1998. "Aural Landscape: Musical Space." *Organised Sound* 3(2): 135–140.

Erlmann, Veit. 2010. *Reason and Resonance: A History of Modern Aurality.* Cambridge, MA: Zone Books.

Feld, Steven. 1994. "From Schizophonia to Schismogenesis: On the Discourses and Commodification Practices of 'World Music' and 'World Beat.'" In *Music Grooves*, by Charles Keil and Steven Feld, 257–289. Chicago: University of Chicago Press.

Feld, Steven. 1996. "Waterfalls of Song: An Acoustemology of Place Resounding in Bosavi, Papua New Guinea." In *Senses of Place*, ed. Steven Feld and Keith H. Basso, 91–135. Santa Fe: School of American Research.

Feld, Steven. 2000. "A Sweet Lullaby for World Music." *Public Culture* 12 (1): 145–171.

Feld, Steven. 2001. *Rainforest Soundwalks: Ambiences of Bosavi Papua New Guinea.* CD. EarthEar.

Feld, Steven. 2012. *Jazz Cosmopolitanism in Accra: Five Musical Years in Ghana.* Durham: Duke University Press.

Fox, Aaron A. 2004. *Real Country: Music and Language in Working Class Culture.* Durham: Duke University Press.

Friedner, Michele, and Stefan Helmreich. 2012. "Sound Studies Meets Deaf Studies." *The Senses and Society* 7(1): 72–86.

Gilroy, Paul. 1993. *The Black Atlantic: Modernity and Double Consciousness.* Cambridge, MA: Harvard University Press.

Goodman, Steve. 2010. *Sonic Warfare: Sound, Affect, and the Ecology of Fear.* Cambridge, MA: MIT Press.

Gray, Lila Ellen. 2011. "Fado's City." *Anthropology and Humanism* 36(2): 141–163.

Grimshaw, Mark. 2011. "Sound and Player Immersion in Digital Games." In *The Oxford Handbook of Sound Studies*, ed. Trevor Pinch and Karin Bijsterveld, 347–366. New York: Oxford University Press.

Guilbault, Jocelyne. 1993. *Zouk: World Music in the West Indies.* Chicago: University of Chicago Press.

Harvey, David. 2006. "Space as a Keyword." In *David Harvey: A Critical Reader*, 270–294. Oxford: Blackwell.

Helmreich, Stefan. 2010. "Listening against Soundscapes." *Anthropology News* 51(9): 10.

Hennion, Antoine. 1989. "An Intermediary between Production and Consumption: The Producer of Popular Music." *Science, Technology and Human Values* 14(4): 400.

Henriques, Julian. 2003. "Sonic Dominance and the Reggae Sound System Session." In *The Auditory Culture Reader*, ed. Michael Bull and Les Back, 451–480. Oxford: Berg.

Henriques, Julian. 2010. "The Vibrations of Affect and Their Propagation on a Night Out on Kingston's Dancehall Scene." *Body and Society* 16(1): 57–89.

Henriques, Julian. 2011. *Sonic Bodies: Reggae Sound Systems, Performance Techniques and Ways of Knowing*. London: Continuum.

Hirschkind, Charles. 2006. *The Ethical Soundscape: Cassette Sermons and Islamic Counterpublics*. New York: Columbia University Press.

Ihde, Don. 2007 [1976]. *Listening and Voice: Phenomenologies of Sound*. 2nd ed. Albany: State University of New York Press.

Inayat Khan, Hidayat. 1996. *The Mysticism of Sound and Music*. Boston: Shambhala.

Ingold, Tim. 2000. "Stop, Look and Listen! Vision, Hearing and Human Movement." In *The Perception of the Environment: Essays in Livelihood, Dwelling and Skill*, 243–287. London: Psychology Press.

Kelman, Ari Y. 2010. "Rethinking the Soundscape: A Critical Genealogy of a Key Term in Sound Studies." *Senses and Society* 5(2): 212–234.

LaBelle, Brandon. 2010. *Acoustic Territories: Sound Culture and Everyday Life*. London: Continuum.

Lee, Tong Soon. 1999. "Technology and the Production of Islamic Space: The Call to Prayer in Singapore." *Ethnomusicology* 43(1): 86–100.

Lefebvre, Henri. 1991. *The Production of Space*. Trans. Donald Nicholson-Smith. Oxford: Blackwell.

Massey, Doreen. 1991. "A Global Sense of Place." In *Space, Place, and Gender*, 146–156. Minneapolis: University of Minnesota Press.

McLuhan, Marshall. 1960. "Five Sovereign Fingers Taxed the Breath." In *Explorations in Communication: An Anthology*, ed. Marshall McLuhan and Edmund Snow Carpenter, 65–70. Boston: Beacon Press.

McLuhan, Marshall. 2004. "Visual and Acoustic Space." In *Audio Culture*, ed. Christoph Cox and Daniel Warner, 67–72. New York: Continuum.

Meintjes, Louise. 1990. "Paul Simon's *Graceland*, South Africa, and Mediation of Musical Meaning." *Ethnomusicology* 34(1): 37–74.

Meintjes, Louise. 2003. *Sound of Africa!: Making Music Zulu in a South African Studio*. Durham: Duke University Press.

Merleau-Ponty, Maurice. 1958. *Phenomenology of Perception*. Trans. Colin Smith. London: Routledge.

Moehn, Fredrick J. 2005. " 'The Disc Is Not the Avenue': Schismogenetic Mimesis in Samba Recording." In *Wired for Sound: Engineering and Technologies in Sonic Cultures*, ed. Paul D. Greene and Thomas Porcello, 47–83. Middletown: Wesleyan University Press.

Morgan, Robert P. 1980. "Musical Time/Musical Space." *Critical Inquiry* 6(3): 527–538.

Novak, David. 2008. "2.5×6 Metres of Space: Japanese Music Coffeehouses and Experimental Practices of Listening." *Popular Music* 27(1): 15.

Novak, David. 2013. *Japanoise: Music at the Edge of Circulation*. Durham: Duke University Press.

Ochoa Gautier, Ana Maria. 2006. "Sonic Transculturation, Epistemologies of Purification and the Aural Public Sphere in Latin America." *Social Identities* 12(6): 803–825.

Ong, Walter J. 2002. *Orality and Literacy: The Technologizing of the Word*. 2nd ed. London: Routledge.

Ouzounian, Gascia. 2007. "Visualizing Acoustic Space." *Circuit: Musiques Contemporaines* 17(3): 45–56.

Picker, John M. 2003. *Victorian Soundscapes*. New York: Oxford University Press.

Pijanowski, Bryan C., Luis J. Villanueva-Rivera, Sarah L. Dumyahn, Almo Farina, Bernie L. Krause, Brian M. Napoletano, Stuart H. Gage, and Nadia Pieretti. 2011. "Soundscape Ecology: The Science of Sound in the Landscape." *BioScience* 61(3): 203–216.

Porcello, Thomas. 2004. "Speaking of Sound: Language and the Professionalization of Sound-Recording Engineers." *Social Studies of Science* 34(5): 733–758.

Porcello, Thomas. 2005. "Music Mediated as Live in Austin: Sound, Technology, and Recording Practice." In *Wired for Sound: Engineering and Technologies in Sonic Cultures*, ed. Paul D. Greene and Thomas Porcello, 103–117. Middletown: Wesleyan University Press.

Rice, Tom. 2013. "Broadcasting the Body: The 'Private' Made 'Public' in Hospital Soundscapes." In *Music, Sound and Space: Transformations of Public and Private Experience*, ed. Georgina Born, 169–185. Cambridge: Cambridge University Press.

Saeed, Abdullah. 2012. *The Qur'an: An Introduction*. London: Routledge.

Sakakeeny, Matt. 2010. "Under the Bridge: An Orientation to Soundscapes in New Orleans." *Ethnomusicology* 54(1): 1–27.

Schafer, R. Murray. 1969. *The New Soundscape: A Handbook for the Modern Music Teacher*. Scarborough, Ontario: Berandol Music.

Schafer, R. Murray. 1977. *The Tuning of the World*. New York: Knopf.

Smalley, Denis. 2007. "Space-Form and the Acousmatic Image." *Organised Sound* 12(1): 35–58.

Soja, Edward W. 1989. *Postmodern Geographies: The Reassertion of Space in Critical Social Theory*. New York: Verso.

Solomon, Thomas. 2000. "Dueling Landscapes: Singing Places and Identities in Highland Bolivia." *Ethnomusicology* 44(2): 257–280.

Southworth, Michael. 1969. "The Sonic Environment of Cities." *Environment and Behavior* 1(1): 49–70.

Sterne, Jonathan. 1997. "Sounds Like the Mall of America: Programmed Music and the Architectonics of Commercial Space." *Ethnomusicology* 41(1): 22–50.

Sterne, Jonathan. 2003. *The Audible Past: Cultural Origins of Sound Reproduction*. Durham: Duke University Press.

Sterne, Jonathan. 2011. "The Theology of Sound: A Critique of Orality." *Canadian Journal of Communication* 36(2): 207–225.

Sterne, Jonathan. 2012a. "Part II: Space, Sites, Scapes." In *The Sound Studies Reader*, ed. Jonathan Sterne. New York: Routledge.

Sterne, Jonathan. 2012b. "Sonic Imaginations." In *The Sound Studies Reader*, ed. Jonathan Sterne, 1–18. New York: Routledge.

Stokes, Martin, ed. 1994. *Ethnicity, Identity, and Music: The Musical Construction of Place*. Oxford: Berg.

Stokes, Martin. 2004. "Music and the Global Order." *Annual Review of Anthropology* 33: 47–72.

Taylor, Timothy D. 1997. *Global Pop: World Music, World Markets*. London: Routledge.

Théberge, Paul. 2004. "The Network Studio: Historical and Technological Paths to a New Ideal in Music Making." *Social Studies of Science* 34(5): 759–781.

Thompson, Emily. 2002. *The Soundscape of Modernity: Architectural Acoustics and the Culture of Listening in America, 1900–1933*. Cambridge, MA: MIT Press.

Truax, Barry. 2001. *Acoustic Communication*: Oxford: Greenwood Publishing Group.

Tsing, Anna. 2000. The Global Situation. *Cultural Anthropology* 15(3): 327–360.

Tuan, Yi-fu. 1977. *Space and Place: The Perspective of Experience*. Minneapolis: University of Minnesota Press.

Valiquet, Patrick. 2012. "The Spatialisation of Stereophony: Taking Positions in Post-war Electroacoustic Music." *International Review of the Aesthetics and Sociology of Music* 43: 403–421.

Weheliye, Alexander G. 2005. *Phonographies: Grooves in Sonic Afro-Modernity*. Durham: Duke University Press.

Williams, Raymond. 1983. *Keywords: A Vocabulary of Culture and Society*. 2nd ed. New York: Oxford University Press.

Wishart, Trevor. 1986. "Sound Symbols and Landscapes." In *The Language of Electroacoustic Music*, ed. Simon Emmerson, 41–60. London: Macmillan Press.

Wrightson, Kendall. 2000. "An Introduction to Acoustic Ecology." *Soundscape: The Journal of Acoustic Ecology* 1(1): 10–13.

Zak, Albin. 2001. *The Poetics of Rock: Cutting Tracks, Making Records*. Berkeley: University of California Press.

Zuckerkandl, Victor. 1956. *Sound and Symbol*. New York: Pantheon Books.

synthesis

"Synthesis" commonly refers to a consolidation of discrete parts into a whole. It is often paired, conceptually and practically, with the reciprocal process of analysis, which entails the separation or isolation of constituent elements in a whole entity or system. In popular and experimental music cultures, the idea of synthesis is typically materialized in the form and action of a synthesizer: an electronic musical instrument designed to synthesize sounds. Synthesized sounds and synthesizer instruments are routinely associated with notions of the synthetic: contrasted to the so-called natural sounds of acoustic instruments or ecological domains and considered to be artificial substitutes or imitations of them. Such associations have a long history, as electronic and synthesized sounds and synthetic materials emerged alongside one another in contexts of nineteenth-century scientific research and industrial capitalism. Attributes of synthesized sounds, like amplitude and decay, also trace to nineteenth-century graphical methods, whereby sounds were analogized to living bodies in motion through the common figure of the waveform. The history of sound synthesis thus manifests the renewable promises of technologies to improve on what presents itself in nature, and the enduring cultural fascinations and fears of lively and unpredictable characteristics of new technologies, which may exceed human controls.

This essay begins by tracing how the concept of synthesis, and its travels through cultural fields, helped to engender the possibility of synthesizing sound. It then sketches a lineage of kindred devices and instruments that preceded commercially available synthesizers and discusses how cultural ideas of synthesis and synthetics informed ways that inventors and musicians shaped synthesizer instruments and sounds. I conclude with a more speculative claim about how synthesis reveals relations among cultural histories, sonic epistemologies, and the audible contours of electronic sounds and soundscapes.

Meanings and Materials

The term "synthesis" surfaced in seventeenth- and eighteenth-century philosophy to refer to the action of proceeding in thought from causes to effects, or from principles to their consequences. In the early eighteenth century, contemporaneous with Newton's writings, "synthesis" began to appear in medical and chemistry texts to refer to the unification of parts by application of scientific techniques. "Synthesis" was defined in a 1706 text on surgery as "that Method whereby the divided Parts are re-united, as in Wounds" (OED: "synthesis"). Before this point, the concept of synthesis existed in the comparatively immaterial realm of logic; now, it was mapped onto the material of the human body and made tangible through scientific practice. This was an important shift that anticipated the articulation of synthesis to sound and music technologies.

Sound synthesis is indebted to concepts in mathematics and physics that emerged in the early nineteenth century. In the 1820s, Joseph Fourier developed the idea that periodic waveforms can be deconstructed into many simple sine waves of various amplitudes, frequencies, and phases (Roads 1996: 1075–1076). In the early 1840s, Georg Ohm applied Fourier's theory to the properties of musical tones and perception, proposing that "all musical tones are periodic [and] every motion of the air which corresponds to a complex musical tone . . . is capable of being analyzed into a sum of simple pendular vibrations, and to each simple vibration corresponds a simple tone which the ear may hear" (Miller 1937: 62; see also Roads 1996: 545).

Hermann von Helmholtz's experiments in physiology and acoustics tested out these nascent theories of sound synthesis and extended them in his landmark treatise, *On the Sensations of Tone* (1885). Helmholtz built on Ohm's theories to argue that the quality of a tone depends on the number and relative strength of its constituent partial tones. He demonstrated this theory with a tuning fork apparatus that was further refined by the instrument maker Rudolph Koenig in the 1870s (Pantalony 2004). The work of Helmholtz and Koenig ushered in the technological possibility of synthesized sound, suggesting that any sound could be analyzed into component parts and then synthesized anew based on this information (Helmholtz 1885; Holmes 2002: 13–14; Peters 2004: 183).

As Helmholtz conducted his experiments, the concept of synthesis was infiltrating a variety of scientific fields. In chemistry, it referred to techniques for the production of compounds from elements; in physics, it described the composition of white light from constituent colors (OED, "synthesis"). Synthesis techniques also manifested in other new devices. One of the first documented technologies to be called a synthesizer was Lord Kelvin's mechanical device to predict the tides, developed in the 1870s. Kelvin's harmonic synthesizer did not generate sound, but in demonstrating the synthesis of a waveform from its component elements it influenced the design of subsequent instruments devoted to the analysis and synthesis of sound waves (Miller 1937: 110–111).

Electronic tones were produced as early as the 1830s (Page 1837; Davies 1984, 667–669), but it was not until the late nineteenth century that methods of harnessing electricity to synthesize composite sounds took hold. The inventor Thaddeus Cahill combined insights from Helmholtz's work with novel techniques of electronic tone generation when developing his instrument the Telharmonium in the 1890s. In his 1897 patent, Cahill wrote of the "electrical vibrations corresponding to the different elemental tones desired," and explained: "out of them I synthesize composite electrical vibrations answering to the different notes and chords required" (Cahill 1897: 2; see also Holmes 2002: 44–47). This usage arguably justifies the Telharmonium's colloquial designation as "the first synthesizer" employed for musical purposes (Williston 2000).

Although a handful of experimental electronic musical instruments emerged in the late nineteenth and early twentieth centuries that can be considered as precursors of the modern synthesizer (Rhea 1979; Davies 1984; Martel 2012), the terms "synthesis" and "synthesizer" were applied to musical devices only sporadically until midcentury. In communications research, speech synthesis techniques flourished in the 1930s and 1940s (Dudley 1940, 1949, 1955). The fields of music and communication were brought together in the work of Harry Olson and colleagues at RCA Laboratories in Princeton, New Jersey, who embraced and popularized the idea of sound synthesis in the 1950s. Comparing earlier theories by Fourier and Helmholtz to Norbert Wiener's *Cybernetics* and Claude Shannon and Warren Weaver's *The Mathematical Theory of Communication*, Olson and his colleagues concluded that the analysis and synthesis of musical sound was analogous to the process of decoding and coding a signal in a communication channel (Olson and Belar 1950: 5). Effectively, they updated Helmholtz's ideas of synthesis, which had emerged through analogies among waveforms based on graphical methods, to an idea of synthesis suitable for a cybernetic era, where a multiplicity of forms could be expressed as patterns of data on the punched-paper coding system of the RCA synthesizer instruments (Manning 1985: 103; Hayles 1999: 98).

From the 1950s on, synthesis techniques and synthesizer instruments were adopted and refined by composers, musicians, and inventors around the world (Young 1989; Guilbault 1993; Born 1995; Chadabe 1997; Théberge 1997; Meintjes 2003; Best 2005; Demers 2010; Niebur 2010). In the 1960s and after, synthesizer design and manufacturing companies emerged in the United States, United Kingdom, Russia, and Japan and underwent various patterns of growth, recession, and resurgence (Johnstone 1994; Takahashi 2000; Pinch and Trocco 2002; Reiffenstein 2006; Mishra 2009; James 2013; Smirnov 2013). RCA did much to register the term "synthesizer" in the public imagination through numerous popular and professional publications in the 1950s that described its synthesizers' design and functions ("Electronic synthesizer" 1955; Plumb 1955a, b) and through instructional content on a 1955 demonstration record that was marketed to the general public and sold upward of sixty-five hundred copies (The Sounds and Music 1955; Synthesizer records sold n.d. [c. 1957]). The term "synthesizer" then moved into widespread circulation in U.S. popular culture following Robert Moog's adoption of it for his mass-marketed keyboard instruments in the late 1960s.

There are numerous methods of sound synthesis: of these, additive and subtractive synthesis techniques informed the design of most electronic musical instruments and synthesizers through the 1970s. Additive synthesis is based on the concept that a complex waveform can be approximated by the sum of many simple waveforms; it informs the design of instruments such as Cahill's Telharmonium at the turn of the twentieth century and the Hammond electronic organs popular in the mid-twentieth century. Subtractive synthesis techniques, which were popularized by Homer Dudley's vocoder system for synthesizing speech at the 1936 World's Fair and continued to inform the designs of many analog synthesizers through the 1970s and beyond, are based on a premise that a wide range of timbral variations can be achieved by the controlled removal or attenuation of harmonic frequencies from a basic waveform. A classic technique of subtractive synthesis involves the independent regulation of the pitch, volume, and timbre of waveform, as controlled by an oscillator, amplifier, and filter, respectively. Many techniques for synthesizing sound have emerged in recent decades, including physical modeling, granular synthesis, and numerous other digital synthesis methods (Roads 1996: 134, 163–169, 197–198, 265–267).

At the same time, historians have applied the concept of synthesis liberally and retrospectively when identifying precursors to modern devices—such as the instruments of Helmholtz, Cahill, and others, as well as Wolfgang von Kempelen's eighteenth-century speaking machine, which some refer to as the "first speech synthesizer" (see DEAFNESS). The proliferation of so-called first synthesizers across historical accounts suggests that modern synthesis techniques have numerous conceptual roots and technological precursors. Indeed, "synthesis" proves to be an expansive term that can refer to any of the specific methods listed above and more; it also circulates in the present as a generic term that can signify any mechanical or electronic production of sound.

Synthetic Sounds and Lively Bodies

Synthesizers now make themselves heard all over the place: they are behind the sounds of countless popular music hooks and bass lines, scaled down to the format of mobile phone apps, and celebrated in documentary films (Fjellestad 2005; Harrison 2005; Fantinatto 2013; Truss 2013). The term itself did not settle into mainstream usage unchallenged. Both Robert Moog and Don Buchla resisted adopting the term "synthesizer" for their electronic musical instruments in the late 1960s. Moog initially wished to distinguish his more compact, voltage-controlled machines from the room-sized, punched paper–controlled RCA synthesizer (Pinch 2008: 472 n. 14). But he conceded that RCA had made the word familiar, and he considered it well suited for characterizing his "complete systems" for sound generation. The Moog catalog began to incorporate the word "synthesizer" in 1967 (Moog 1996: 21; Pinch and Trocco 2002: 67–68). Buchla disliked the connotation of "synthetics" as imitative substitutes and consequently avoided applying the word "synthesizer" to his electronic musical instruments in favor of names like "Electric Music Box" (Buchla 1997: 2–3; Pinch and Trocco 2002: 41). He believed that electronic musical instruments were better directed toward the exploration of new sonic possibilities, such as complex timbral variations, rather than toward imitative functions (Buchla 1997: 3). Referencing the pervasive marketing of synthesizers since the 1970s for their capacities to emulate acoustic instruments, the composer David Dunn has echoed Buchla's position, arguing that the term "synthesizer" is "a gross misnomer . . . more the result of a conceptual confusion emanating from industrial nonsense about how these instruments 'imitate' traditional acoustic ones" (1992: 19).

This "conceptual confusion" arguably persists because synthesized sounds evolved in relation to an industrial history of synthetic substitutes. The conceptual and technical possibility of synthesizing sound, which emerged from Helmholtz's research in the late 1800s and was taken up by early electronic instrument inventors such as Cahill, coincided with developments of various synthetic substances through similar applications of scientific methods. For example, following advances in organic chemistry in the late nineteenth century, developments of synthetic dyes were increasingly applied to consumer products. The idea of synthesis took on new connotations as public opinion registered the meanings and merits of synthetic materials. Synthetic materials were understood to be "manmade" imitations of natural substances, produced by processes of analysis and synthesis. This held two conflicting connotations. On the one hand there was suspicion that synthetic materials were not as good as natural ones. On the other, a certain faith in science and technology cultivated expectations that the synthetic could exceed the natural and provide a better, brighter, more durable substitute (OED: "synthetic"; "Synthetic sugar," 1944).

As social and technological processes of sound reproduction produced the very ideas of "original" and "copy" (Sterne 2003), the emergence of sound synthesis techniques produced audible, interdependent categories of "natural" and "artificial" sounds. This unfolded in the context of debates about synthetic and natural materials happening across cultural fields (Smulyan 2007: 44–45; OED, "synthetic"). Some inventors and musicians embraced synthesized sound as a means of transcending bodily limitations in performance, since myriad sound-producing tasks could be delegated to electronic signals or machine processes. Synthesizers promised to mimic, or even sound better than, a human performer (Olson and Belar 1955: 595; Plumb 1955b; Holmes 2002: 12). At the same time, there were concerns over what this delegation meant for conventional ideas of musicianship and creative authority. Was technology "somehow false or falsifying" when mediating acts of musical expression (Frith 1986: 265, quoted in Théberge 1997: 2)? Or, if synthesized sounds were too "realistic," would synthesizers put musicians out of work (Taubman 1955a, b; Strongin 1969)? Synthesized sounds thus exemplified broader debates about the roles of emerging technologies in musical practice and the place of science and technologies in everyday life.

While nature and artifice are well-worn topics for twenty-first-century readers familiar with cultural theory, these categories held great significance to the inventors, musicians, and listeners who greeted new sound synthesis technologies over the last century. Indeed, stories of synthesized sound in practice are often marked by movements around and across perceived boundaries of nature and artifice, of human and machine, and of what counts as fully human in the course of human histories. Many inventors of electronic musical instruments have devised and revised touch-sensitive interfaces in efforts to humanize expressive possibilities of otherwise unwavering electronic tones (Chadabe 1997: 14; Holmes 2002). Disco and house music producers, and their dance floor interpreters, have heard in "unnatural" (i.e., not acoustic) electronic beats and synthesized strings a sonic metaphor for queer identities and communities (Dyer 1990; Currid 1995; Gilbert and Pearson 1999: 61–66, 91). R & B musicians have taken up the vocoder and other explicitly technologized voice synthesis effects to challenge cultural inscriptions of black subjects and voices as "the epitome of embodiment" and authentic "soul" (Weheliye 2002: 30–31). In these examples, sonic artifice—as it is so marked by distinctive timbral and tone-shaping dimensions of synthesized sound— is a machine-produced veneer that always reflects back on human conditions, relations, desires. Synthesized sounds themselves are complex naturecultures—instances of the imploded and deeply interwoven categories of natural and cultural, "where the fleshy body and the human histories are always and everywhere enmeshed in the tissue of interrelationship where all the relators aren't human" (Haraway and Goodeve 2000: 106).

As a corollary of their synthetic connotations, synthesized sounds are also associated with notions of otherworldliness and alien or artificial forms of life. As early as the 1950s, composers of film scores, television jingles, and experimental radio plays in the United States and United Kingdom utilized percolating electronic sounds to signify outer space or alien life forms (Taylor 2001: 72–95; Wierzbicki 2005). A *Daily Tribune* headline on the RCA synthesizer succinctly registered how listeners perceived synthesized sound in terms of artifice and alterity: "Electronic Synthesizer 'Makes' Music; Gives Sounds Never Heard on Earth" (1955).

Synthesized sounds began their association with notions of life and liveliness a century earlier, through graphical methods and the dynamic figure of the waveform. By the late nineteenth century, scientists had distilled the organic processes of plants, animals, and humans—as well as the forms of electronic sounds—into a universal language of waveform representations. Electrical activity was a common, animating presence that enabled scientists to analogize myriad forms to one other and describe them with the same terms, like amplitude and decay. The shape of a waveform signified lively matter in motion, like the extension of a moving body into space and its variations over time, held still for observation and analysis (Brain 2002; Rodgers 2011: 518–521).

Moreover, techniques of sound analysis and synthesis developed alongside new scientific practices for analyzing dead bodies and producing diagnoses in nineteenth-century medicine. As autopsies and dissections of bodies became routine, perceptions of the relationship of life and death changed (Foucault 1994: 142; Curtis 2004: 229–234). Medical practitioners gained increasing authority to extend life artificially through applied knowledge or techniques. Diagnoses and plans for the sustenance of living bodies were synthesized from aggregated information about a corpse, as analyses of body parts and bodily processes in isolation made possible the restoration of a living whole. Likewise, the graphical distillation of sound waves into waveform representations endeavored to hold sounds still, like forms of life to be broken down by analysis. The expert analytic techniques of acoustic researchers, together with the animating force of electricity, made possible the synthesis of new, dynamic waveforms, and technoscientific dreams of creation permeated the realm of electronic sounds.

Synthesized sounds thus grew as lively, synthetic wonders, embodying both the technical achievements of scientific practice and the unsettling potential of laboratory creations to resist containment—like Frankenstein's monster—and become more than the sum of their parts. The latter tendency is on display in the matter of unstable oscillators, which are at once a technical "problem" and a celebrated aesthetic feature throughout the history of synthesizer instruments. Synthesizer designers and performers have long grappled with "audible drift," the tendency of analog oscillators to fluctuate and go out of tune, due to environmental conditions or wear (Chadabe 1997: 157). Stable oscillators were a notable feature that electronics manufacturers marketed to synthesizer designers (Belar 1949), which competing synthesizer companies in turn marketed to consumers. Yet some artists embrace the fact that no two analog synthesizers are alike and that each one manifests an individual character and lifelike quirks. Describing her relationship to an old analog synthesizer, the electronic music composer Mira Calix concludes: "when it goes off on its own accord I find it quite interesting. They're like little creatures, you know, they breathe" (Rodgers 2010: 131).

Machine Logics and Sonic Epistemologies

Synthesis is a means of generating new sounds based on prior knowledge of sound, and each synthesizer thus "brings with it a particular logic," a means of ordering or making sense of the world (Greene 2005: 5). The logic of an instrument's design and use is informed by social history and prevailing cultural metaphors and meanings (Waksman 2001; Sterne 2003; Rodgers 2011). An instrument's applications in creative practice may rework the "script" that its design presents (Akrich 1992 [1987]) and, concurrently, alternate instrument designs embody the multiple and culturally varying ways of knowing sound (Diamond 1994).

Jessica Rylan, a noise musician and synthesizer designer who runs her own musical instrument company called Flower Electronics, provides an example of how knowledge about sound inhabits the material forms and functions of synthesizer instruments. In an interview we did in 2006, she observed that the so-called fundamental parameters of sound have played a defining role in synthesizer designs and techniques. Conventional synthesis, Rylan explained, is characterized by "this very scientific approach to sound, like, What are the fundamental parameters of sound? Volume, pitch, and timbre." She continued: "What a joke that is! It has nothing to do with anything" (Rodgers 2010: 147). These "fundamental parameters of sound" do have to do with something, namely Helmholtz's analogies of eyes and ears, and of light and sound waves. In the 1860s, Helmholtz theorized that loudness, pitch, and timbre corresponded to the primary properties of color: brightness, hue, and saturation (Helmholtz 1885: 18–19; Lenoir 1994: 198–199). His resolution of sound into these basic elements, in connection with a logic of resolving complex waveforms into simpler sine waves, laid an epistemological foundation for synthesis techniques. Helmholtz's tripartite structure of sound also shaped subsequent designs of analog synthesizers, which in their simplest form have three separate modules—an oscillator, filter, and amplifier—devoted to regulating these three constituent elements of sound. Rylan's critique is that Helmholtz's model of perception and approach to analyzing sounds need not determine the form of synthesizers to the extent that it has across the history of electronic instrument design.

Rylan departs from a Helmholtzian logic to design synthesizers that generate sounds and patterns that remind her of things in the world that evoke her curiosity, such as the varying sizes and ever-shifting temporal organization of raindrops. She incorporates unpredictable and chaotic elements into her designs of analog circuits, in contrast to what she describes as the "top-down," orderly approach of Helmholtz and followers. As Jonathan Sterne and I have noted elsewhere: "the Helmholtzian approach creates sound by breaking it into components and imitating and manipulating them. The Rylanian approach begins from an experience of sound and undertakes synthesis to approach and modulate it" (Sterne and Rodgers 2011: 45). Rylan centers the hearer's experience of sound versus positioning sound as an external phenomenon to be analyzed and controlled by the performer (Rodgers 2010: 145–47).

Rylan's approach also foregrounds the complexity of overlapping sounds in the world, whereby the act of synthesizing sounds—an exercise in setting chaotic and unpredictable patterns in motion—proceeds as a dynamic "sequence of interconnections" (Dunn 1992, 19). As the technical writer and historian of electronic musical instruments Tom Rhea has observed, the process of synthesis contains an implicit question: "What makes up this totality of sound that we hear?" (1979: 4). Rylan's work seems to propose that sounds are not individually discrete wholes with rationally ordered and consistent internal structures; instead, the "totality of sound" to be heard and resynthesized is a whole world of complex systems and interactions. Synthesis, then, is not merely a means of creating of novel electronic sounds. It also directs us to a charged moment: that fleeting "interruption of time" (4) that follows a retrospective analysis and precedes a new synthesis. Through this opening, we may listen for the cultural histories and sonic epistemologies that reside within technological forms, and for logics of part-whole relations and complex systems that frame the contours of everyday soundscapes.

Note

Thanks to Jonathan Sterne, Mara Mills, the graduate students in Digital Musics at Dartmouth College in winter 2013, and the editors and anonymous reviewers of this book for their helpful feedback.

References

Akrich, Madeleine. 1992 [1987]. "The De-scription of Technical Objects." In *Shaping Technology/Building Society: Studies in Sociotechnical Change*, ed. W. E. Bijker and J. Law, 205–224. Cambridge, MA: MIT Press.

Belar, Herbert. 1949. List adapted from *Electronics Buyers Guide*, June 1949. Herbert Belar Collection. David Sarnoff Library, Princeton University.

Best, Curwen. 2005. *Culture @ the Cutting Edge: Tracking Caribbean Popular Music*. Chapel Hill, NC: University of the West Indies Press.

Born, Georgina. 1995. *Rationalizing Culture: IRCAM, Boulez, and the Institutionalization of the Musical Avant-Garde*. Berkeley: University of California Press.

Brain, Robert M. 2002. "Representation on the Line: Graphic Recording Instruments and Scientific Modernism." In *From Energy to Information: Representation in Science and Technology, Art, and Literature*, ed. B. Clarke and L. Dalrymple Henderson, 155–177. Stanford: Stanford University Press.

Buchla, Don. 1997. Interview with Trevor Pinch and Frank Trocco. Analogue Music Synthesizer Oral History Project, 1996–1998. Archives Center, National Museum of American History, Washington, DC.

Cahill, Thaddeus. 1897. Art of and Apparatus for Generating and Distributing Music Electrically, US Patent 580,035, April 6.

Chadabe, Joel. 1997. *Electric Sound: The Past and Promise of Electronic Music*. Upper Saddle River: Prentice Hall.

Currid, Brian. 1995. " 'We Are Family': House Music and Queer Performativity." In *Cruising The Performative: Interventions into the Representation of Ethnicity, Nationality, and Sexuality*, ed. S.-E. Case, P. Brett, and S. L. Foster, 165–196. Bloomington: Indiana University Press.

Curtis, Scott. 2004. "Still/Moving: Digital Imaging and Medical Hermeneutics." In *Memory Bytes: History, Technology, and Digital Culture*, ed. L. Rabinovitz and A. Geil, 218–254. Durham: Duke University Press.

Davies, Hugh. 1984. "Electronic Instruments." In *The New Grove Dictionary of Musical Instruments*, ed. S. Sadie, 657–690. London: Macmillan.

Demers, Joanna. 2010. *Listening through the Noise: The Aesthetics of Experimental Electronic Music*. Oxford: Oxford University Press.

Diamond, Beverley. 1994. *Visions of Sound: Musical Instruments of First Nation Communities in Northeastern America*. Chicago: University of Chicago Press.

Dudley, Homer. 1940, March 1. "The Vocoder—Electrical Re-creation of Speech," Presented October 17, 1939, before a Joint Meeting of the Society of Motion Picture Engineers with the New York Electrical Society, New York. *Society of Motion Picture and Television Engineers Motion Imaging Journal* 34(3): 272–278.

Dudley, Homer. 1949. Speech Analysis and Synthesis System. US Patent 2,466,880, April 12.

Dudley, Homer. 1955. "Fundamentals of Speech Synthesis." *Journal of the Audio Engineering Society* 3(4) (October): 170–185.

Dunn, David. 1992. "A History of Electronic Music Pioneers." In *Eigenwelt der Apparatewelt: Pioneers of Electronic Art*, catalog of exhibition in Ars Electronica 1992 festival, Linz,

Austria, curated by W. and S. Vasulka, available at www.davidddunn.com/~david/Index2.htm, accessed August 15, 2014.

Dyer, Richard. 1990. "In Defence of Disco." In *On Record: Rock, Pop, and the Written Word*, ed. S. Frith and A. Goodwin, 410–418. New York: Pantheon Books.

"Electronic Synthesizer 'Makes' Music: Gives Sounds Never Heard on Earth." 1955, February 1. *Daily Tribune*.

Fantinatto, Robert, dir. 2013. *I Dream of Wires: The Modular Synthesizer Documentary*. Available at the documentary's website, http://idreamofwires.org, accessed August 15, 2014.

Fjellestad, Hans, dir. 2005. *Moog*. Plexifilm.

Foucault, Michel. 1994. *The Order of Things: An Archaeology of the Human Sciences*. New York: Vintage Books.

Frith, Simon. 1986. "Art versus Technology: The Strange Case of Popular Music." *Media, Culture and Society* 8(3): 263–279.

Gilbert, Jeremy, and Ewan Pearson. 1999. *Discographies: Dance Music, Culture, and the Politics of Sound*. London: Routledge.

Greene, Paul D. 2005. "Introduction: Wired Sound and Sonic Cultures." In *Wired for Sound: Engineering and Technologies in Sonic Cultures*, ed. P. D. Greene and T. Porcello, 1–22. Middletown: Wesleyan University Press.

Guilbault, Jocelyne. 1993. *Zouk: World Music in the West Indies*. Chicago: University of Chicago Press.

Haraway, Donna Jeanne, and Thyrza Nichols Goodeve. 2000. *How Like a Leaf: An Interview with Thyrza Nichols Goodeve*. New York: Routledge.

Harrison, Nate. 2005. *Bassline Baseline*. Video essay. Available at Nate Harrison website, http://nkhstudio.com/pages/popup_bassline.html, accessed September 28, 2014.

Hayles, N. Katherine. 1999. *How We Became Posthuman: Virtual Bodies in Cybernetics, Literature, and Informatics*. Chicago: University of Chicago Press.

Helmholtz, Hermann von. 1885. *On the Sensations of Tone as a Physiological Basis for the Theory of Music*. 2nd English ed. Trans. Alexander J. Ellis. New York: Longmans, Green.

Holmes, Thom. 2002. *Electronic and Experimental Music: Pioneers in Technology and Composition*. 2nd ed. New York: Routledge.

James, Al. 2013, April. "The Secret World of Modular Synthesizers." *Sound on Sound*, available at www.soundonsound.com/sos/apr13/articles/modular-synths.htm, accessed September 28, 2014.

Johnstone, Robert. 1994. *The Sound of One Chip Clapping: Yamaha and FM synthesis*. Cambridge, MA: MIT Japan Program, Massachusetts Institute of Technology.

Lenoir, Timothy. 1994. "Helmholtz and the Materialities of Communication." *Osiris* 9: 185–207.

Manning, Peter. 1985. *Electronic and Computer Music*. Oxford: Clarendon Press.

Martel, Caroline, dir. 2012. *Wavemakers/Le Chant des Ondes*. National Film Board of Canada.

Meintjes, Louise. 2003. *Sound of Africa!: Making Music Zulu in a South African Studio*. Durham: Duke University Press.

Miller, Dayton Clarence. 1937. *The Science of Musical Sounds*. 2nd ed. New York: Macmillan.

Mishra, Jyoti. 2009, April. "The SOS Guide to Choosing a Modular Synth." *Sound on Sound*, available at www.soundonsound.com/sos/apro9/articles/goingmodular.htm, accessed September 28, 2014.

Moog, Robert. 1996. Interview with Trevor Pinch and Frank Trocco. Analogue Music Synthesizer Oral History Project, 1996–1998. Archives Center, National Museum of American History, Washington, DC.

Niebur, Louis. 2010. *Special Sound: The Creation and Legacy of the BBC Radiophonic Workshop.* Oxford: Oxford University Press.

Olson, Harry F., and Herbert Belar. 1950. "Preliminary Investigation of Modern Communication Theories Applied to Records and Music." Herbert Belar Collection. David Sarnoff Library, Princeton University.

Olson, Harry F., and Herbert Belar. 1955. "Electronic Music Synthesizer." *Journal of the Acoustic Society of America* 27(3): 595–612.

Oxford English Dictionary. 2000. Oxford: Oxford University Press. Available at http://www.oed.com, accessed September 28, 2014.

Page, C. G. 1837. "The Production of Galvanic Music." *American Journal of Science and Arts* 32 (July): 396–397.

Pantalony, David. 2004. "Rudolph Koenig's Instruments for Studying Vowel Sounds." *American Journal of Psychology* 117(3): 425–442.

Peters, John Durham. 2004. "Helmholtz, Edison, and Sound History." In *Memory Bytes: History, Technology, and Digital Culture,* ed. L. Rabinovitz and A. Geil, 177–198. Durham: Duke University Press.

Pinch, Trevor. 2008. "Technology and Institutions: Living in a Material World." *Theory and Society* 37: 461–483.

Pinch, Trevor J., and Frank Trocco. 2002. *Analog Days: The Invention and Impact of the Moog Synthesizer.* Cambridge, MA: Harvard University Press.

Plumb, Robert K. 1955a. "Electronic Device Can Duplicate Every Sound." *New York Times*, February 1.

Plumb, Robert K. 1955b. "Electronic Synthesizer Produces Good Music and May Later Imitate Human Speech." *New York Times*, February 6.

Reiffenstein, Tim. 2006. "Codification, Patents and the Geography of Knowledge Transfer in the Electronic Musical Instrument Industry." *Canadian Geographer/Le Géographe Canadien* 50(3): 298–318.

Rhea, Tom. 1988 [1979]. "The First Synthesizer." In *Synthesizer Basics: The Musician's Reference for Creating, Performing, and Recording Electronic Music—Compiled from the Pages of Keyboard Magazine,* rev. ed., ed. B. Hurtig, 4. Milwaukee: Hal Leonard Corporation.

Roads, Curtis. 1996. *The Computer Music Tutorial.* Cambridge, MA: MIT Press.

Rodgers, Tara. 2010. *Pink Noises: Women on Electronic Music and Sound.* Durham: Duke University Press.

Rodgers, Tara. 2011. " 'What, for Me, Constitutes Life in a Sound?': Electronic Sounds as Lively and Differentiated Individuals." In "Sound Clash: Listening to American Studies," ed. K. Keeling and J. Kun, special issue, *American Quarterly* 63(3): 509–530.

Smirnov, Andrey. 2013. *Sound in Z: Experiments in Sound and Electronic Music in Early 20th-Century Russia.* Köln: Walther König.

Smulyan, Susan. 2007. "The Magic of Nylon: The Struggle over Gender and Consumption." Chapter 2 in *Popular Ideologies: Mass Culture at Mid-Century*, 41–71. Philadelphia: University of Pennsylvania Press.

The Sounds and Music of the RCA Electronic Music Synthesizer. 1955. RCA Victor. LM-1922 (LP).

Sterne, Jonathan. 2003. *The Audible Past: Cultural Origins of Sound Reproduction.* Durham: Duke University Press.

Sterne, Jonathan, and Tara Rodgers. 2011. "The Poetics of Signal Processing." In "The Sense of Sound," ed. R. Chow and J. Steintrager, special issue, *differences* 22(3): 31–53.

Strongin, Theodore. 1969. "Electronic—but with Soul." *New York Times*, September 7, D40.

Synthesizer records sold. n.d. [c. 1957]. Note. Harry F. Olson Collection. David Sarnoff Library, Princeton University.

"Synthetic Sugar." 1944. *New York Times*, June 4.

Takahashi, Yuzo. 2000. "A Network of Tinkerers: The Advent of the Radio and Television Receiver Industry in Japan." *Technology and Culture* 41(3): 460–484.

Taubman, Howard. 1955a. "Machines and Men." *New York Times*, February 6, X9.

Taubman, Howard. 1955b. "Synthesized Piano Music Found to Have a Tone Matching a Grand's." *New York Times*, February 1, 35.

Taylor, Timothy D. 2001. *Strange Sounds: Music, Technology and Culture.* New York: Routledge.

Théberge, Paul. 1997. *Any Sound You Can Imagine: Making Music/Consuming Technology.* Middleton, CT: Wesleyan University Press.

The Sounds and Music of the RCA Electronic Music Synthesizer. 1955. RCA Victor. LM-1922 (LP).

Truss, Si. 2013, February 14. "The Best iPad/iPhone iOS Synths in the World Today." *MusicRadar*, available at www.musicradar.com/news/tech/the-best-ipad-iphone-ios-synths-in-the-world-today-571053/1, accessed September 28, 2014.

Waksman, Steve. 2001. *Instruments of Desire: The Electric Guitar and the Shaping of Musical Experience.* Cambridge, MA: Harvard University Press.

Weheliye, Alexander G. 2002. " 'Feenin': Posthuman Voices in Contemporary Black Popular Music." *Social Text* (20)2: 21–47.

Wierzbicki, James Eugene. 2005. *Louis and Bebe Barron's Forbidden Planet: A Film Score Guide.* Scarecrow film score guides no. 4. Lanham: Scarecrow Press.

Williston, Jay. 2000. "Thaddeus Cahill's Telharmonium." Synthmuseum.com, available at www.synthmuseum.com/magazine/0102jw.html, accessed September 28, 2014.

Young, Gayle. 1989. *The Sackbut Blues: Hugh Le Caine, Pioneer in Electronic Music.* Ottawa: National Museum of Science and Technology.

transduction

In the received account, sound is a form of energy transmitted through a medium. Often, that energy moves across or between media—from an antenna to a receiver, from an amplifier to an ear, from the lightness of air to the thickness of water. With such crossings, sound is *transduced*. The word comes from Latin *transducere*, "to lead across, transfer," out of *trans*, "across, to or on the farther side of, beyond, over" + *ducere*, "to lead." A loudspeaker is a transducer. A microphone is a transducer. A telephone is a transducer. During the twentieth century, the human ear came itself to be described as a transducer.

Transduction names how sound changes as it traverses media, as it undergoes transformations in its energetic substrate (from electrical to mechanical, for example), as it goes through transubstantiations that modulate both its matter and meaning. When an antenna converts electromagnetic waves into electrical signals and when those are converted via a loudspeaker into patterns of air pressure, we have a chain of transductions, material transformations that are also changes in how a signal can be apprehended and interpreted.

The OED defines a *transducer* as "any device by which variations in one physical quantity (e.g. pressure, brightness) are quantitatively converted into variations in another (e.g. voltage, position)." An early appearance of the word comes in 1923 in the *Bell System Technical Journal*, in an article titled "Transient Oscillations in Electric Wave-Filters": "the spectrum of the interference presented to the terminals of the selective network will be modified by the characteristics of the 'transducer,' over which the disturbances are transmitted" (Carson and Zobel 1923: 24 n. 19). In 1924, the word arrives in an audio context in *Transmission Circuits for Telephonic Communication* (Johnson 1924). In verb form, to *transduce* means "to alter the physical nature or medium of (a signal); to convert variations in (a medium) into corresponding variations in another medium" (OED).[1]

Transduction first entered sound studies with Jonathan Sterne's 2003 book *The Audible Past: Cultural Origins of Sound Reproduction*. There, Sterne described transduction—and particularly its mechanical manifestation as tympanic oscillation in the ear (that is, as the vibration of the eardrum)—as the originating principle for modern sound reproduction. Prior to the emergence of the transductive idiom, sound was understood through its production (in vocal articulation, in vibrations of strings) rather than through its reception (in ears). Sterne's recognition of this transductive shift set the concept on its way into sound studies. He went on to say that "even though transducers operate on a very simple set of physical principles, they are also cultural artifacts" (2003: 22). It is this dual identity that has made transduction so good to think with and that has permitted sound scholars to join science and technology studies with media and cultural studies.

In what follows, I review uses of transduction in sound studies. I propose that the growing popularity of the term is reinforced by its promise to unite the material with the semiotic, an aspiration of science and technology studies, media studies, and anthropology (at least) since the 1990s, when scholars began to worry that the symbolic and linguistic dimensions of cultural practice were eclipsing attention to the material, physical, and technological world. Transduction, a term of art within the science of sound itself, has also been an appealing concept because it narrows the distance between cultural analysis and technical description, offering a conceptual language partially shared between scholars in the humanities and in engineering and science circles. Such overlapping terminology has afforded to sound studies scholars a productive complicity with the worlds they seek to describe—as well as a way to critique such worlds on something like their own terms. The fact that the term also turns out to have a heritage in 1960s proto-poststructuralist process philosophy—chiefly in the work of Gilbert Simondon, who was concerned with how to theorize being and becoming—keeps questions of phenomenology and experience in play, questions of keen interest to those in sound studies who wish to theorize what it means to encounter sound as an unfolding event. I conclude by calling for thinking beyond transduction.

From Science and Technology Studies to Sound Studies

One starting point for sound studies has been science and technology studies, a field dedicated to analyzing the social, political, and economic conditions surrounding and suffusing technoscientific practice (see Bijsterveld and Pinch 2012 for this lineage). Since the 1980s and 1990s, science studies has been preoccupied with how to hold simultaneously in view both the semiotic and the material features of scientific activities and artifacts (see Donna Haraway 1997 on the "material-semiotic"). *Transduction* might be heard as an analytic that answers to this demand.

Start with an account of technologically realized sound: Julian Henriques's article "Sonic Dominance and Reggae Sound System Sessions" (2003). In this analysis of the room- and body-shaking bass of reggae and dub sound systems, Henriques suggests "the aural is both a medium for oral or musical codes of communication, as well as a material thing in and of itself. You feel both the air as a gaseous liquid medium that 'carries' the sound and hear the waveform of the shape of the sound" (460). With the amped up loudspeaker, the listener experiences transduction on the dance floor: "the human body can be considered as a sensory transducer," experiencing the "transformation [of] sonic energy to kinetic energy" (468). Henriques continues:

> My use of the term transduction, as a connection or homology between physical and social circuits, flows and fields, is not intended as any kind of reductionism. . . . This concept of transduction again exemplifies how the condition of sonic dominance can reveal the often hidden functioning of the senses. At each point of transduction, electromagnetic, sonic, or cultural, one thing changes into another. This creates a surplus. Transduction describes a process of transcending the dualities of form/content, pattern/substance, body/mind, and matter/spirit. A transducer is a device for achieving escape velocity to leave the world of either/or and enter the world of either or both. (469)

In this usage, transduction describes sound as meaningful and material, reaching across (while also exceeding) sensory, cognitive registers.

Experiences of sonic immersion, then, are made possible by structures of transduction. To think further about how this is so, let me move now from the field of the dance floor to the scientific field. In my article "An Anthropologist Underwater: Immersive Soundscapes, Submarine Cyborgs, and

Transductive Ethnography" (2007; see also Helmreich 2009), I employ the notion of transduction to get underneath sometimes too-easy accounts of sonic "immersion." In 2004, I dove to the ocean floor in the three-person research submersible *Alvin*. After having been immersed in a patch of the Pacific inside a titanium sphere, immersed ethnographically in the particulars of a cultural practice, and immersed in the sounds of sonar and the surrounding sea, I came to wonder how immersion—as a sense of presence and immediacy—was produced. I found revelatory the analytic of *transduction*—the transmutation and conversion of signals across media, which, when accomplished seamlessly, produces a sense of effortless presence, of "immersion." For scientists inside *Alvin* to have a sense of being located in a space of sound, signals had to be transduced from the outside water into our interior air. We were situated in a sound world made available to us through hydrophones—microphones made of material sufficiently denser than water to allow propagating waves to be impeded and then relayed. The possibility of us imagining ourselves immersed in a submarine soundscape *depended* on transduction.[2]

Transduction should remind auditors of the physical, infrastructural conditions that support the texture and temper of sounds we take to be meaningful. Extending the argument to experience more generally, I have argued for a *transductive anthropology*, one that listens closely for telltale distortions and resistances, turbulence that might reveal the conditions beneath any self-evident "presence."

Shift now from the scientific field to the scientific laboratory. In her "Screaming Yeast: Sonocytology, Cytoplasmic Milieus, and Cellular Subjectivities" (2009), Sophia Roosth examined the field of "sonocytology," pioneered by UCLA chemist Jim Gimzewski. Sonocytology is a practice dedicated to bringing the vibrations of cells into human audibility (basically by turning up the volume; they vibrate in the humanly audible range but very, very quietly). One of Gimzewski's collaborators reports that the "frequency of the yeast cells the researchers tested has always been in the same high range, 'about a C-sharp to D above middle C in terms of music' . . . sprinkling alcohol on a yeast cell to kill it raises the pitch" (Wheeler 2004: 32). In her reading of this practice, Roosth showed that turning up the volume on cellular vibration was a transduction that summoned up human sympathy and anxiety. Were these yeasty creatures suffering? Were these high-pitched noises they made something like screams of pain? This instance of transduction, as in the submarine example,

worked on human sentiment to the extent that its own operation was occluded; laboratory auditors were transported into the immersive subcel-
lular soundscape that Gimzewski described as resonating with "a kind of
music." Transduction, in other words, vanished as the mediating operation that permitted researchers to believe they were "hearing" a genuine
auditory emanation from the world of yeast.

Henriques, Helmreich, and Roosth each point to how transduction as
a technical operation summons up experiential realness, that is, a sense
of being in the unmediated auditory presence of a sensation or feeling.
Helmreich and Roosth sought further to reveal how transduction is the
result of *work*, of labor that, when done well, produces a sense of seam-
less presence, presence we should not take for granted but rather should
inquire into as itself a technical artifact.

More recently, transduction has begun to animate discussions of the
boundaries of sound as such, challenging, among other things, the bor-
ders we put around vibratory phenomena. In 2012, Michele Friedner and I
examined the work of artist Wendy Jacob, who in 2009 built a transducing
floor, a platform that could seat some thirty people. At an MIT conference
called "Waves and Signs," Jacob ran low-frequency vibrations through the
floor so that hearing and deaf people could join in experiences that rendered hearing and feeling as overlapping, kindred sensory modes (compare Connor 2004). Transduction undergirds what cultural theorist and
dubstep artist Steve Goodman (2010) has called "unsound," vibration that
exists below the threshold of human hearing. The point in these works is
not that sound—or, for that matter, vibration (see Trower 2012)—is "really" transductive but that transduction affords a way into thinking about
the infrastructures through which the vibrating world is nowadays apprehended. Those infrastructures are historically specific and include such
technologies as dance floors, hydrophones, stereos, cochlear implants,
and the situated bodies of persons positioned to enjoy and make aesthetic
sense of such phenomena as thumping and humming bass frequencies.

The Philosophical Milieu

The sound studies works I have flagged call on earlier discussions of
transduction in continental philosophy. *Transduction* began its career in
the humanities when it migrated from engineering into phenomenology

and political philosophy. In those domains, transduction was not immediately taken up in a sonic register but was treated as a vehicle for conceptualizing processes of thinking and doing. For phenomenologist Gilbert Simondon, transduction "maps out the actual course that invention follows, which is neither inductive nor deductive but rather transductive, meaning that it corresponds to a discovery of the dimensions according to which a problematic can be defined" (1992 [1964]: 313).

Simondon's was a call to think about transduction as a logical operation. More, transduction "denotes a process—be it physical, biological, mental or social—in which an activity gradually sets itself in motion, propagating within a given area, through a structuration of the different zones of the area over which it operates. Each region of the structure that is constituted in this way then serves to constitute the next one to such an extent that at the very time this structuration is effected there is a progressive modification taking place in tandem with it" (313). To think transductively, for Simondon, was to inquire into the meaning of such words as *milieu*, that French coinage that places us variously in preexisting circumstances or in worlds summoned forth by our very emplacements, though always (as the word means in French) "in the middle" (see Canguilhem 1952). "Transduction," wrote Gilles Deleuze and Félix Guattari, would be "the manner in which one milieu serves as the basis for another, or conversely is established atop another milieu, dissipates in it or is constituted in it" (1987: 313). Philosopher of media Adrian Mackenzie, in his *Transductions: Bodies and Machines at Speed*, put it this way: "to think transductively is to mediate between different orders, to place heterogeneous realities in contact, and to become something different" (2002: 18). Such interpretations found their way quickly into sound studies writing on transduction (Henriques refers to both Simondon and Mackenzie), infusing this technical term with philosophical resonance.[3]

Moving against Transduction

Transduction does not solve sound studies' puzzles about materiality and meaning, but it does help think through the scene of transductive technologies, as well as the temporality of sound in experience. In Mark Hansen's work on media, for example, "the medium perhaps names the very transduction between the organism and the environment that constitutes life as essentially technical" (2006: 300). Transduction, understood as the transformation of energy, helps to explain composer Michel Chion's claim that sound "unscrolls itself, manifests itself within time, and is a living process, energy in action" (Chion 1990: 65).[4]

It is important to understand the limits of the concept. Transduction would seem beside the point in getting at the sonic ecologies of social worlds like those studied by ethnographer-of-rainforest-music-and-sound Steven Feld (2003); in the Papua New Guinea he studied, distance and presence are otherwise materialized, through the synonymy of upward and outward sounding through the canopied forestscape. Transduction may not work to think about Paul Stoller's work on Songhay possession, about which he writes: "for the Songhay, the 'cries' of the monochord violin and the 'clacks' of the gourd drum *are* the voices of the ancestors, voices filled with the power of the past" (2011: 112). Though one can imagine transduction being employed to understand these phenomena, it seems to me that the historical and technical specificity of the term attaches it more logically to cases that have at their heart technoscientific—and even electric, electronic, and electromagnetic—infrastructural instantiations.

More to the point, transduction is not the really real material substrate of sound. It is not the really real to a now revealed-to-be-phantasmatic immersion. Transduction is a representational recipe with its own rhetorical, historical, and technical starting points. One of the key assumptions packed into transduction is that sound *moves*. The analytic of transduction embeds a traveling model of sound. (Recall *transducere*, "to lead across, transfer," out of *trans*, "across, to or on the farther side of, beyond, over" + *ducere*, "to lead.") But as Jonathan Sterne and Tara Rodgers (2011) suggest, the "travel" of sound is a metaphor:

[The movement of sound], so central to almost all representations of signal processing, itself has roots in ideas about travel and voyage that inflect Western epistemologies of sound more broadly. In late nineteenth- and early twentieth-century texts that were foundational to the fields of acoustics and electroacoustics, and to ideas and machines of sound synthesis, sound was defined as fluid disturbances that initiate sensory pleasures and affects. It was also figured as a journey of vibrating particles that voyage back and forth, outward and home again. . . . Sound and electricity were both understood as fluid media and were conceptually linked to each other through water-wave metaphors and associated terms such as current, channel, and flow. (45)

But the metaphor of sound as movement does not necessarily or directly correspond with its materiality. As philosopher Casey O'Callaghan writes, "the claim that sounds travel turns out to be an unnecessary and, indeed, undesirable commitment for a theory of sounds" (2007: 28). For O'Callaghan, sounds are *individual events*. Sounds have persistence and duration, but it is not therefore correct to say that they "travel." Waves may travel, but sounds do not. They become present at reception. Even the most basic description of sound (as "traveling"—that is, as *transduced*) may be cross-contaminated, crosscut with leading questions as sound cuts across spaces, materials, and infrastructures. We should think, then, not with transduction, but across it.

Notes

1. The OED reports another early appearance of the verb form in 1949, in a textbook titled *Acoustic Measurements*. Transduction as a process noun pops up earlier, in a 1947 article in the *Journal of the Acoustical Society of America*.

2. As composers such as Michael Redolfi know; his "Sonic Waters," recorded underwater, is full of spatializing sleights-of-sound that create immersive experience through highly transduced hydrophonic operations (see Helmreich 2012).

3. *Transduction* has a range of nonsonic meanings. In biology, it refers to "the transfer of genetic material from one cell to another by a virus or virus-like particle" (OED). In physiology, it has been used to gloss a common logic across the senses (Shepherd and Corey 1992). In Piaget's psychology, to describe "[c]hildish transduction" as "opposed to adult deduction . . . Transduction is, in the first place, purely a mental experiment, by which we mean that it begins by simply reproducing in imagination events such as they are or could be presented by immediate reality" (2001 [1927]: 293). In the genre of anthropology known as cultural ecology, to describe the function of ritual: in his 1971 "Ritual, Sanctity, and Cybernetics," Roy Rappaport, describing how the slaughter of pigs by the Tsembaga Maring of New Guinea calibrates to larger-scale dynamics of ecological conflict between Maring-speaking groups, argued that the ritual cycle "operates as a transducer—a device which transmits energy or information from one subsystem into another" (1971: 61). In linguistic anthropology, transduction has been proposed as a way to add texture to the notion of translation: "much of what goes into connecting an actual source-language expression to a target-language one is like . . . a transduction of energy" (Silverstein 2003: 84). For other usages, see Barad (2001), Myers (2006), Whitelaw (2009), Tracy (2010), and Brunner and Fritsch (2011).

4. And if sound is transduced, then perhaps it too is an organism? See Dorin's (2003) discussion of Steve Reich's description of his process-based compositions as "organisms."

References

Barad, Karen. 2001. "Performing Culture/Performing Nature: Using the Piezoelectric Crystal of Ultrasound Technologies as a Transducer Between Science Studies and Queer Theories." In *Digital Anatomy*, ed. Christina Lammar, 98–114. Vienna: Turia & Kant.

Bijsterveld, Karin, and Trevor Pinch, eds. 2012. *The Oxford Handbook of Sound Studies*. Oxford: Oxford University Press.

Brunner, Christoph, and Jonas Fritsch. 2011. "Interactive Environments as Fields of Transduction." *Fibreculture* 18, available at http://eighteen.fibreculturejournal. org/2011/10/09/fcj-124-interactive-environments-as-fields-of-transduction/, accessed September 8, 2014.

Canguilhem, Georges. 2001 [1952]. "The Living and Its Milieu," translated from the French by John Savage, *Grey Room* 3: 7–31.

Carson, John R., and Otto J. Zobel. 1923. "Transient Oscillations in Electric Wave-Filters." *Bell System Technical Journal* 2(3): 1–52.

Chion, Michel. "Un langage pour décrire les sons," *Programm-Bulletin du G.R.M* 16: 39–75. Translation in Jean-Jacques Nattiez, *Music and Discourse: Toward a Semiology of Music*, translated from the French by Carolyn Abbate (Princeton, NJ: Princeton University Press, 1990).

Connor, Steven. 2004. "Edison's Teeth: Touching Hearing." In *Hearing Cultures: Essays on Sound, Listening and Modernity*, ed. Veit Erlmann, 153–172. New York: Berg.

Deleuze, Gilles, and Félix Guattari. 1987. *A Thousand Plateaus: Capitalism and Schizophrenia*. Minneapolis: University of Minnesota Press.

Dorin, Alan. 2003. "Artifact and Artifice: Views on Life." *Artificial Life* 9: 79–87.

Feld, Steven. 2003. "A Rainforest Acoustemology." In *The Auditory Culture Reader*, ed. Michael Bull and Les Back, 223–240. Oxford: Berg.

Friedner, Michelle, and Stefan Helmreich. 2012. "Sound Studies Meets Deaf Studies." *Senses and Society* 7(1): 72–86.

Goodman, Steve. 2010. *Sonic Warfare: Sound, Affect, and the Ecology of Fear*. Cambridge, MA: MIT Press.

Hansen, Mark B. N. 2006. "Media Theory." *Theory, Culture and Society* 23: 297–306.

Haraway, Donna. 1997. *Modest_Witness@Second_Millennium.FemaleMan©_Meets_Onco Mouse™: Feminism and Technoscience*. New York: Routledge.

Helmreich, Stefan. 2007. "An Anthropologist Underwater: Immersive Soundscapes, Submarine Cyborgs, and Transductive Ethnography." *American Ethnologist* 34(4): 621–641.

Helmreich, Stefan. 2009. "Submarine Sound." *The Wire* 302: 30–31.

Helmreich, Stefan. 2012. "Underwater Music: Tuning Composition to the Sounds of Science." In *The Oxford Handbook of Sound Studies*, ed. Karin Bijsterveld and Trevor Pinch, 151–175. Oxford: Oxford University Press.

Henriques, Julian F. 2003. "Sonic Dominance and Reggae Sound System Sessions." In *The Auditory Culture Reader*, ed. Michael Bull and Les Back, 451–480. Oxford: Berg.

Johnson, K. S. 1924. *Transmission Circuits for Telephonic Communication: Methods of Analysis and Design*. New York: D. Van Nostrand Company, Inc.

Mackenzie, Adrian. 2002. *Transductions: Bodies and Machines at Speed*. London: Continuum.

Myers, Natasha. 2006. "Animating Mechanism: Animations and the Propagation of Affect in the Lively Arts of Protein Modeling." *Science Studies* 19(2): 6–30.

O'Callaghan, Casey. 2007. *Sounds: A Philosophical Theory*. Oxford: Oxford University Press.

Piaget, Jean. 2001 [1927]. *The Child's Conception of Physical Causality*. New Brunswick: Transaction.

Rappaport, Roy. 1971. "Ritual, Sanctity, and Cybernetics." *American Anthropologist* 73(1): 59–76.

Redolfi, Michel. 1989. *Sonic Waters #2 (Underwater Music) 1983–1989*. Hat Hut Records, Therwil, Switzerland.

Roosth, Sophia. 2009. "Screaming Yeast: Sonocytology, Cytoplasmic Milieus, and Cellular Subjectivities." *Critical Inquiry* 35: 332–350.

Shepherd, G. M., and D. P. Corey. 1992. "Sensational Science. Sensory Transduction: 45th Annual Symposium of the Society of General Physiologists, Marine Biological Laboratory, Woods Hole, MA, USA, September 5–8, 1991." *New Biologist* 4(1): 48–52.

Silverstein, Michael. 2003. "Translation, Transduction, Transformation: Skating 'Glossando' on Thin Semiotic Ice." In *Translating Cultures: Perspectives on Translation and Anthropology*, ed. Paula G. Rubel and Abraham Rosman, 75–105. Oxford: Berg.

Simondon, Gilbert. 1992 [1964]. "The Genesis of the Individual." Translated from the French by Mark Cohen and Sanford Kwinter. In *Incorporations*, ed. Jonathan Crary and Sanford Kwinter, 296–319. New York: Zone.

Sterne, Jonathan. 2003. *The Audible Past: Cultural Origins of Sound Reproduction*. Durham: Duke University Press.

Sterne, Jonathan, and Tara Rodgers. 2011. "The Poetics of Signal Processing." *differences* 22 (2 and 3): 31–53.

Stoller, Paul. 2011. *The Taste of Ethnographic Things: The Senses in Anthropology*. Philadelphia, PA: University of Pennsylvania Press.

Tracy, Megan. 2010. "The Mutability of Melamine: A Transductive Account of a Scandal." *Anthropology Today* 26(6): 4–8.

Trower, Shelly. 2012. *Senses of Vibration: A History of the Pleasure and Pain of Sound*. New York: Continuum.

Wheeler, Mark. 2004. "Signal Discovery?" *Smithsonian Magazine* 34: 30–32.

Whitelaw, Mitchell. 2009, May 3. "Transduction, Transmateriality, and Expanded Computing." Entry in *The Teeming Void* (blog), available at http://teemingvoid.blogspot.com/2009/01/transduction-transmateriality-and.html, accessed August 15, 2014.

voice

Voice is both a sonic and material phenomenon and a powerful metaphor, and this is what makes it complex and interesting. The material, sonic experience of voice—learning to gurgle, laugh, scream, speak, sing, and to listen to others doing so—seems to be natural and universal. But such experiences occur within culturally and historically specific contexts. Sonic and material experiences of voice are never independent of the cultural meanings attributed to sound, to the body, and particularly to the voice itself. For example, when, in the film *The King's Speech*, the stuttering Bertie declares "I have a voice!" we hear this as a profound moment of self-realization and self-assertion, not simply a declaration of fact. With such a declaration, Bertie activates a host of culturally salient associations between voice and individuality, authorship, agency, authority, and power—associations that are made daily in our common parlance: we "find" our "voice" or discover an "inner voice"; we "have a voice" in matters or "give voice to" our ideas; we "voice concern" and are "vocal" in our opinions.

A brief look at the *Oxford English Dictionary* shows us that the most basic, literal meaning of "voice"—"the sound produced by the vocal organs of humans or animals, considered as a general fact/phenomenon"—is secondary in importance to a meaning that fuses a basic, literal sense to the notion of voice as an index or signal of identity: sound produced by *and characteristic of* a specific person/animal. Almost before we can speak of the sound itself, we attribute the voice to someone or something. Attributing voice to nonhuman entities (the collective, the mechanical, musical instruments) is a powerful way of making them intelligible, of endowing them with will and agency. We speak of the "voice of the people," "the voice of history," "the voice of reason," "the voice of authority," "the voice of God"; the "Voice of America"; we "voice" the notes of a piano or the melodic lines of a composition, or we appreciate the "voice" of a particular instrument.

If we spoke a language in which there were perhaps multiple words for "voice" but none with these kinds of associations, or lived in a society where public speaking was not associated with personal agency and political power, then the declaration "I have a voice!" would make little sense. Terms relating to voice in other languages might well reveal different sorts of associations, and would be an area ripe for further study. But an important first step in denaturalizing the category of voice is to understand the common and naturalized meanings it has in English and, by extension, in the Euro-Western context. While the sonorous and material aspects of voice typically serve as the constitutive outside when "voice" is invoked in discourses about personal agency, cultural authenticity, and political power, they themselves often remain beyond the reach of critical analysis.

Here I will first give a brief sense of where these ideas have come from and discuss some critical responses to the binaries that underlie them. I will then outline four ways of understanding the production of voices— through materiality, technological mediation, performance/performativity, and voicing—which can help us to understand the cultural and historical specificity of vocal practices and ideas about voice without relying on familiar assumptions.

Voice in the Western Cultural Imagination

The Western metaphysical and linguistic traditions have bequeathed us two powerful ideas about voice. One is the idea of voice as guarantor of truth and self-presence, from which springs the familiar idea that the voice expresses self and identity and that agency consists in having a voice. This is coupled with the idea that the sonic and material aspects of the voice are separable from and subordinate to its referential content or message, an assumption that underlies much of modern linguistic ideology. The model of the speaking subject assumed by Rousseau and Locke embodies all of our notions of voice as presence, authenticity, agency, rationality, will, and self. Such a model, perhaps paradoxically, treats the sonic, material aspects of voice as secondary and as potentially disruptive to the sovereignty of the subject. One possible response to this is to valorize the second term of the binary, the sounding, material voice; thus, the "maternal voice" could be imagined by French feminists in the 1980s as a kind of haven that resists representation (Kristeva 1980; Irigaray

1985), and the source of musical enjoyment could be declared not to be in the melodies or words themselves but in the realm of material vocality, or what Roland Barthes (1991 [1982]) famously called "the grain of the voice." Another possible response, elaborated within the deconstructive and psychoanalytic traditions, is to play on the vulnerability of the sovereign subject, theorizing the voice as an excess that can potentially disrupt self-presence and signification (Derrida 1974; Lacan 1989; Dolar 1996, 2006; Žižek 1996).

The binary set up in Western philosophical and linguistic thought between the signifying, authorial voice and bodily, material vocality was closely articulated with a social project central to Euro-Western modernity. One of the ways the subject of the European Enlightenment identified himself was by differentiating his language—rational language, purified of unnecessary associations and suited to expressing "universal" concepts—from the language of the lower-class folk, which was mired in custom and superstition. Purifying language meant privileging referentiality over other functions of language, creating an opposition between content and form and privileging the former (de Certeau 1988; Bauman and Briggs 2003). Such an idea would eventually became the basis of Saussure's distinction between *langue* as a system of signs—identified as the object of linguistic study—and *parole* as actually occurring speech that needed to be excluded in order to form a science of language (see LANGUAGE).

In the Western cultural imagination, this binary between a signifying voice and a vocality that is outside of referential meaning is recursively elaborated in other contrasts: human versus animal; language versus music; male versus female. The female voice has played a particularly important role in Western cultural production as a vehicle for presenting inarticulate vocality (Tolbert 2001). In genres ranging from literature to opera to classic Hollywood film, the female voice is repeatedly staged as an excessive but powerless vocality that is controlled by authorial male voices (Silverman 1988; Lawrence 1991; Dunn and Jones 1995; Frank 1995). However, critical attention to vocal practice and performance and the power of sound can challenge well-worn narratives of gendered power and voice (Abbate 1991; Andre 2006).

Materiality

The materiality of voice has to do with the sound itself as well as with the bodily process of producing and attending to voices. When we consider the musical voice as a sonic phenomenon, not merely as a vehicle for words or music, timbre—commonly referred to as voice quality or tone color, or colloquially referred to as an instrument's or vocalist's "sound"—becomes central. Perhaps because words used to describe timbre—such as "warm," "bright," "open," "husky," "gruff," "creaky"—are seemingly subjective and highly culturally variable, they are also an extremely socially meaningful aspect of vocal sound and performance (Cusick 1999; Fales 2002; Porcello 2002; Sundar 2007). The materiality of the voice is also a feature of spoken language. Linguistic variation, a classic topic within sociolinguistics, is a sonic vocal phenomenon with powerful social meanings and effects, as are intonational patterns and other "prosodic" features of language such as timbre, pitch, and volume (McConnell-Ginet 1978; Mendoza-Denton 2008). Particular vocal practices may originate in a very specific kind of event but then become generalized as vocal "gestures" that can be used to project a certain status for the speaker, retaining some aspect of the original situation in their sonic iconicity (Irvine 1990; Harkness 2011).

Voices are not only sonic phenomena; they are material, in the sense that they are produced through bodily actions. The term "vocal practices" is helpful in opening up this aspect of the materiality of the voice because it requires us to consider what is being done with the body, with space, and, as I will show, with technology, to produce the voice. Vocal practices include the bodily knowledge and training required to produce a particular sound: the "internal choreography" involved in shaping the vocal tract each time a singer sings or a person speaks (Poynton 1996, 1999; Eidsheim 2009; Harkness 2013). Musical vocal practices that are developed in particular times and places, such as "singing like a guy" in 1990s Western pop, or singing French *melodie* at the turn of the twentieth century, are modes of discipline that come to be naturalized and endowed with social meanings (Potter 1998; Cusick 1999; Stark 2003; Bergeron 2010). Vocal practices can also include the external choreography and staging that are aspects of performance. How are voices performed in relation to bodies? Just as singers "place" their voices in varying ways inside their bodies and vocal tracts, they also construct an association between the vocal sound they are producing and the image they project, a project that may be more or less self-conscious but is never simply "natural." Does a singer grunt and flail on stage or stand still with eyes screwed shut?

Technological Mediation

Mediating technologies, broadly defined, are crucial in this project of matching voices with bodies. Technologies of sound reproduction, broadcasting, transmission, and amplification draw attention to powers and possibilities of voices separated from their "original" bodies or voices produced at least partly through nonhuman sources such as microphones, the vocoder, or musical instruments said to have a "vocal" sound (Peters 1999; Dickinson 2001; Sterne 2003; Smith 2008). Michel Chion has most famously theorized the power of the *acousmêtre* in film, the voice without a visible representation of its source (Chion 1999). This concept opens the door to exploring the always-constructed relationship between voices and bodies, particularly in media contexts: for instance, the racial and gender politics of matching voices with bodies in film (Siefert 1995; Maurice 2002; Taylor 2009; Bucholz 2011) or the juxtaposition of globally circulating images with local voices and subjectivities (Boellstorff 2003).

Technologies also inspire powerful ways of conceptualizing the voice and its powers. For example, FM radio helps to create a genre called "direct speech" in newly democratic Nepal, an improvised voice communication network in 1990s Indonesia allows people to imagine themselves as equal members of a public, or the microphone in 1950s India allows female singers to produce a voice heard as "pure" and "chaste" (Kunreuther 2006, 2010, 2014; Weidman 2006; Barker 2008; see also Inoue 2011). Friedrich Kittler's (1990) concept of a "discourse network," which combines the material conditions that make communication possible with the forms of authority, power, and discipline that surround them, very usefully draws attention to the fact that metaphysical and metaphorical ideas about voice emerge from the material practices and technologies through which voices become audible in particular contexts.

Performance and Performativity

Studies of the poetics and politics of spoken and sung forms have emphasized vocal practices as creative expressions of social and cultural identity. But appreciating the creativity of vocal practices need not be limited to the model of the creative individual "expressing" him- or herself. The issue of voice and its relationship to agency and resistance explicitly grounds important theoretical explorations of voice under conditions of domination (Spivak 1988; Scott 1990; Sinha 1996). Related to this is a sense of vocal practice as "speaking back" to larger structures of power: hegemonic societal norms, oppressive political and economic situations, or commodified mass culture (Basso 1979; Abu-Lughod 1988; Bernstein 2003; Wilce 2003; Feld et al. 2004; Fox 2004; Samuels 2004). Studying vocal practices that occur within a social field and are thus directed at an audience invites us to hear vocal practices as performances, productively complicating a simple notion of expression with multiple possibilities for *voicing*, as I discuss in the next section.

A strain of linguistic-anthropological research has been concerned with the ways in which vocal modalities signal different social statuses, states of being, and life stages, stressing the iconic and indexical aspects of the sounding voice (Urban 1985; Irvine 1990; Graham 1995). This claim is different from the idea that vocal practices express identity; it gives a sense instead of their constitutive power (Sugarman 1997; Inoue 2006). It shades into a perspective that emphasizes vocal practices as naturalized modes of discipline where the repeated enactment of a vocal practice helps bring into being a social category and a subject position: what Bourdieu referred to as the "symbolic power" of language, Austin conceptualized as "doing things" with words, and Butler more broadly theorized as "performativity." For example, politicians in mid-twentieth-century Tamil-speaking South India constituted a new authoritative subjectivity linked with a specific oratorical style in which public speaking was less about expressing meanings or conveying information than it was about generating political power through the act of orating itself (Bate 2004, 2009). The latter perspective moves beyond the notion of social or cultural identities that are expressed by vocal practice to make the claim that particular vocal practices enable certain social identities and subject positions.

Voicing

The assumed linking of a voice with an identity or a single person overlooks the fact that speakers may have many different kinds of relationships to their own voices or words, or that a single "voice" may in fact be collectively produced (Bakhtin 1981; Goffman 1981). The concept of *voicing* draws attention to the fact that "speakers are not unified entities, and their words are not transparent expressions of subjective experience" (Keane 2000: 271). Voicing emphasizes the strategic and politically charged nature of the way voices are constructed both in formal and everyday performances. As Jane Hill shows in her classic study of the "voice system" of a Mexican peasant's narrative, a speaker may be inhabiting others' voices and words and artfully orchestrating a multitude of voices to tell his story (Hill 1995). Vocal practices (for example, using Spanish words in an otherwise Mexicano linguistic context) provide the material and sonic bases for techniques of voicing, which in turn produce new ways that voices come to be "typified," identified with socially recognized characters (Agha 2005; Keane 2011). Voice is also a central but undertheorized element that can give us insight into the sonic and affective aspects of interpellation, which Althusser theorized as the process by which subjects recognize themselves as implicated in ideologies that "call" or "hail" them.

Attention to textual and performed techniques of voicing, which imply particular models of circulation and reception, originality and reproduction, allows scholars to explore the ways in which the attribution of voices complicates the often assumed equation of voice with representation and agency. What, for instance, do we do with singers who insist that they are only reproducing what someone else composed? The concept of voicing may help to break down the dichotomy often drawn between "having a voice" and being silent or silenced by suggesting ways to interpret voices that are highly audible and public but not agentive in a classic sense (Majumdar 2001; Weidman 2003, 2011; see also SILENCE). As an example, I turn here to my recent research on singers in the South Indian Tamil-language film industry—a context at once familiar through the global media circulation of Bollywood song and dance, and strange because it is embedded in a set of culturally specific social relations that confound many Euro-Western assumptions about performance and the relationship between voice and self.

Female Voices in the Public Sphere

In the popular film industries of India, voices in the song-dance sequences are provided by "playback singers"—known as such because their voices are first recorded in the studio and then "played back" on the set to be lip-synched by actors and actresses. Emerging as a profession in the 1950s, playback singing afforded women new ways to be audible and visible in the public sphere. The singers active in the 1950s and 1960s achieved celebrity status, cultivating a distinctive new vocal sound that became strongly identified with Indian modernity. Playback singers of this generation confound many of our expectations about voice. Although they were in the business of singing for many different on-screen characters, they placed great value on the recognition of their voices by audiences; although they were stars, they were purposely not glamorous; and though live stage appearances were crucial for them, they adopted a rigid, nonemotive performing style. As such they were able to command a great deal of affect while displaying almost none themselves.

One of the more interesting moments of my fieldwork in Chennai, the center of the South Indian Tamil language film industry, occurred during a conversation in 2009 with the well-known playback singer S. Janaki, then in her early seventies. In discussing the nature of performance and the role of the performer, she had sharply disagreed with her daughter-in-law, a young dancer, who stressed that in order to perform well "I must forget myself" and "become one with the character I am portraying"—a perspective that seems relatively familiar. Janaki maintained, by contrast, that in singing on stage or in the studio "you must not forget who you are." To lose oneself in expressive performance was entirely in contradiction to the mode of performance she, and others of her generation, had carefully cultivated. Janaki was known for her ability to produce numerous different kinds of voices while barely moving, with no facial expression and no physical gestures. "For us [playback singers]," she maintained, "the acting is all in the throat."

Such vocal practices can be seen as a mode of discipline in which the female playback singer produces herself as a "respectable" female performer, one who sings but does not act. By emphasizing their difference from actresses, female playback singers inserted themselves into an ideology in which the female voice was identified as a site of purity, in contrast to the female body, which was subject to fashion and the consuming gaze of audiences. But this wasn't just any female voice; it had to sound a certain way. Produced by a very specific internal choreography, it was higher in pitch than any preceding female vocal genres and had a pure, consistent timbre. Sounds of bodily materiality such as breathiness, speaking, laughing, sighing, or crying were separated out from the singing voice and confined to "effects" that were performed only occasionally and in highly stylized ways.

Far from interfering with the purity of the female singing voice, recording and sound amplification technologies were seen as enabling and enhancing it. These singers' vocal sound and performing personae were products of the closely held microphone, without which they would not have been audible beyond a close range. On stage, the microphone enabled these singers to sing without projecting: that is, without appearing to put their bodies into the performance. It presented the possibility of inhabiting the stage, and by extension the public sphere, as a respectable woman.

While the microphone enabled a new kind of voice, sound recording provided a model for a new kind of performer. The playback singer was not a singing actress, a classical singer, or a singer-songwriter—kinds of performers who would be expected to show emotional involvement with what they were singing. Playback singers were cast in a strictly reproductive role, as vocalizers of what others had written and composed, indeed as a kind of sound reproduction technology themselves. Although playback singers played an essential role in the shaping and realization of songs that were often composed with them in mind and given to them in only skeletal form during rehearsal and recording sessions, their live performances emphasized their role as mere mediums for the "playing back" of songs. They were supposed to sound the same as their recordings, and, like a sound recording played over and over again, their voices were never supposed to change.

But the notion of "singing in one's own voice" that these singers employed did not carry the same connotations of intentional, authorly performance that we generally associate with the term "voice." Not changing one's voice, in this case, was equated with an *absence* of the kind of mannered performance required for "mimicry" but was not necessarily associated with expression, selfhood, and artistic agency. It was a concept of "voice" and "voice recognition" defined with reference to technological fidelity rather than expressive subjectivity. The image of respectable distance and detachment— the poker-faced poise these singers maintained in performance—allowed for the indeterminacy of their relationship to the material they performed by leaving ambiguous the conditions of their authorship and agency, intentionality and interiority: all those things we commonsensically associate with "having a voice" or "singing in one's own voice."

Conclusion

From the perspective of Euro-Western oppositions between a masculinized, signifying, authorial voice and a feminized, sonic, and material vocality, it would be easy to dismiss these singers as mere reproducers who lacked creative agency. But in doing so I believe we would be missing a great deal of their societal significance, for these voices, and their reliability, are highly valued and invested with great affective power in modern India. The mediating technologies involved in playback singing—sound recording, microphones, and the cinematic matching of image and sound—not only disrupt expected relationships between sound and image, voice and body, and person and presence but help to constitute other, less familiar ways of conceiving of voice and subjectivity.

Playback singers encourage us to apply a critical, denaturalizing perspective to voice more generally. They remind us that voice as a sonic and material phenomenon is inevitably embedded in social relations that shape how voices are produced, felt, and heard. Paying careful attention to vocal sound, as well as to how the acts of singing and performing are conceptualized, can yield insight into how vocal practices enable the emergence of new roles and new subjectivities in various sociopolitical contexts.

References

Abbate, Carolyn. 1991. *Unsung Voices: Opera and Musical Narrative in the Nineteenth Century*. Princeton: Princeton University Press.

Abu-Lughod, Lila. 1988. *Veiled Sentiments: Honor and Poetry in a Bedouin Society*. Berkeley: University of California Press.

Agha, Asif. 2005. "Voice, Footing, Enregisterment." *Journal of Linguistic Anthropology* 15(1): 38–59.

Althusser, Louis. 1971. "Ideology and Ideological State Apparatuses." In *Lenin and Philosophy and Other Essays*, 121–176. New York: Monthly Review Press.

Andre, Naomi. 2006. *Voicing Gender: Castrati, Travesti, and the Second Woman in Early Nineteenth-Century Italian Opera*. Bloomington: Indiana University Press.

Austin, J. L. 1962. *How to Do Things with Words*. Ed. J. O. Urmson. Oxford: Clarendon.

Bakhtin, Mikhail. 1981. *The Dialogic Imagination: Four Essays*. Trans. Caryl Emerson and Michael Holquist. Ed. Michael Holquist. Austin: University of Texas Press.

Barker, Joshua. 2008. "Playing with Publics: Technology, Talk, and Sociability in Indonesia." *Language and Communication* 28: 127–142.

Barthes, Roland. 1991 [1982]. "Music's Body." In *The Responsibility of Forms*, trans. Richard Howard, 245–312. Berkeley: University of California Press.

Basso, Keith. 1979. *Portraits of the Whiteman: Linguistic Play and Cultural Symbols among the Western Apache*. Cambridge: Cambridge University Press.

Bate, Bernard. 2004. "Shifting Subjects: Elocutionary Revolution and Democracy in Eighteenth-Century America and Twentieth-Century India." *Language and Communication* 24: 339–353.

Bate, Bernard. 2009. *Tamil Oratory and the Dravidian Aesthetic*. New York: Columbia University Press.

Bauman, Richard, and Charles Briggs. 2003. *Voices of Modernity: Language Ideologies and the Politics of Inequality*. Cambridge: Cambridge University Press.

Bergeron, Katherine. 2010. *Voice Lessons: French Melodie in the Belle Epoque*. Oxford: Oxford University Press.

Bernstein, Jane, ed. 2003. *Women's Voices across Musical Worlds*. Boston: Northeastern University Press.

Boellstorff, Tom. 2003. "Dubbing Culture: Indonesian Lesbi and Gay Subjectivities in an Already Globalized World." *American Ethnologist* 30(2): 225–242.

Bourdieu, Pierre. 1991. *Language and Symbolic Power*, ed. John Thompson. Cambridge, MA: Harvard University Press.

Bucholtz, Mary. 2011. "Race and the Re-embodied Voice in Hollywood Film." *Language and Communication* 31: 255–265.

Butler, Judith. 1997. *Excitable Speech: A Politics of the Performative* New York: Routledge.

Chion, Michel. 1999. *The Voice in Cinema*. Ed. and trans. Claudia Gorbman. New York: Columbia University Press.

Cusick, Suzanne. 1999. "On Musical Performances of Gender and Sex." In *Audible Traces: Gender, Identity, and Music*, ed. Elaine Barkin and Lydia Hammessley, 25–48. Zurich: Carciofoli Verlagshaus.

de Certeau, Michel. 1988. *The Writing of History*. Trans. Tom Conley. New York: Columbia University Press.

Derrida, Jacques. 1974. *Of Grammatology*. Trans. Gayatri Spivak. Baltimore: Johns Hopkins Press.

Dickinson, Kay. 2001. " 'Believe'? Vocoders, Digitalized Female Identity and Camp." *Popular Music* 20(3): 333–347.

Dolar, Mladen. 1996. "The Object Voice." In *Gaze and Voice as Love Objects*, ed. S. Žižek and R. Salecl, 7–31. Durham: Duke University Press.

Dolar, Mladen. 2006. *A Voice and Nothing More*. Cambridge, MA: MIT Press.

Duncan, Michele. 2004. "The Operatic Scandal of the Singing Body: Voice, Presence, Performativity." *Cambridge Opera Journal* 16(3): 283–306.

Dunn, Leslie, and Nancy Jones, eds. 1995. *Embodied Voices: Representing Female Vocality in Western Culture*. Cambridge: Cambridge University Press.

Eckert, Penelope. 2000. *Linguistic Variation as Social Practice: The Linguistic Construction of Identity in Belten High*. Malden, MA: Blackwell.

Eidsheim, Nina. 2009. "Synthesizing Race: Towards an Analysis of the Performativity of Vocal Timbre." *Trans* 13.

Fales, Cornelia. 2002. "The Paradox of Timbre." *Ethnomusicology* 46(1): 56–95.

Feld, Steven. 2012 [1982]. *Sound and Sentiment: Birds, Weeping, Poetics, and Song in Kaluli Expression*. 2nd ed. Durham: Duke University Press.

Feld, Steven, and Aaron Fox. 1994. "Music and Language." *Annual Review of Anthropology* 23: 25–53.

Feld, Steven, Aaron Fox, Thomas Porcello, and David Samuels. 2004. "Vocal Anthropology." In *A Companion to Linguistic Anthropology*, ed. A. Duranti, 321–345. Malden, MA: Blackwell.

Fox, Aaron. 2004. *Real Country: Music and Language in Working Class Culture.* Durham: Duke University Press.

Frank, Felicia Miller. 1995. *The Mechanical Song: Women, Voice, and the Artificial in 19th-Century French Narrative.* Stanford: Stanford University Press.

Goffman, Erving. 1981. *Forms of Talk.* Philadelphia: University of Pennsylvania Press.

Graham, Laura. 1995. *Performing Dreams: Discourses of Immortality among the Zavante of Central Brazil.* Austin: University of Texas Press.

Harkness, Nicholas. 2011. "Culture and Interdiscursivity in Korean Fricative Voice Gestures." *Journal of Linguistic Anthropology* 21(1): 99–123.

Harkness, Nicholas. 2013. *Songs of Seoul: An Ethnography of Voice and Voicing in Christian South Korea.* Berkeley: University of California Press.

Hill, Jane. 1985. "The Grammar of Consciousness and the Consciousness of Grammar." *American Ethnologist* 12: 725–737.

Hill, Jane. 1995. "Voices of Don Gabriel: Responsibility and Self in a Modern Mexicano Narrative." In *The Dialogic Emergence of Culture*, ed. D. Tedlock and B. Mannheim, 97–147. Champaign-Urbana: University of Illinois Press.

Inoue, Miyako. 2006. *Vicarious Language: Gender and Linguistic Modernity in Japan.* Berkeley: University of California Press.

Inoue, Miyako. 2011. "Stenography and Ventriloquism in Late Nineteenth Century Japan." *Language and Communication* 31: 181–190.

Irigaray, Luce. 1985. *This Sex Which Is Not One.* Trans. Catherine Porter. Ithaca: Cornell University Press.

Irvine, Judith. 1990. "Registering Affect: Heteroglossia in the Linguistic Expression of Emotion." In *Language and the Politics of Emotion*, ed. C. Lutz and L. Abu-Lughod, 126–161. Cambridge: Cambridge University Press.

Keane, Webb. 2000. "Voice." *Journal of Linguistic Anthropology* 9(1–2): 271–273.

Keane, Webb. 2011. "Indexing Voice: A Morality Tale." *Journal of Linguistic Anthropology* 21(2): 166–178.

Kittler, Friedrich. 1990. *Discourse Networks 1800/1900.* Stanford: Stanford University Press.

Kristeva, Julia. 1980. *Desire in Language: A Semiotic Approach to Literature and Art.* New York: Columbia University Press.

Kunreuther, Laura. 2006. "Technologies of the Voice: FM Radio, Telephone, and the Nepali Diaspora in Kathmandu." *Cultural Anthropology* 21(3): 323–353.

Kunreuther, Laura. 2010. "Transparent Media: Radio, Voice, and Ideologies of Directness in Postdemocratic Nepal." *Journal of Linguistic Anthropology* 20(2): 334–351.

Kunreuther, Laura. 2014. *Voicing Subjects: Public Intimacy and Mediation in Kathmandu.* Berkeley: University of California Press.

Lacan, Jacques. 1989. *Ecrits: A Selection.* Trans A. Sheridan. London: Tavistock/Routledge.

Lawrence, Amy. 1991. *Echo and Narcissus: Women's Voices in Classical Hollywood Cinema.* Berkeley: University of California Press.

Locke, John. 1959 [1690]. *An Essay Concerning Human Understanding.* 2 vols. New York: Dover.

Majumdar, Neepa. 2001. "The Embodied Voice: Song Sequences and Stardom in Popular Hindi Cinema." In *Soundtrack Available: Essays on Film and Popular Music*, ed. P. Wojcik and A. Knight, 161–181. Durham: Duke University Press.

Maurice, Alice. 2002. "Cinema at Its Source: Synchronizing Race and Sound in the Early Talkies." *Camera Obscura* 49 (17,1): 1–71.

McConnell-Ginet, Sally. 1978. "Intonation in a Man's World." *Signs* 3(3): 541–559.

Mendoza-Denton, Norma. 2008. *Homegirls: Language and Cultural Practice among Latina Youth Gangs*. Malden, MA: Wiley-Blackwell.

Peters, John D. 1999. *Speaking into the Air: A History of the Idea of Communication*. Chicago: University of Chicago Press.

Porcello, Thomas. 2002. "Music Mediated as Live in Austin: Sound, Technology, and Recording Practice." *City and Society* 14(11): 69–86.

Potter, John. 1998. *Vocal Authority: Singing Style and Ideology*. Cambridge: Cambridge University Press.

Poynton, Cate. 1996. "Giving Voice." In *Pedagogy, Technology, and the Body*, ed. Erica McWilliam and Peter Taylor, 103–112. New York: Peter Lang.

Poynton, Cate. 1999. "Talking Like a Girl." In *Musics and Feminisms*, ed. Sally Macarthur and Cate Poynton, 119–128. Sydney: Australian Music Centre.

Rousseau, Jean-Jacques. 1990 [1781]. "Essay on the Origin of Languages and Writings Related to Music." In *The Collected Writings of Rousseau*, ed. Roger Masters and Christopher Kelly, vol. 7. Hanover: University Press of New England.

Samuels, David. 2004. *Putting a Song on Top of It: Expression and Identity on the San Carlos Apache Reservation*. Tucson: University of Arizona Press.

Saussure, Ferdinand de. 1998 [1921]. *Course in General Linguistics*. Chicago: Open Court.

Schlicter, Annette. 2011. "Do Voices Matter? Vocality, Materiality, Gender Performativity." *Body and Society* 17(1): 31–52.

Scott, James. 1990. "Voice under Domination." In *Domination and the Arts of Resistance: Hidden Transcripts*, 136–182. New Haven: Yale University Press.

Siefert, Marsha. 1995. "Image/Music/Voice: Song Dubbing in Hollywood Musicals." *Journal of Communication* 45(2): 44–64.

Silverman, Kaja. 1988. *The Acoustic Mirror: The Female Voice in Psychoanalysis and Cinema*. Bloomington: Indiana University Press.

Sinha, Mrinhalini. 1996. "Gender in the Critiques of Colonialism and Nationalism: Locating the 'Indian Woman.'" In *Feminism and History*, ed. Joan Scott, 477–504. New York: Oxford University Press.

Smith, Jacob. 2008. *Vocal Tracks: Performance and Sound Media*. Berkeley: University of California Press.

Spivak, Gayatri. 1988. "Can the Subaltern Speak?" In *Marxism and the Interpretation of Culture*, ed. Cary Nelson and Lawrence Grossberg, 271–313. Urbana: University of Illinois Press.

Srivastava, Sanjay. 2006. "The Voice of the Nation and the Five-Year Plan Hero: Speculations on Gender, Space, and Popular Culture." In *Fingerprinting Popular Culture: The Mythic and the Iconic in Indian Cinema*, 122–155. New Delhi: Oxford University Press.

Stark, James. 2003. *Bel Canto: A History of Vocal Pedagogy*. Toronto: University of Toronto Press.

Sterne, Jonathan. 2003. *The Audible Past: Cultural Origins of Sound Reproduction*. Durham: Duke University Press.

Sugarman, Jane. 1997. *Engendering Song: Singing and Subjectivity at Prespa Albanian Weddings*. Chicago: University of Chicago Press.

Sundar, Pavitra. 2007. "Meri Awaz Suno: Women, Vocality, and Nation in Hindi Cinema." *Meridians* 8(1): 144–179.

Taylor, Jessica. 2009. "Speaking Shadows: A History of the Voice in the Transition from Silent to Sound Film in the United States." *Journal of Linguistic Anthropology* 19(1): 1–20.

Tolbert, Elizabeth. 2001. "The Enigma of Music, the Voice of Reason: 'Music,' 'Language,' and Becoming Human." *New Literary History* 32: 451–465.

Urban, Greg. 1985. "The Semiotics of Two Speech Styles in Shokleng." in *Semiotic Mediation*, ed. Mertz and Parmentier, 311–329. New York: Academic Press.

Weidman, Amanda. 2003. "Gender and the Politics of Voice: Colonial Modernity and Classical Music in South India." *Cultural Anthropology* 18 (2): 194–232.

Weidman, Amanda. 2006. *Singing the Classical, Voicing the Modern: The Postcolonial Politics of Music in South India*. Durham: Duke University Press.

Weidman, Amanda. 2011. "Anthropology and the Voice." *Anthropology News* 52(1): 13.

Wilce, James. 2003. *Eloquence in Trouble: The Poetics and Politics of Complaint in Rural Bangladesh*. Oxford: Oxford University Press.

Žižek, Slavoj. 1996. "I Hear You with My Eyes, or, The Invisible Master." In *Gaze and Voice as Love Objects*, ed. S. Zizek and R. Salecl, 90–126. Durham: Duke University Press.

contributors

ANDREW J. EISENBERG received his Ph.D. in ethnomusicology from Columbia University in 2009 and is currently Visiting Assistant Professor of Music at NYU, Abu Dhabi. He has carried out extensive research on sound and social relations in Mombasa, Kenya, with the support of Fulbright and the Social Science Research Council; and on the music recording industry in Nairobi, Kenya, under the European Research Council–funded "Music, Digitization, Mediation" research program. Among his recent publications is the article "Hip Hop and Cultural Citizenship on Kenya's 'Swahili Coast'," which won the 2013 Richard Waterman prize from the Popular Music Section of the Society for Ethnomusicology. He is now completing a monograph based on his research in Mombasa, Kenya, entitled *Sound and Citizenship: Islam, Aurality, and Social Belonging on the Kenyan Coast*.

VEIT ERLMANN is an anthropologist/ethnomusicologist and the Endowed Chair of Music History at the University of Texas at Austin. He has won numerous prizes, including the Alan P. Merriam award for the best English monograph in ethnomusicology and the Mercator Prize of the German Research Foundation DFG. He has published widely on music and popular culture in South Africa, including *African Stars* (1991), *Nightsong* (1996), and *Music, Modernity and the Global Imagination* (1999). His most recent publication is *Reason and Resonance: A History of Modern Aurality* (2010). Currently he is working on a book on intellectual property law in South Africa that will be published by Duke University Press.

PATRICK FEASTER is Media Preservation Specialist for the Media Digitization and Preservation Initiative at Indiana University at Bloomington. Feaster is the author of the award-winning *Pictures of Sound: One Thousand Years of Educed Audio, 980–1980* (2012), and has received three Grammy nominations for his work on historical albums including *Actionable Offenses: Indecent Phonograph Recordings from the 1890s* and *Debate '08: Taft and Bryan Campaign on the Edison Phonograph*. A co-founder of the First Sounds Initiative and current president of the Association for Recorded

Sound Collections, he has played a central role in identifying, playing back, and contextualizing many of the world's oldest surviving sound recordings.

STEVEN FELD is a musician, filmmaker, and Distinguished Professor Emeritus of Anthropology at the University of New Mexico. His documentary sound art CDs include *Voices of the Rainforest*, *The Time of Bells 1–5*, *Suikinkutsu*, and *The Castaways Project*, and his feature films include *Hallelujah!* and *A Por Por Funeral for Ashirifie*. He is author of *Jazz Cosmopolitanism in Accra* (2012) and *Sound and Sentiment* (3rd ed., 2012); co-author of *Music Grooves* (1994) and *Bosavi-English-Tok Pisin Dictionary* (1998); editor and translator of Jean Rouch's *Ciné-Ethnography* (2003); and co-editor of *Senses of Place* (1996). His current writing concerns schizophonia, intervocality, and acoustemology, and his current feature film project explores the performance and politics of musical marionettes in Ghana.

DANIEL FISHER is assistant professor of Anthropology at the University of California, Berkeley. He has conducted long-term ethnographic research on media and sound production in Northern Australia and shorter-term ethnographic field projects on musical media in Peru and New York City. He is co-editor of *Radio Fields: Anthropology and Wireless Sound in the 21st Century* (2012) and is currently completing a monograph focused on the mediatization of voice and sound in Aboriginal Australia.

STEFAN HELMREICH is the Elting E. Morison Professor of Anthropology at MIT. His research has examined the works and lives of contemporary biologists thinking through the limits of "life" as a category of analysis. He is the author of *Alien Ocean: Anthropological Voyages in Microbial Seas* (2009), a study of marine biologists working in realms usually out of sight and reach: the microscopic world, the deep sea, and oceans outside national sovereignty. *Sounding the Limits of Life: Essays in the Anthropology of Biology and Beyond* is forthcoming. This book as well as a series of forthcoming articles track the cultural circulation of such abstractions as "water," "sound," and "waves."

CHARLES HIRSCHKIND is associate professor of Anthropology at the University of California, Berkeley. He is the author of the award-winning *The Ethical Soundscape: Cassette Sermons and Islamic Counterpublics* (2006) and co-editor (with David Scott) of *Powers of the Secular Modern: Talal Asad and his Interlocutors* (2006). His current project is based in southern Spain and explores some of the different ways in which Europe's Islamic past inhabits its present, unsettling contemporary efforts to secure Europe's Christian civilizational identity.

DEBORAH KAPCHAN is associate professor of Performance Studies at New York University. A Guggenheim fellow, she is the author of *Gender on the Market: Moroccan Women and the Revoicing of Tradition* (1996), and *Traveling Spirit Masters: Moroccan Music and Trance in the Global Marketplace* (2007). In addition to her numerous articles on sound, narrative, and poetics, she is also the editor of and contributor to two collections of essays: *Cultural Heritage in Transit: Cultural Rights as Human Rights* (2014), and *Theorizing Sound Writing* (under review). She is translating and editing a volume entitled *Poetic Justice: An Anthology of Moroccan Contemporary Poetry*.

MARA MILLS is assistant professor of Media, Culture, and Communication at New York University, working at the intersection of disability studies and media studies. She is completing a book (*On the Phone: Deafness and Communication Engineering*) on the significance of deafness and hardness of hearing to the emergence of "communication engineering" in early-twentieth-century telephony. Articles from this project can be found in *Social Text*, *differences*, the *IEEE Annals of the History of Computing*, *The Oxford Handbook of Sound Studies*, and *The Oxford Handbook of Mobile Music Studies*. Her second book project, *Print Disability and New Reading Formats*, examines the reformatting of print over the course of the past century by blind and other print disabled readers, with a focus on Talking Books and electronic reading machines. With John Tresch, Mills is the co-editor of a recent issue of *Grey Room* on the "audiovisual."

JOHN MOWITT holds the Leadership Chair in the Critical Humanities at the University of Leeds. He was formerly a professor in the department of Cultural Studies and Comparative Literature at the University of Minnesota. His publications range widely over the fields of culture, politics, and theory. In 2008 he collaborated with the composer Jarrod Fowler to transfigure his 2002 book, *Percussion: Drumming, Beating, Striking*, from a printed to a sonic text/performance, "*Percussion*" *as Percussion*. His *Radio: Essays in Bad Reception* appeared in 2011, and *Sounds: The Ambient Humanities* in 2015. In addition, he is a senior co-editor of the journal, *Cultural Critique*.

DAVID NOVAK is associate professor of Music at the University of California, Santa Barbara, with affiliations in Anthropology, Film and Media Studies, and East Asian Languages and Cultural Studies, and co-director of the Center for the Interdisciplinary Study of Music. His work deals with the globalization of popular music, remediation, protest culture, and social practices of listening. Novak is the author of the award-winning *Japanoise: Music at the Edge of Circulation* (2013), as well as recent essays and sound recordings in Public Culture, Cultural Anthropology, Sensory Studies, and The Wire. His current research focuses on the roles of music, sound, and noise in the antinuclear movement in post–3.11 Japan.

ANA MARÍA OCHOA GAUTIER is professor and director of the Center for Ethnomusicology in the Department of Music at Columbia University. She is the author of Entre los deseos y los derechos: Un ensayo crítico sobre políticas culturales (2003), Músicas locales en tiempos de globalización (2003), and Aurality: Listening and Knowledge in Nineteenth-Century Colombia (2014). She is now working on understandings of sound and indigeneity in northern South America and on a short book on silence.

THOMAS PORCELLO is professor of Anthropology and associate dean of Strategic Planning and Academic Resources at Vassar College. Porcello is co-editor of Wired for Sound: Engineering and Technologies in Sonic Cultures (2004). He has co-authored reviews on the senses and the anthropology of sound for Annual Reviews of Anthropology, and his essays and reviews have appeared in Ethnomusicology Forum, Anthropological Quarterly, American Anthropologist, Ethnomusicology, and Social Studies of Science among others. Porcello's current research examines the sonic dimensions of live, broadcast, and virtual sports competitions and events.

TOM RICE is a lecturer in Anthropology at Exeter University. He specializes in auditory culture and works in particular on the sound environments of institutions. In 2013 he published a book on his research into listening practices in the hospital setting entitled Hearing and the Hospital: Sound, Listening, Knowledge and Experience. The book was shortlisted for the Foundation for the Sociology of Health and Illness Book Prize 2014. As well as writing and teaching on sound Rice has produced audio pieces including a documentary for BBC Radio 4 about the relationship between music and water titled The Art of Water Music.

TARA RODGERS is a composer, historian, and critic of electronic music. She holds an MFA in Electronic Music from Mills College and a Ph.D. in Communication Studies from McGill University. She has presented work at the Tate Modern, the Museum of Contemporary Canadian Art, on the Le Tigre Remix album, and in many other forums. She is the author of numerous essays on music, technology, and culture, and of Pink Noises: Women on Electronic Music and Sound (2010), which won the 2011 Pauline Alderman Book Award from the International Alliance for Women in Music. She currently serves on the editorial boards of Leonardo Music Journal and Women & Music.

MATT SAKAKEENY is an ethnomusicologist, journalist, and musician, and associate professor of Music at Tulane University. He is the author of the book Roll

With It: *Brass Bands in the Streets of New Orleans* (2013) and articles in *Ethnomusicology,* *Black Music Research Journal,* and other publications. Sakakeeny holds a Bachelor of Music from Peabody Conservatory (1994) and a Ph.D. in Ethnomusicology from Columbia University.

DAVID SAMUELS is associate professor of Music at New York University and has worked broadly on issues of music, language, and expressive culture. His research includes topics in poetics and semiotics, history and memory, technology, and Native American and popular culture. He is the author of *Putting a Song on Top of It:* *Expression and Identity on the San Carlos Apache Reservation* (2004), and his articles on music, language, and sound have appeared in such journals as *American Ethnologist,* *Cultural Anthropology,* *Journal of American Folklore,* *Semiotica,* and *Language and Society.* More recently, his research interests have turned to various issues of vernacular modernities: cultural and linguistic revitalization, the multiple legacies of missionary activity among Native American communities, and the intertwined histories of musical and ethical philosophies.

MARK M. SMITH is Carolina Distinguished Professor of History at the University of South Carolina. He is author or editor of over a dozen books. His most recent is *The Smell of Battle, The Taste of Siege: A Sensory History of the Civil War* (2014). He is general editor of Studies in Sensory History and of Cambridge Studies on the American South. His work has been featured in the *New York Times,* the *Times of London,* the *Boston Globe, Brain, Science,* and the *Chronicle of Higher Education,* and he is a regular book reviewer for the *Wall Street Journal.*

BENJAMIN STEEGE is assistant professor in the Department of Music at Columbia University. He studies the history of music theory and aesthetics in the nineteenth and twentieth centuries, with particular attention to early modernism. His book *Helmholtz and the Modern Listener* was published in 2012, and his articles have appeared in *Journal of the American Musicological Society, Journal of Music Theory, Current Musicology,* and elsewhere. Steege has recently received research fellowships from the Alexander von Humboldt Foundation, the National Endowment for the Humanities, and the Radcliffe Institute for Advanced Study. His current work focuses on the contest between psychological and antipsychological views of music in the twentieth century.

JONATHAN STERNE is professor and James McGill Chair in Culture and Technology in the Department of Art History and Communication Studies at McGill University. He is author of *MP3: The Meaning of a Format* (2012), *The Audible Past: Cultural Origins of Sound Reproduction* (2003), and numerous articles on media, technologies, and the politics of culture. He is also editor of *The Sound Studies Reader* (2012). His new projects consider instruments and instrumentalities; histories of signal processing; and the intersections of disability, technology, and perception.

AMANDA WEIDMAN is associate professor of Anthropology at Bryn Mawr College. Her publications include *Singing the Classical, Voicing the Modern: The Postcolonial Politics of Music in South India* (2006), as well as articles on performance, embodiment, and technological mediation in relation to South Indian classical music, film songs, and historic South Indian sound recordings, and a review article on voice for the *Annual Review of Anthropology*. She is currently working on a book on playback singing in relation to the cultural politics of gender in South India from post-independence to the post-liberalization period.

index

body (*continued*)
resonance and, 178, 180–81; synthesis and, 213; transduction and, 224; voice and, 235–36, 239. *See also* deafness; hearing
Bonet, Juan Pablo, 46
Booth, S., 92
Born, Georgina, 5–6
Bourdieu, Pierre, 101–2, 118, 237
Brecht, Bertholt, 154
Brown, Lee B., 146
Buchla, Don, 212
Bull, Michael, 5–6, 106, 197
Butler, Judith, 237

Cage, John: compositions by, 3, 112, 127, 155, 185; music definition by, 197; on noise, 125; on silence, 183, 184–85
Cahill, Thaddeus, 210, 211
Carpenter, Edmund, 195
Cassirer, Ernst, 13
Cavarero, Adriana, 114
Chidester, David, 166–67
Chion, Michel, 82–84, 104, 228, 236
Chladni, E. F. F., 26, 30n5
chora, the, 33–34, 81, 82, 84, 84–85n11
cinema: *acousmêtre* and, 236; playback singing and, 238–41; silence and, 185–86; soundtracks, 96n4; verbal art and, 93; voice and, 82–84
circulation, 130–31, 199–200, 201–2
Clarke, Eric, 103, 196
colonialism and postcolonialism: music and, 120; radio and, 153, 156–57; religion and, 165; scientific standardization and, 25; silence and, 187
Connell, John, 199
context, social/cultural: hearing and, 72, 73–74; listening and, 61–62, 101–2, 103; music and, 103, 113, 116, 118–20; noise and, 59, 61, 70, 126, 127, 129, 130–31, 131–33; radio and, 151, 153–60; silence and, 189; sound reproduction and, 58–59, 144; synthesis and, 213–14, 216; voice and, 232–33, 235, 237, 238, 241

Corbin, Alain, 60, 170, 198
Cusick, Suzanne, 122

deafness, 3, **45–53**; Aristotle on, 65–66, 74n1; deaf identities, 45, 47, 51; as disability, 50–51, 52; silence and, 194; sound studies and, 28; technology and, 3, 45, 48–53, 69, 186; visualism and, 82, 84. *See also* sign language
Deleuze, Gilles, 199, 227
Derrida, Jacques, 81, 85n1, 180
Descartes, René, 177, 178
Dewey, John, 12, 13
disability studies, 52, 73–74, 82. *See also* deafness
Du Bois, W. E. B., 82, 117
Duverney, Joseph-Guichard, 178, 179

ears: as composite organs, 52; hearing definitions and, 65, 68; as hearing technology, 22, 69, 71; as passive, 79; scientific inquiry into, 46, 49, 142, 178, 179, 180–81; as transducers, 222, 223
echo, 3, 34, **55–62**
ecomusicology, 8
Edison, Thomas A., 142–43, 144
eduction, 146–47
Eisenberg, Andrew J., 193, 247
Eisenberg, Evan, 146
Eisler, Hanns, 79
Ellis, Alexander, 117
Eno, Brian, 40–41
Erlmann, Veit, 175, 247
ethnography: of listening, 104–8; music studies and, 118–19; of public sound, 131–33, 168–69, 200–202; of radio production, 157–60; recording technology and, 58, 94–96, 197–98, 238–41; reflexivity and, 107–8; salvage ethnography, 58, 118; of senses, 17–19, 34–42, 104–8; sound studies, contributions to, 7, 201–2
ethnomusicology: anthropology of sound and, 14; place and, 198–99; postcolonial critiques of, 120; relativ-

ism and, 113, 116, 118; soundscape
concept and, 197–98; sound studies
and, 6
Eurocentrism, 113, 116, 117, 118, 127, 130

Fanon, Frantz, 157
Feaster, Patrick, 61, 139, 147, 247–48
feedback, 38, 200
Feld, Steven, 248; acoustemology, 4, 12,
19, 152, 198; anthropology of sound
and, 6, 14, 15, 16, 17, 120–21; listening,
body and, 18, 101–2; recordings by, 4,
17, 18, 121; on religious soundmaking, 171; transduction and, 4, 228; on
voice, 92. See also acoustemology
film. See cinema
Fisher, Daniel, 151, 248
Foucault, Michel, 84, 134n3
Friedner, Michele, 52, 226

Galileo Galilei, 176
Gibson, Chris, 199
Gilroy, Paul, 199–200
Gimzewski, Jim, 225, 226
Gitelman, Lisa, 121
Goodman, David, 103
Goodman, Steve, 226
Gopinath, Sumanth, 5–6, 91
Greenblatt, Stephen, 175–76
Grosz, Elizabeth, 183
Guattari, Félix, 199, 227

Hansen, Mark, 227–28
Haraway, Donna, 13, 15, 17, 19, 214
Harris, Roy, 80, 143
Harvey, David, 194–95, 202
Havelock, Eric, 66, 140–41
hearing, **65–74**; acoustics and, 22; deafness as variety of, 53; hearing damage,
73–74; historical variations in, 52; vs.
listening, 68–69, 71, 84, 99; as metaphor, 1; scientific study of, 68, 69–70,
72, 73, 74, 178, 179; sound and, 82,
193; vs. vision, 65–67, 166, 195. See also
aurality; deafness; ears; listening

Heidegger, Martin, 71, 154–55, 180
Heinicke, Samuel, 47, 82
Helmholtz, Hermann von: acoustics,
popularization of, 27, 28–29, 30n10,
69; music and, 115, 178–79; periodic
vs. nonperiodic sound, 127; synthesis
and, 209, 210, 213; translation of, 117;
tripartite structure of sound, 216–17
Helmreich, Stefan, 4, 15, 52, 222, 224–25,
226, 248
Henriques, Julian, 224, 226
Herbert, R., 103
Hill, Jane, 238
Hirschkind, Charles, 165, 248
Hui, Alexandra, 69
Humphries, Tom, 49

iconicity, 90–91, 92, 94–95, 96n4, 237
Ihde, Don: on audiovisual litany, 67; on
auditory attention, 82; on spatiality,
195, 196; on technology, 40, 102; on
visualism, 78–79, 79–80, 81, 82
image, **78–85**. See also vision/the visual
immersion, 66, 67, 197, 200, 224–25,
229n2
indexicality, 90–91, 92, 94–95, 96n4,
237
inscription: eduction of, 147; of music,
113, 114, 116–17, 118, 119, 121, 141;
noise and, 129, 131; phonography and,
121, 139–40, 141, 142, 143–44; scientific
study of sound and, 49; synthesis and,
214–15; textual descriptions of sound,
3, 56, 57, 60–61, 61–62, 139–41
interspecies relations, 8, 13, 18

Jakobson, Roman, 89, 92–93, 95

Kahn, Douglas, 126, 172n1
Kaluli of Papua New Guinea, 4, 6, 15–19,
101–2, 121, 168, 228
Kapchan, Deborah, 33, 249
Katz, Mark, 5, 144
Kelvin, Lord William Thompson, 210
Kenyan sound spaces, 200–202

objectivity, 67, 107–8, 118
O'Callaghan, Casey, 229
Ochoa Gautier, Ana María, 181, 250
ocularcentrism, 176
Ong, Walter, 66, 195
onomatopoeia, 88, 90, 94
ontologies of sound, 12–14, 37–38, 41, 85n1, 171, 193–95, 202n1
orality, 66
Osaka, Japan, Kamagasaki area of, 131–33
otherness: acoustemology and, 15, 17, 19; body and, 33; hearing-vision differences and, 67; music and, 117; resonance and, 177, 181

Peirce, Charles Sanders, 72, 89–91
performance and performativity, 36, 41, 118–19, 236–37, 237–38, 239–40
performatives, 89, 93–94, 95
Peters, John Durham, 48–49, 143
phenomenology: acoustemology and, 4; anthropology of sound and, 6, 16; embodiment of sound and, 39–40; hearing and, 67, 166–67; relationality and, 19; resonance and, 180; spatiality of sound and, 195–96; transduction and, 223, 226–27. See also Ihde, Don
phonetics, 28, 46, 48–49, 51, 92
phonography, 139–48, 200; as inscription, 121, 139–40, 141–42, 143–44; as sound reproduction, 142–47; as sound writing, 139–41, 144, 147
phonology, 28, 91, 92
phonotactics, 91
Pinch, Trevor, 107
Pitman, Isaac, 141
place/emplacement: acoustemology and, 16, 17–18, 198; acoustics and, 25, 30n7; hospital listening, 104–8; space and, 198–99
Plato, 114, 115
playback singers, 238–41
poetics: of Aboriginal radio, 158–59; acoustemology and, 18–19; anthro-

pology of sound concept and, 14, 16; Jakobsonian poetics, 92–93, 95; of Nepali indirectness, 160n4; of place, 198–99; voice and, 92, 236–37
Porcello, Thomas, 7, 87, 94, 250
postcolonialism. See colonialism and postcolonialism
psychoacoustics, 23, 68, 69, 72, 101, 186
Pythagoras, 24, 114, 167

quiet, 28, 60–61, 129, 132

radio, 151–60; adaptation of sound technologies for, 70; audiovisual litany and, 67; colonialism and, 153, 156–57; de-naturalization of, 155–56, 160; as distraction, 71; indigenous radio, 157–60; listening and, 100, 103, 153; naturalization of, 154–56; noise and, 128, 129; social context and, 151, 153–60; voice and, 160n4, 236
Rameau, Jean-Philippe, 114–15, 178
Rancière, Jacques, 84
Rayleigh, Lord (John William Strutt), 27, 30n7
RCA Laboratories, 210–11, 212, 214
recording and playback, 139–48; acoustemology and, 17, 18; circulation and, 199–200; commodification of sound and, 120, 121–22; vs. eduction, 146–47; graphic inscription, 49, 141–42, 143; historical inquiry and, 3, 55, 56, 57, 58–60, 62; noise and, 128–29; phonogenicity and, 145, 147; as reproduction of sounds, 139–40, 142–45, 146; schizophonia and, 197–98; silence and, 185–86; space and, 195; transduction and, 4; verbal art and, 93; voice and, 239–41. See also inscription; phonography; technological mediation
Reé, Jonathan, 46, 82
relationality, 12–15, 13–14, 19, 41, 126, 194–95, 199. See also acoustemology

religion, **165–72**; listening and, 167–68, 186–87; music and, 115–16, 169; nonspatial hearing and, 193; religious soundmaking, 168–71; secularism and, 171–72; silence and, 165, 186–87, 194; spatiality of sound and, 200–202
resonance, **175–81**
Rice, Tom, 99, 250
ringtones, 90–91
Rodgers, Tara, 208, 217, 228–29, 250
Roosth, Sophia, 225–26
Rosenblith, Walter, 46
Rothenbuhler, Eric, 143
Rousseau, Jean-Jacques, 88, 96n2, 233
Russolo, Luigi, 127
Rylan, Jessica, 216–17

Sachs, Curt, 119–20
Sakakeeny, Matt, 1, 112, 250–51
Samuels, David, 87, 251
Saussure, Ferdinand de, 80–81, 88, 90, 234
Sauveur, Joseph, 24–25, 46, 114–15
Schaeffer, Pierre, 83, 84, 155
Schafer, R. Murray: on radio, 153; schizophonia, 197–98; soundscapes and, 7, 120–21, 197, 224–25; sound studies origins and, 7, 28, 120–21; urban noise, 129, 134n5, 187; visual-auditory binary, 195; World Soundscape Project, 14–15, 134n5, 146, 197. See also soundscape
schizophonia, 197–98
Schmidt, Eric Leigh, 171–72, 186–87
Schütz, Alfred, 13
Schwartz, Hillel, 52, 56, 169
science and technology studies, 4, 7, 223, 224–26
scientific inquiry: ears, 46, 49, 142, 178, 179, 180–81; hearing, 68, 69–70, 72, 73, 74, 178, 179; music, 5, 113, 114–15, 176, 177, 209; sonocytology, 225–26; synthesis concept and, 209–12; vibration, 22, 24–26, 27, 28, 114–15, 177–78, 209. See also acoustics

Scott de Martinville, Édouard-Léon, 142, 143, 148n5
signification: as central to language, 87–88, 90; chora concept and, 84–85n1; Helmholtz's theory and, 179; listening and, 175; Peircean semiotics and, 89–91; resonance and, 181; sound-image concept and, 80–81; vs. voice, 234; writing and, 140
sign languages, 3, 47–48, 49, 51, 82, 96n1
silence, **183–89**; John Cage on, 3, 112, 183, 184–85; contemporary sound studies and, 28; cultural context and, 189; music and, 115, 184–86; vs. noise, 129–30; religion and, 165, 186–87, 194; silencing, 186–88, 238; vs. soundlessness, 194, 202n2
Simondon, Gilbert, 223, 227
Smith, Bruce R., 55, 56
Smith, Mark M., 55, 251
sound art, 9, 52, 127, 154
sound demos (activism), 133, 134n8, 134n9
sound knowledge, 34, 38, 42
soundscape, 7; vs. acoustemology, 15; as acoustic ecology, 197–99; architectural acoustics and, 60–61; critique of concept, 197, 224–25; cultural context and, 72; music and, 120–21, 185–86, 197; noise and, 129, 134n5, 187; recording and playback and, 146; religious sound bodies and, 36
sound studies (as discipline), 3, 4, 5–8, 28–29, 112–13, 120–21, 201–2
soundtracks, 71, 83, 96n4, 196
space, **193–202**; architectural acoustics and, 61, 70; despatialization of sound and, 193–94; music studies and, 5–6; phenomenal field and, 195–96; radio and, 154–55; technological mediation and, 193–94, 196–98, 199–200; territory and, 199
speech: deafness and, 46, 47, 48–49; language and, 81, 87, 88; music and, 115; performatives, 93–94; religion and, 166–67, 170; scientific study of

Printed and bound by CPI Group (UK) Ltd, Croydon, CR0 4YY

25/03/2025

14647325-0002